THE FANTASY OF J. R. R. TOLKIEN

The Fantasy of
J. R. R. TOLKIEN

MYTHOPOEIA AND THE
RECOVERY OF CREATION

Robert J. Dobie

Foreword by Bradley J. Birzer

The Catholic University of America Press
Washington, D.C.

Copyright © 2024

The Catholic University of America Press

All rights reserved

Cataloging-in-Publication Data is available from the Library of Congress

ISBN (paperback): 978-08132-3815-9
ISBN (ebook): 978-08132-3816-6

IN MEMORIAM:

Margaret Rose Dobie (1936–2018)

CONTENTS

Abbreviations	ix
Foreword by Bradley J. Birzer	xi
Preface	xv
Introduction: Of Niggle, Mythopoeia, and the Secret Fire	1
Chapter 1. Creation, Sub-creation, and Recovery	25
Chapter 2. "The Fall, Mortality, and the Machine"	47
Chapter 3. The Recovery of Language	77
Chapter 4. The Recovery of Nature	105
Chapter 5. The Recovery of Fellowship	135
Chapter 6. The Recovery of Virtue	159
Chapter 7. The Recovery of Eternity	179
Chapter 8. The Recovery of Hope	209
Bibliography	241
Index	251

ABBREVIATIONS

Ainu   *The Ainulindalë (The Silmarillion)*

Akal   *The Akallabêth (The Silmarillion)*

Conf.   *Confessiones* (Augustine)

CP   *Consolation of Philosophy* (Boethius)

De ver. *Questiones disputatae de veritate* (Thomas Aquinas)

FR   *The Fellowship of the Ring*

Letters *The Letters of J. R. R. Tolkien*

MC   *The Monsters and the Critics*

MR   *Morgoth's Ring: The Later Silmarillion*

QS   *The Quenta Silmarillion*

RK   *The Return of the King*

RP   *The Rings of Power and the Third Age (The Silmarillion)*

SD   *Sauron Defeated: The End of the Third Age*

S.Th.   *Summa theologiae* (Thomas Aquinas)

TL   *Tree and Leaf*

TT   *The Two Towers*

Vala   *The Valaquenta (The Silmarillion)*

FOREWORD

September 1977 was a momentous month in my household in central Kansas. On September 6, I turned ten, a great age for any boy. On September 15, Houghton Mifflin published J. R. R. Tolkien's *The Silmarillion*, edited by his son, Christopher. It had been, I would find out later, a long time in the making. A week later, on September 23, my mom gave my oldest brother, Kevin, a copy of *The Silmarillion* to celebrate his 18th birthday. I still remember the moment well, and I was especially taken with the cover art—"The Mountain Path" by Tolkien himself—and the fold-out map in the back of the book.

There was something about that cover that especially grabbed ahold of my imagination. I wanted so desperately to travel into that world, to explore its deepest depths, and to scale its highest heights. Even though I was too young to understand what was happening, I repeatedly tried to read *The Silmarillion*, but I never got farther than the creation account, the "Ainulindalë." Again, though, I read it so many times as a young boy that it somehow became a part of me, even as a pre-teen. To this day, I can't read the first chapter of Genesis (a core text I have the privilege to teach to college freshmen every fall), without thinking of Tolkien's account. Perhaps this has distorted my view of the biblical creation story, but I prefer to think of it as enhancing rather than distorting. It would still be a few years before I purchased a box set of *The Hobbit* and *The Lord of the Rings* with money earned from mowing lawns. But there's no doubt, from 1977 on, I was a dedicated Tolkien admirer, and I soon came to devour every mythic and fictional word he had published. As a junior at the University of Notre Dame I took an excellent course, "Fantasy and Philosophy," and I eagerly chose to write my term paper on Tolkien's Catholicism. A little over a decade later, that paper would become the foundation of my first book.

Needless to write, I've lost count of how many times I've read, reread, and taught Tolkien. It's been a wonderful, never-ending journey, one that began with me obsessing over "The Mountain Path" nearly half a century ago.

It was with no small amount of enthusiasm, then, that I read this book that you now hold in your hands, *The Fantasy of J. R. R. Tolkien: Mythopoeia and the Recovery of Creation*. It is a thing of beauty, overflowing with wisdom. With it, author Robert J. Dobie has made old things new again, rediscovering what makes Tolkien so enticing to so many. Indeed, Dobie is so worthy of his task that his voice, at some level, becomes also Tolkien's voice. Having fully immersed himself in the literature by and about Tolkien, Dobie incorporates works from Tolkien's vast corpus, everything from "Leaf by Niggle" to *The Silmarillion* to the more recently published books such as *The Nature of Middle-earth* edited by Carl Hostetter.

As indicated by the title of his own book, Dobie is especially concerned with the notion of "recovery"—of language, nature, fellowship, virtue, eternity, and, most wonderfully, hope. Such recovery, the author notes, was not only crucial to Tolkien as a mythmaker, but it also remains crucial to us as we weather the whirligig of modern and post-modern culture. By recovery, Dobie means seeing the world as it was meant to be, in an enchanted, sacramental, numinous, and pre-fallen sense. "But art redeems, Tolkien emphasizes, not by creating an imaginary 'never-never land' (or 'utopia' which comes from the Greek for 'no-place'), but to the contrary, by recovering what in our primary world is of an eternal nature and therefore of timeless value, especially within ourselves," Dobie writes. Thus, when we as human beings sub-create, to use a very Tolkienian term, we participate in creation itself.

A few snippets from the book reveal its excellence.

On the Ring:

> Hence, the paradoxes of the Ring: it confers a limitless time span, invisibility, sharpened hearing, and great power; and yet it distorts and obscures the wearer's vision of the world—as Aristotle notes, the sense that is most closely related to thought and intelligence—and mires it down in a sort of vague and hazy fog, making its wearer unable to make clear and necessary distinctions, visible, conceptual, or otherwise. This difference between enhanced power of hearing and diminished powers of sight leads to deception and trickery.[1]

Here, Dobie employs Aristotle well, and he does so with other thinkers—such as Boethius and Eric Voegelin—throughout the book.

On Tom Bombadil:

> Now Tom Bombadil is, of course, a benign being, a great friend to the hobbits. But Tolkien purposely does not make clear what sort of being Tom is: he is not a hobbit, nor a man, elf or dwarf; perhaps he is a Maia, but that, again, is not stated. But perhaps this is precisely the point: the reader must not know what Tom is in order that the nature of things may, as were, speak through him.[2]

Debate on who Tom Bombadil is or what he represents is legion in Tolkienian circles, yet Dobie wisely sidesteps the question, noting that he allows the nature of a thing to be revealed. In *The Fantasy of J. R. R. Tolkien*, Tom speaks for all living things.

On the employment of monsters:

> That is, monsters, as manifestations of the uncanny, give the reader a sense that our primary world is like a small island in a vast sea of realms beyond human sensibility or even intellectual perception. They intimate a vast sea of being and meaning that

---

1 Pages 61–62 below.
2 Page 125 below.

is yet unknowable in purely rational terms. This is especially the case when the monster is a harbinger of evil, as evil itself, as the pure negation or lack of being, goodness, and of course intelligibility, is unknowable in itself.³

Monsters, as such, reveal deep insecurities in our world, taking us into an eldritch realm of the irrational. Further, as it crucial to arguments in western civilization, only goodness possesses true reality. Evil is the lack of something, Dobie sagaciously claims.

On fellowship:

Fellowship, according to Tolkien, is built into the very act of creation of his secondary world; it follows that it is also built, by implication, into the process by which our primary world was and still is created and thus is essential to experiencing and even knowing the world and the things in as they truly are, viz., the gift of a Creator who seeks fellowship with His creatures.⁴

One only has to be reminded of Genesis 1 and the stewardship given to man. As with sub-creation, God, through grace, seeks to cooperate with us and participate in the very building of reality. Again, it is the great strength of Dobie to stress this.

These, of course, represent a mere smattering of delights to be found in this book. But they are representative. In each of these quotes, as he does throughout *The Fantasy of J. R. R. Tolkien*, Dobie perceptively reveals an aspect of Tolkien's thought. Tolkien, to be sure, is endlessly fascinating, but with so many books written about him, he runs the risk of becoming staid. In an act of recovery, though, Dobie offers something deeply interesting. As he notes about Tolkien's writing: "The numinous and enchanted landscapes of Tolkien's fiction are imbued with meaning, purpose, and, hence with moral value that also calls for a moral response." The same could be said of *The Fantasy of J. R. R. Tolkien*. Dobie is to be thanked and congratulated on such an excellent accomplishment.

3 Page 130 below.
4 Page 135 below.

PREFACE

I have been a devoted lover of Middle-earth since, on a gray November day in 1978, I bought at a bookstall in my local mall a copy of *The Fellowship of the Ring* (the paperback Ballantine edition, with the white cover featuring Tolkien's watercolor of Hobbiton and Bag End). I remember taking it home, sitting on my bed, and turning to the first page, "Concerning Hobbits." I was immediately entranced and continued reading through the evening and into the early morning hours. It was, however, difficult going for my twelve-year-old brain: fans of Tolkien who have read *The Lord of the Rings* multiple times often forget what a difficult and challenging work it is to first-time readers. But I persevered: the world I stepped into upon reading this book gave me such a *frisson* of the numinous that I could not put it down. Yes, the book was bewildering; but that only added to its magic and charm as it gave intimations of strange, uncanny powers at work in the world (It also didn't help that the quality of the maps at the back of those old Ballantine editions was very poor—"Where the heck is Isengard?"). I remember in particular, while reading the chapter "The Old Forest," how the woods around my rather ordinary split-level home in a rather ordinary Philadelphia suburb came alive with a strange menace. After reading the last appendix of *The Return of the King*, I immediately turned again to "Concerning Hobbits" at the beginning of *The Fellowship of the Ring* and read through it a second time, then a third. I then went on to read *The Hobbit* and *The Tolkien Reader* and then tried to read *The Silmarillion*, which had just come out a year or two before. But I put it down after only reading a couple dozen pages or so, utterly bewildered and confused ("Where are the hobbits?").

Then high school, college, graduate school, and the scramble to climb the greasy pole of tenure and promotion as a young professor of philosophy came and went, and Tolkien and Midde-earth faded into the distant glow of adolescent nostalgia. But in a turn of events that I am sure many of readers will appreciate, the release of the Peter Jackson film adaptations of *The Lord of the Rings* in 2001, 2002, and 2003 reignited my interest in and love for Tolkien and I reread *The Lord of the Rings*, *The Hobbit*, and (finally!) *The Silmarillion* (this time being able not only to finish it but also thoroughly enjoy it). Seeing this renewed enthusiasm for Tolkien, my then-new wife encouraged me to take advantage of my position as a college professor and offer a course on Tolkien. I resisted, fearing that a personal love and passion would become "mere work." But after a few years of delay, I finally gave in to my wife (always a mark of growing wisdom) and offered a special topics course entitled "J. R. R. Tolkien as Philosopher" at my university. I don't think that I have ever had greater pleasure teaching a course (It was also one of my only classes where, without exception, all the students were uniformly smart, engaged, and enthusiastic.). Teaching this course deepened my appreciation for Tolkien's achievement enormously; it forced me to engage with the entire corpus of Tolkien's work (most of it published posthumously by his son, Christopher) and with scholarship on Tolkien. Most importantly, it was while teaching this course a second and then a third time that the idea for this book came about and its thesis developed. Could I not write a book based on my lecture notes? But I hesitated again: it seemed to me a dilettantish extravagance to write a book on an author and subject outside my own area of expertise (medieval philosophy). I assumed that I would write my Tolkien book when I retired or neared retirement.

But the rather abrupt death of my mother from pancreatic cancer in August of 2018 suddenly made the writing of my Tolkien book urgent. After all, time, death, and eternity are recurring and fundamental themes in Tolkien's work, and thus the writing of this book became in many senses a therapeutic necessity. After clearing some other scholarly projects from my desk, I finally began work on this book in the spring of 2020, just as the COVID-19 pandemic hit. The timing was purely accidental; nevertheless, work on this book during that time was a source of consolation, both for the strange times of the pandemic and for the loss of my mother. I owe much to my wife Aurora, my students, and my colleagues at La Salle University (especially to Br. Michael McGinness, director of the honors program, and to the staff at Connelly Library, most of all the interlibrary loan department) for encouragement and support in writing this book during what was a challenging time. I would also like to thank Dr. Holly Ordway and Word on Fire Academic for generously forwarding to me three months prior to its release a PDF of her book *Tolkien's Faith: A Spiritual Biography*, which I found of invaluable help during the final revisions of the manuscript. But even given all these debts, I do not think that any of the above will take it amiss if I dedicate this book to the memory of my mother.

INTRODUCTION

Of Niggle, Mythopoeia, and the Secret Fire

When teaching my course "J. R. R. Tolkien as Philosopher," the first reading assignment on my syllabus is Tolkien's short story "Leaf by Niggle." At first glance, it would seem to be an odd choice. The story is a highly unusual one for Tolkien and one that usually surprises my students: "Leaf by Niggle" is distinctly set in mid-twentieth-century England and has in it no dragons, elves, dwarves, hobbits, or wizards—none of the creatures we usually associate with Tolkien's creative world. Second, for a writer who claimed on several occasions (as we shall see below) to dislike allegory, "Leaf by Niggle" is for all intents and purposes an allegory. Third, for a writer who objected strongly to biographical interpretations of literary works, "Leaf by Niggle" is clearly autobiographical.

But sometimes the most uncharacteristic works of an author give the reader the deepest insight into his more characteristic work; and

"Leaf by Niggle" is no exception. "Leaf by Niggle" literally came to Tolkien in a dream sometime in 1938 to 1939, just as he was at an impasse in trying to finish the early chapters of his *Hobbit* sequel, which was to become *The Lord of the Rings*.[1] Shortly after writing it down, his "writer's block" seemed to crumble, and he was able to recommence writing *The Lord of the Rings*. The story, therefore, evidently expressed something of profound importance for Tolkien, for it seems to express *in nuce* all the fundamental ideas that he was trying to convey in his fiction. Apparently, it gave him the intellectual clarity that enabled him to get on with and eventually complete his masterwork.

Tree and Leaf

"There was once a little man called Niggle, who had a long journey to make.... He did not want to go, indeed the whole idea was distasteful to him; but he could not get out of it. He knew he would have to start some time, but he did not hurry with his preparation."[2] We immediately encounter in this story a man whose time is short. A journey, a "needful journey" (i.e., death),[3] awaits and calls him.

But who is Niggle, and what does he do? "Niggle was a painter."[4] He was not, Tolkien quickly adds, a great painter. Moreover, he was a painter obsessed with a relatively narrow subject—trees and, in particular, leaves: "He was the sort of painter who can paint leaves better than trees. He used to spend a long time on a single leaf, trying

---

[1] The story was published much later in 1945 in *The Dublin Review*. Humphrey Carpenter, *Tolkien: A Biography* (Boston: Houghton-Mifflin, 2000), 199–200.

[2] *TL*, 93.

[3] Tom Shippey remarks concerning this "necessary journey": "to any Anglo-Saxonist this is bound to recall the Old Northumbrian poem known as Bede's Death-Song." This goes "Before that compelled journey (*néidfaerae*) no man is wiser than he needs to be, in considering, before his departure, what will be judged to his soul after his deathday, good or evil." Tom Shippey, *The Road to Middle-earth: How J. R. R. Tolkien Created a New Mythology* (New York: Houghton-Mifflin, 2003), 93.

[4] *TL*, 93.

to catch its shape, and its sheen, and the glistening of dewdrops on its edges. Yet he wanted to paint a whole tree, with all of its leaves in the same style, and all of them different."[5] Niggle is an artist, but an artist obsessed with detail (Hence the name "Niggle," since "niggling" is an old English word for fussing over details. Here the allegory with Tolkien is quite exact, as Tolkien was famous for his painstaking attention to detail, both in his fiction and in his scholarly work). What is interesting here, however, is that this obsessive attention to detail and to the painting of one leaf in particular leads Niggle out toward the whole tree and the landscape beyond: "Then all round the Tree, and behind it, through gaps in the leaves and boughs, a country began to open out; and there were glimpses of a forest marching over land, and of mountains tipped with snow."[6]

So, Niggle is an artist obsessed with his work. But Tolkien also writes that Niggle "was kind-hearted, in a way."[7] Niggle's kind-heartedness, however, is tested by his neighbor, Parish. Parish has a lame leg and a wife who is often ill; he therefore is constantly asking Niggle for help and favors. Parish is also a gardener who often gives Niggle unsolicited advice on (or criticism of) his own unkept garden, and who, to the great annoyance of Niggle, pays almost no attention to the great painting that Niggle is working on (for, although starting out with individual leaves, it comes to occupy a huge canvas covering almost an entire wall in his shed).

But time for Niggle presses on, and this itself becomes a burden and source of anxiety. Niggle is anxious that he will not finish his great painting before his needful journey. One day after a storm, the roof of his neighbor Parish's house is damaged; moreover, water from the damaged roof is pouring into the bedroom where Parish's wife is lying sick with a fever. Parish asks Niggle if he might be able to go call the doctor and leave a note with the builder (betraying in his demand little hint of gratitude). Although bothered by this request and annoyed that he is being taken away from his work, Niggle makes the journey into

---

5   *TL*, 94.
6   *TL*, 94.
7   *TL*, 93.

town to call the doctor and leave a note with the builder. But in doing so, he falls sick himself (while he learns, to his annoyance, that the illness of Parish's wife has turned out not to have been so serious after all). Niggle takes to bed and become deathly ill.

Soon Niggle's home is visited by an Inspector, who, dressed all in black, finds Niggle's preparation for the floods afflicting the region inadequate. Much to the distress of Niggle, the Inspector points to his painting as something that would be better used for patching up his neighbor's roof! But in the end, it doesn't matter, for a Driver comes to take Niggle away. He does so in such haste that he leaves Niggle no time to pack. The Driver takes Niggle to a train station, where he is quickly bundled onto a train wagon and the train runs "almost at once into a dark tunnel."[8]

Niggle then wakes up in a dim and deserted train station. There a Porter meets him, but, finding him unprepared and without having properly packed his bags, has him bundled off to a workhouse infirmary (a not very subtle allusion to purgatory).[9] There, Niggle is subjected to a rather unpleasant treatment: "The medicine they gave him was bitter. The officials and attendants were unfriendly, silent, and strict; he never saw anyone else, except a very severe doctor, who visited him occasionally. It was more like being in a prison than a hospital."[10] He is put to work at carpentry, "painting bare boards all one plain color." And he is never allowed outside, being kept in the dark for hours "to do some thinking." Where once Niggle took pleasure in painting all the intricate details of a leaf, he now is painting boards only of one color; where once he enjoyed the beauty of natural things—trees and leaves—he is now confined indoors. And yet, through this process of mortification, a slow transformation takes place within Niggle: what is transformed is Niggle's relation to and experience of time:

> At any rate, poor Niggle got no pleasure out of life, not what he had been used to call pleasure. He was certainly not amused. But it could not be denied that he began to have a feeling of—

---

[8] *TL,* 102.

[9] Indeed, Tolkien later referred to *Leaf by Niggle* as his "purgatorial story." See *Letters,* 195.

[10] *TL,* 103.

well, satisfaction: bread rather than jam. He could take up a task the moment one bell rang, and lay it aside promptly the moment the next one went, all tidy and ready to be continued at the right time. He got through quite a lot in a day, now; he finished small things off neatly. He had no "time of his own" (except alone in his bed-cell), and yet he was becoming master of his time; he began to know just what he could do with it. There was no sense of rush. He was quieter inside now, and at resting-time, he could really rest.[11]

In the workhouse infirmary, Niggle's existence becomes one not of mere pleasure but of deep satisfaction (of "bread rather than jam"—one thinks here of the contrary experience of Bilbo, when, after many years of possessing Sauron's Ring, he feels like butter "scraped over too much bread"[12]). But what is the source of this satisfaction? It is that Niggle is now no longer pressed for time. Indeed, the paradox is that he has all the time in the world because he no longer has "time of his own": precisely because he has no time of his own, he is master of his own time.

It therefore seems like no accident that after this transformation of Niggle's consciousness, he is put to hard labor digging and then finally to a period of complete rest. It is then that Niggle hears in the room next to where he is lying in bed a dialogue in which two voices discuss his fate. The First Voice is very severe and asks point blank, "What was the matter with Niggle?" The Second Voice, which Tolkien describes as "gentle, though it was not soft—it was a voice of authority, and sounded at once hopeful and sad," responds with arguments in Niggle's favor: "He was a painter by nature. In a minor way, of course; still, a Leaf by Niggle has a charm of its own. He took a great deal of pains with leaves, just for their own sake. But he never thought that that made him important. There is no note in the Records of his pretending, even to himself, that it excused his neglect of things ordered by the law."[13]

In the end, the First Voice defers to the Second Voice, who recommends now some gentle treatment. And when the First Voice

[11] *TL*, 104.
[12] *FR*, I, 1, 32.
[13] *TL*, 105–6.

finally addresses Niggle directly and asks him if he has anything to say, the first question he asks is about Parish, which greatly pleases the First Voice.

After a short rest, Niggle is again called by the Porter (who, this time, is friendly) and is shown to another railway station. Niggle takes the train, and after a while the train stops at a station leading out to a beautiful, sunny, green country. He sets out down the lane into this lush landscape and, suddenly, to his great surprise and joy, he finds the Tree that he had spent his whole life painting:

> Before him stood the Tree, his Tree, finished. If you could say that of a Tree that was alive, its leaves opening, its branches growing and bending in the wind that Niggle had so often felt or guessed, and had so often failed to catch. He gazed at the Tree, and slowly he lifted his arms and opened them wide.[14]

Upon seeing his Tree, Niggle exclaims: "'It's a gift!'... He was referring to his art, and also to the result; but he was using the word quite literally."[15] There is a rich ambiguity here: it could be the case that Niggle has glimpsed, however imperfectly, the "Platonic Form" of his Tree, which he has tried to reproduce in his painting; or it could be that it is Niggle's art that created the Tree, which was then brought into existence by a gratuitous act of grace. In any case, Niggle inspects his Tree further:

> He went on looking at the Tree. All the leaves he had ever laboured at were there, as he had imagined them rather than as he had made them; and there were others that had only budded in his mind, and many that might have budded, if only he had had the time. Nothing was written on them, they were just exquisite leaves, yet they were dated as clear as a calendar. Some of the most beautiful—and the most characteristic, the most perfect examples of the Niggle style—were seen to have been produced in collaboration with Mr. Parish: there was no other way of putting it.[16]

14 *TL*, 109–10.
15 *TL*, 110.
16 *TL*, 110.

Every leaf "is dated," preserved in its temporal uniqueness and individuality, and yet is seen now in relation to the living and timeless unity of the Tree. Indeed, the Tree is overflowing with life: birds are building in the Tree, singing, mating, hatching, growing wings, and flying away. In the distance, Mountains and a Forest loom. In other words, far from being limited and contained, static and lifeless, the eternal, real Tree opens out onto an infinity of vistas, of landscapes, worlds, and stories, which "did not seem to belong to the picture, or only as a link to something else, a glimpse through the trees of something different, a further stage: another picture."[17] The real Tree preserves every moment of time and yet transcends every one of them.

But the main thought that Niggle has is, "Where is Parish?": "'Of course!' he said. 'What I need is Parish. There are lots of things about earth, plants, and trees that he knows and I don't. This place cannot be left just as my private park. I need help and advice: I ought to have got it sooner.'"[18] And before long, Parish himself greets Niggle in this beautiful countryside. Soon the two are working together, but this time not only as close friends; each takes on what were once the characteristics of the other: "As they worked together, it became plain that Niggle was now the better of the two at ordering his time and getting things done. Oddly enough, it was Niggle who became absorbed in building and gardening, while Parish often wandered about looking at the trees, and especially at the Tree."[19]

After spending some time in exploring the country, Niggle and Parish meet a man whom they take to be a Shepherd. He offers to guide them into the distant country. Parish refuses, saying that he must wait for his wife. But before Niggle sets out, Parish asks the Shepherd the name of the country that he and Niggle are caring for, and he responds:

17   *TL*, 111.
18   *TL*, 111–12.
19   *TL*, 112. As Craig Bernthal observes concerning this passage, "Niggle has two important insights: that the art is not really just his, to own, but part of a larger creative process to be shared.... Second, this dependency implies that others can and probably must contribute. Help and advice are fundamental to creation, which cannot happen without them." Craig Bernthal, *Tolkien's Sacramental Vision: Discerning the Holy in Middle Earth* (Kettering, OH: Angelico Press, 2014), 78.

> "Don't you know? ... It is Niggle's Country. It is Niggle's Picture, or most of it: a little of it is now Parish's Garden." "Niggle's Picture!" said Parish in astonishment ... "But it did not look like this then, not *real*," said Parish. "No, it was only a glimpse then," said the man; "but you might have caught the glimpse, if you had ever thought it worth while to try."[20]

In the last section of the story a certain town counselor by the name of Tompkins discusses Niggle and his work with a local schoolmaster by the name of Atkins. Niggle, of course, by this time has long been gone. Atkins shows a certain appreciation of Niggle's artistic gifts, but Tompkins has nothing but contempt and scorn for Niggle's work: "There is plenty of scope for bold young men not afraid of new ideas and new methods. None of this old-fashioned stuff. Private day-dreaming. He could not have designed a telling poster to save his life."[21] Back in the supposedly real world, doctrines of utility and progress have no use for the inherent beauty and goodness of things; indeed, they deny that inherent beauty and goodness exist. Eventually, all of Niggle's work except for a lone painting of a leaf perishes. This lone painting languishes for some time in a quiet, forgotten corner of the local art museum before that museum too is destroyed in a fire.

But Niggle and Parish, in their new country that is also eminently and truly their own, are oblivious to their own earthly oblivion. They give

---

20 *TL*, 114–15. "In Niggle's life, there are two worlds: the inner, creative world, where he begins to paint his leaf and create the country that surrounds it; and the outer, 'real', world, full of what Niggle calls 'interruptions'—the neighbor who calls to ask a favor, the errands that must be run in town, the garden that requires tending.... Tolkien reveals that though the two worlds seem to oppose each other at times, both play a necessary role in what he saw as man's search for truth, or the state of perfection before the fall. In other words, a juxtaposition of reality and fantasy is necessary in mythmaking." Michaela Baltasar, "J. R. R. Tolkien: A Rediscovery of Myth," in *Tolkien and the Invention of Myth: A Reader*, ed. Jane Chance (Lexington, KY: University Press of Kentucky, 2004), 29. Thus, true art or sub-creation, far from being self-indulgent nonsense, is for Tolkien a glimpse into a wider and higher reality. Or it has a character that can best be described as "sacramental," i.e., that of a material reality charged with meaning.

21 *TL*, 116.

their region a name, Niggle's Parish in the Bay. And when the Second Voice tells the First Voice that the Porter now calls their station by that name, the First Voice asks: "What did they say?" The Second Voice responds: "They both laughed. Laughed—the Mountains rang with it!"[22]

Of Secret Fire and Mythopoeia

As was noted earlier, Tolkien stated several times that he disliked allegory, most famously in the foreword to the second edition of *The Lord of the Rings*: "But I cordially dislike allegory in all its manifestations, and always have done so since I grew old and wary enough to detect its presence. I much prefer history, true or feigned, with its varied applicability to the thought and experience of readers. I think that many confuse 'applicability' with 'allegory'; but the one resides in the freedom of the reader, and the other in the purposed domination of the author."[23] For Tolkien, a good story should stand on its own and not be a proxy for abstract ideas. Hence, Tolkien said that he preferred history, "true or feigned," insofar as it focuses on the concrete actions of individuals.

But as is usual with Tolkien, he modifies considerably his rather harsh condemnations of allegory elsewhere. For example, in his long, well-known letter to Milton Waldman, whom he was trying to persuade, after completing *The Lord of the Rings*, to publish that work together with *The Silmarillion*, Tolkien expresses, as usual, his "dislike" for "conscious and intentional allegory." Nevertheless, Tolkien goes on to say, "the more 'life' a story has the more readily will it be susceptible of allegorical interpretations: while the better a deliberate allegory is made the more nearly will it be acceptable just as a story."[24] This is an important concession: the more living a story is—the more it touches upon the most fundamental truths and desires of human existence—the more the story is susceptible to allegory. So in a way, the better the story is, the more life a story has, the more allegorical it becomes. It follows

---

22 *TL*, 118.
23 *FR*, xxiv.
24 *Letters*, 145.

that even our very lives, insofar as they are living stories, are allegories as well; they are, indeed, *living* allegories:

> What appreciative readers have got out of the work [*The Lord of the Rings*] or seen in it has seemed fair enough, even when I do not agree with it. Always excepting, of course, any "interpretations" in the mode of simple allegory: that is, the particular and the topical. In a larger sense, it is I suppose impossible to write any "story" that is not allegorical in proportion as it "comes to life"; since each of us is an allegory, embodying in a particular tale and clothed in the garments of time and place, universal truth and everlasting life.[25]

Each of our lives enacts, whether we know it or not, universal and eternal truths and values as well as "everlasting life." Indeed, our lives would be unintelligible otherwise, and art and story would be impossible. Therefore, to the degree a story manifests these universal truths and eternal life, it actually takes on more life and applicability. Hence, we have a paradox: the more a story is applicable to our lives in all their particularity, the more universal it becomes and the more it transcends our own individual lives. That is why Tolkien can remark in reaction to W. H. Auden's review of *The Return of the King*: "The story is not about JRRT at all, and is at no point an attempt to allegorize his experience of life—for that is what the objectifying of his subjective experience in a tale must mean, if anything."[26] The story is not about JRRT precisely because it reflects, not JRRT as "this man," but because it reflects the "universal" and the "eternal" in JRRT and in every man, woman, and rational creature.

We see this movement in "Leaf by Niggle." Niggle moves from a life where he is very short on time, isolated or even in conflict with his neighbor, Parish, and obsessed with painting single, ephemeral leaves. Yet, as he moves through death, purgatory, and purification, he finally moves into a realm of eternal and universal truth and value where the particular is not negated but affirmed and preserved in a higher mode

---

25 *Letters*, 212.
26 *Letters*, 239.

of life that is free of time. The leaves he painted in this life turn out to be expressions or manifestations of an actual, living Tree in a real and actual country in which every moment of his life is perceived in a living and dynamic now; and Niggle discovers in the end that this country could not have been discovered without the help of his neighbor, Parish, and that the enjoyment of his own country could not be attained without fellowship with him.[27] As Carson Halloway observes, "Leaf by Niggle" shows the act of sub-creation as an act of redemption: indeed, in the story, the sub-creator's art is shown to be more real than the primary world itself.[28]

Furthermore, as Tom Shippey notes concerning the ending of "Leaf by Niggle," there is a narrative bifurcation in the story: "The real world, the live world, dismisses and forgets Niggle: from that point of view, Niggle's story is a tragedy. The *other* real world, the world after death, turns to 'eucatastrophe.'"[29] Thus, "'Leaf by Niggle' ends as a comedy, even a 'divine comedy', on more levels than one. But while it looks forward to 'divine comedy' it incorporates and springs from a sense of earthly tragedy: failure, anxiety, and frustration."[30] Through art there is redemption of all earthly tragedy brought about by our fall into pride and lust for power and, through those vices, a greed for and grasping after time and a false immortality (or serial longevity). But art redeems, Tolkien emphasizes, not by creating an imaginary "never-never land" (or "utopia," which comes from the Greek for "no-place"), but to the contrary, by recovering what in our primary world is of an eternal nature and therefore of timeless value, especially within ourselves.

---

[27] Just to be clear, "Niggle's Parish" is not an allegory for heaven in Tolkien's story; rather it is another, higher stage of purgatory: "God is not there, and while the place is pure and good, with no stain of sin, it is not complete." Austin M. Freeman, *Tolkien Dogmatics: Theology through Mythology with the Maker of Middle-earth* (Bellingham, WA: Lexham Press, 2022), 334.

[28] Carson L. Holloway, "Redeeming Sub-Creation," in *The Ring and the Cross: Christianity and The Lord of the Rings*, ed. Paul E. Kerry (Madison, NJ: Fairleigh Dickinson University Press, 2011), 189–90.

[29] Tom Shippey, *J. R. R. Tolkien: Author of the Century* (New York: Houghton-Mifflin, 2000), 276.

[30] Shippey, *J. R. R. Tolkien: Author of the Century*, 277.

As is clear, Niggle stands for Tolkien, and it is evident from the story that Tolkien thought that his fiction was opening up to us an undiscovered country. Or better, that he was *recovering* for us a country that is already ours, just as "Niggle's Parish" is already Niggle's and Parish's. The point of all of Tolkien's fantasy seems to be to recover the world as creation: a world of beings that are inherently meaningful because created in wisdom and love by a wise and good Creator whose fundamental desire is to share that creation with us and which our sub-creative efforts only imitate and participate in:

> Those who believe in a personal God, Creator, do not think the Universe is in itself worshipful, though devoted study of it may be one of the ways of honouring Him. And while as living creatures we are (in part) within it and part of it, our ideas of God and ways of expressing them will be largely derived from contemplating the world about us. (Though there is also revelation both addressed to all men and to particular persons.)[31]

Thus, the secondary world that Tolkien creates is an enchanted and numinous one, in which the meaningfulness of all things shines out, for that is what the primary world is to eyes that have been cleansed from the effects of triteness and familiarity. But, Tolkien claims, he is able to achieve this recovery only by cutting out any overt and obvious references to anything like religion in our own primary world. Thus, in a letter to a Jesuit friend who remarked to Tolkien how much Catholic imagery there is in *The Lord of the Rings*, he responds:

> *The Lord of the Rings* is of course a fundamentally religious and Catholic work; unconsciously so at first, but consciously in the revision. That is why I have not put in, or have cut out, practically all references to anything like "religion," to cults or practices, in the imaginary world. For the religious element is absorbed into the story and the symbolism.[32]

---

31 *Letters*, 400.
32 *Letters*, 172.

The reasons that Tolkien gives for omitting overt references to Christianity I shall examine closely in the next chapter; but suffice it to say here that the whole goal of his fiction, as Tolkien sees it, is precisely to "absorb" the "religious element"—and really any meaningful element—into the story and into the world it represents. The whole goal of Middle-earth is to recover for us a sense and understanding of our own primary world as a meaningful creative act. His fiction, Tolkien seems to be saying, is not really fiction, but is a revelation of a world that is just as real as, if not more real than, our primary world. This real world is simply our own world viewed with new and fresh eyes; the secondary world of fantasy is the *truth* of the primary world.

Thus, at the heart of every genuine and living creative work of art is a living principle, what Tolkien calls the "Secret Fire" or "Flame Imperishable." This refers to the principle or spark that not only gives a story life, but does so because it imitates and even participates in the principle or spark that gives life and intelligibility to all that is living and meaningful in our primary world. As Tolkien remarks concerning the Flame Imperishable in his posthumously published book, *Morgoth's Ring*, the relation of the Creator to his creation is exactly analogous to that of the author with the product of his art:

> This [the "Flame Imperishable"] appears to mean the Creative activity of Eru (in some sense distinct from or within Him), by which things could be given a "real" and independent (though derivative and created) existence. The Flame Imperishable is sent out from Eru, to dwell in the heart of the world, and the world then Is, on the same plane as the Ainur, and they can enter into it. But this is not, of course, the same as the re-entry of Eru to defeat Melkor. It refers rather to the mystery of "authorship," by which the author, while remaining "outside" and independent of his work, also "indwells" in it, on its derivative plane, below that of his own being, as the source and guarantee of its being.[33]

---

[33] *MR*, 345.

The more life a story has, then, the more it reflects and *derives its own life from* the life within creation, which, of course, derives its narrative or temporal life from the eternal life of its author or creator. For, as Tolkien here notes, his fiction reflects in a sense the "mystery of 'authorship,'" which itself reflects the mystery of being: that all beings are inherently meaningful, but the source of their meaning also lies outside them, a paradox that can only be understood by analogy with a story where the author is both everywhere in the story giving it shape, structure, and meaning, but also being totally outside it as well, since he cannot—ordinarily—be a character within the story.[34] In other words, as Tolkien asserted in a letter written toward the end of his life to a schoolgirl who asked him about the meaning of life, the purpose of art is to allow all creatures to express their love of the one who created them:

> So it may be said that the chief purpose of life, for any one of us, is to increase according to our capacity our knowledge of God by all the means we have, and to be moved by it to praise and thanks. To do as we say in the *Gloria in Excelsis*: Laudamus te, benedicimus te, adoramus te, glorificamus te, gratias agimus tibi propter magnam gloriam tuam.... And in moments of exaltation, we may call on all created things to join in our chorus, speaking on their behalf, as is done in Psalm 148, and in The Song of the Three Children in Daniel II. PRAISE THE LORD ... all mountains and hills, all orchards and forests, all things that creep and birds on the wing.[35]

---

34 This living principle or Secret Fire Tolkien admitted, when pressed, was indeed the Holy Spirit, the person of the divine Trinity who is the source of life and inspiration within creation. Bradley J. Birzer, *J. R. R. Tolkien's Sanctifying Myth: Understanding Middle-earth* (Wilmington, DE: ISI Books, 2003), 62. Austin Freeman, however, offers caution here: the Secret Fire in Tolkien's legendarium is not a person and thus it cannot be identified with the Holy Spirit so neatly. Freeman, *Tolkien Dogmatics*, 34–36. This is probably as good a place as any to alert the reader to the fact that Tolkien had the habit of making strong, categorical statements about his work or his intentions, which he later qualified or modified considerably elsewhere. It is therefore always prudent not to take Tolkien's statements about his work immediately and uncritically at face value.

35 *Letters*, 400.

The essential purpose of all art, then, is to allow creatures themselves to speak on their own behalf the praise of their Creator and to tell in their own words the story of salvation from evil—a story in which they are essential characters and in which and from which our own stories acquire significance and meaning. In the end, the distinctions between primary and secondary world, self and world, life and allegory, particular and universal are transcended in good art. But this transcendence is predicated upon and presupposes a primal distinction: that between creature and creator, creation and sub-creation, the story and the mind of the author.

Tolkien gave particular expression to these ideas in his didactic poem "Mythopoeia," which he wrote in the early 1930s, soon after the conversion to Christianity of his friend C. S. Lewis. The poem summarizes the arguments that Tolkien used during a long conversation that he and a fellow friend, Hugo Dyson, had with Lewis in September of 1931—a conversation that was the catalyst for the latter's conversion. Its arguments are against a certain Misomythus's ("Hater of Myth's") materialist-scientific view of the world. It is an attempt to summarize, appropriately enough in poetic form, the case for the truth of myth and of Christianity as true myth. It also gives us, in many ways, the key to his story "Leaf by Niggle."[36] In essence, its argument is that human beings are by nature myth-making animals (hence, the word "mythopoeia"); it follows that nature, or even existence itself, is a matter of myth-making: that the fabric of reality, the structure of being itself, is an intelligible story made by a creative intelligence: "Tolkien puts the discussion of myth squarely within the theological context of a doctrine of creation. If the natural world demonstrated the presence of God, it was quite logical to expect myths, ancestral tales about the world, to also reflect the presence of the Creator of the world and of stories."[37]

---

36 "'Leaf by Niggle' represents the same perspective on myth as Tolkien's 'Mythopoeia'. It is both a springboard into fantasy and the end result of fantasy." Yannick Imbert, *From Imagination to Faërie: Tolkien's Thomist Fantasy* (Eugene, OR: Pickwick Publications, 2022), 174–75.

37 Imbert goes on to say, "myth-making is testimony, not to an evolutionary dimension of human thought but to an intrinsic quality of human beings.... This is precisely why, continues Philomythus, naming is a decidedly mythic thing: 'trees

It is significant, I think, that Tolkien begins "Mythopoeia" with trees: "Yet trees are not 'trees' until so named and seen— / and never were so named, till those had been / who speech's involuted breath unfurled, / faint echo and dim picture of the world."[38] That trees—or indeed any other things—truly are what they are is only due to language; and thus things and language are co-eval. Language is not, as most moderns would have it, an arbitrary layering of sense on meaningless sensations: words stir in the mind a deep feeling of kinship with the life and death of trees, beasts, and stars, from which the human mind, over time, separates out meaning and thing: "digging the foreknown from experience / and panning the vein of spirit out of sense."[39] But, Tolkien's poem continues, the modern mind separates sense from thing so entirely that "There is no firmament, / only a void, unless a jewelled tent / myth-woven and elf-patterned; and no earth, / unless the mother's womb whence all have birth."[40] A tree is not a tree as such without language; only through language can it be what it truly is. But, by the same token, language cannot exist, cannot have anything to express or enunciate, without the material tree, the thing itself. Language and things are entwined at their roots.

The fashioning of myth and fantasy, then, is not mere idle wish fulfillment to defeat ugly fact: "All wishes are not idle, nor in vain / fulfillment we devise—for pain is pain, / nor for itself to be desired, but ill; / or else to strive or to subdue the will / alike were graceless; and of Evil this / alone is deadly certain: Evil is."[41] The fashioning of myth and fantasy responds to a natural and necessary need to recover the primal meanings of things and of the linguistic world in which those meanings are revealed. And far from being a denial of evil, myth and fantasy make it their primary theme, demonstrating the hard and irreducible reality of evil, but also making sense of it in the larger

---

are not trees until so named and seen'. Naming, describing the world, not always as it is seen, but as it is: that is the calling of the myth-maker." Imbert, *From Imagination to Faërie*, 131.

38 *TL*, 86.
39 *TL*, 86.
40 *TL*, 87.
41 *TL*, 88.

meaning of things themselves. Indeed, myth-making presupposes evil and pain as its motivating drive to recover the reality of things. This recovery, Tolkien continues, is even more urgent in our age, dominated as it is by the Machine:

> Blessed are the legend-makers with their rhyme
> of things not found within recorded time.
> It is not they that have forgot the Night,
> or bid us flee to organized delight,
> in lotus-isles of economic bliss
> forswearing souls to gain a Circe-kiss
> (and counterfeit at that, machine-produced,
> bogus seduction of the twice-seduced).[42]

Indeed, if "escapism," with all of its negative connotations, can be applied to anything, it can be applied most appropriately to the Machine and modern life, whose only goals are comfort, security, and pleasure and thus separation from, even isolation from, the reality of the world (which includes evil). By contrast, the myth-maker, by taking evil deadly seriously, does not retreat in despair ("They have seen Death and ultimate defeat, / and yet they would not in despair retreat."[43]), for they see that things have in themselves a sense or direction, whereas modern men and women only have progress—to nowhere: "I will not walk with your progressive apes, / erect and sapient. Before them gapes / the dark abyss to which their progress tends."[44] For ultimately, Tolkien argues, "Salvation changes not, nor yet destroys, / garden nor gardener, children nor their toys. / Evil it will not see, for evil lies / not in God's picture but in crooked eyes, / not in the source but in malicious choice, / and not in sound but in the tuneless voice."[45] The crooked eyes that Tolkien refers to here—the eyes that cannot see the fundamental goodness, beauty, and meaningfulness of the world—are ones that have separated the realm of language and meaning from reality.

42 *TL*, 88.
43 *TL*, 88.
44 *TL*, 89.
45 *TL*, 90.

Why Another Book on Tolkien?

The works of Tolkien have only grown in popularity over the years, especially after the release and almost ecstatic reception of Peter Jackson's film adaptations of *The Lord of the Rings* in 2001, 2002, and 2003. And the number of books about Tolkien and his work has only grown exponentially since. So why write (and read) another book on Tolkien? I can give three reasons.

First, to read Tolkien is to find an almost limitless applicability to the many and various problems and questions that contemporary men and women face and raise. And as the human condition changes and faces new problems and challenges, the scope for the applicability of Tolkien's fiction changes and even expands accordingly. Thus, a book on Tolkien's work is by definition always timely.[46]

Second, there has been something of a renaissance in recent years of books and articles studying the philosophical and theological ideas that underlie Tolkien's fantasy,[47] not to mention the profound influence Tolkien's Catholic faith had on the composition and development of his literary work.[48] In particular, recent studies have shown the great

---

[46] It should also be noted that, although bits and pieces of Tolkien's manuscripts continue to be published from time to time (most recently, for example, *The Nature of Middle-earth* in 2021), the great bulk of his previously unpublished writings are now easily available in editions meticulously edited by his son, Christopher. Books on Tolkien and his *oeuvre* can now, therefore, take full advantage of the almost-complete availability of his writings related to his Middle-earth legendarium.

[47] Most notably, Craig Bernthal, *Tolkien's Sacramental Vision*; Bradley Birzer, *J. R. R. Tolkien's Sanctifying Myth*; Stratford Caldecott, *The Power of the Ring: The Spiritual Vision Behind* The Lord of the Rings *and* The Hobbit (New York: Crossroad Publishing, 2012); Matthew Dickerson, *A Hobbit Journey: Discovering the Enchantment of J. R. R. Tolkien's Middle-earth* (Grand Rapids, MI: Brazos Press, 2012); Peter Kreeft, *The Philosophy of Tolkien: The Worldview Behind* The Lord of the Rings (San Francisco: Ignatius Press, 2005); Joseph Pearce, *Tolkien, Man and Myth: A Literary Life* (San Francisco: Ignatius Press, 1998); and Elizabeth A. Whittingham, *The Evolution of Tolkien's Mythology: A Study of the History of Middle-earth* (Jefferson, NC: MacFarland, 2008).

[48] Holly Ordway recounts in fascinating detail the depth and strength of

affinity between the worldview of Tolkien's fantasy and various strands of medieval philosophy, above all Christian Neoplatonism,[49] but also the philosophy of Thomas Aquinas and Thomism.[50] And these studies themselves follow in the wake of much scholarship examining the important and, in some cases, decisive role that Tolkien's work as a scholar of medieval literature played in the development and writing of his fiction.[51] All these works have contributed to a much deeper, more nuanced understanding of the philosophical and theological riches that underlie much of Tolkien's fiction.

Tolkien's commitment to his Catholic faith in her book *Tolkien's Faith: A Spiritual Biography* (Elk Grove Village, IL: Word on Fire Academic, 2023).

49 In particular, see Verlyn Flieger, *Splintered Light: Logos and Language in Tolkien's World*, rev. ed. (Kent: Kent State University Press, 2002); Mary Carman Rose, "The Christian Platonism of C. S. Lewis, J. R. R. Tolkien and Charles Williams," in *Neoplatonism and Christian Thought*, ed. Dominic J. O'Meara (Albany, NY: SUNY Press, 1982), 203–12; John Houghton, "Augustine in the Cottage of Lost Play: The *Ainulindalë* as Asterisk Cosmogony," in *Tolkien the Medievalist*, ed. Jane Chance (New York: Routledge, 2003), 171–82; and most recently, Michael John Halsall, *Creation and Beauty in Tolkien's Catholic Vision: A Study in the Influence of Neoplatonism in J. R. R. Tolkien's Philosophy of Life as "Being and Gift"* (Eugene, OR: Pickwick Publications, 2020). Rose identifies these Neoplatonic elements as consisting in a commitment to the reality and availability of supersensory aspects of creation, to modes of our coming to know these aspects of creation, and to the ideal copresence of truth, beauty, and goodness in all aspects of creation: "It is the belief that the mundane world is not man's true home and that during life in this world the hope for the next life provides a steadying, leavening influence." Rose, "Christian Platonism," 210. Halsall also identifies the strong influence of Boethius's *Consolation of Philosophy* on the metaphysics of Middle-earth and, even more interestingly, the possible influence of the early medieval Neoplatonic Irish philosopher, John Scotus Eriugena (flourished early to mid-ninth century) on Tolkien's metaphysical imagination, in particular the notion of a Celtic "Otherworld," to which Eriugena gives philosophical expression and support (we'll have more to say of this notion later). Unfortunately, as Halsall admits, we have no solid evidence that Tolkien read the works of Eriugena directly.

50 See Jonathan S. McIntosh, *The Flame Imperishable: Tolkien, St. Thomas, and the Metaphysics of Faërie* (Kettering, OH: Angelico Press, 2017). See also the book cited earlier by Yannick Imbert, *From Imagination to Faerie: Tolkien's Thomist Fantasy*.

51 See Jane Chance, ed., *Tolkien the Medievalist* (New York: Routledge, 2003).

There is another stream of Tolkien criticism that we may broadly call "critical" or "postmodern" insofar as it analyzes Tolkien's fiction in terms of the structures of power and material interests inherent in language and the literary tradition. Such criticism of Tolkien is not as foreign to his intentions and interests as one might at first think. As Peter Candler remarks, Tolkien shared with the Postmodernists the contention that "philology (understood broadly as 'the love for words') returns one to the inescapably linguistic character of all revelation and truth," even if, for Tolkien, this also points "to a certain conception of the human being as fundamentally sacramental in its created participation in the life of the Trinity."[52] As Jane Chance remarks in her book on the importance of power, both moral and political, in Tolkien's fantasy: "The power of truth and its liberation from hegemony are indeed the great themes of *Rings*."[53] Holly Ordway has demonstrated that Tolkien was not the musty fuddy-duddy that Humphrey Carpenter's popular biography portrays, but a man deeply engaged with and knowledgeable of modernity, particularly modern fiction, even if he was highly critical of it as well.[54] Nevertheless, postmodern criticism often makes too many assumptions that, Tolkien asserts either explicitly (in his letters) or implicitly (in his fiction), are dubious if not false.[55] In particular

---

[52] Peter M. Candler, Jr., "Tolkien or Nietzsche; Philology and Nihilism" in *Tolkien among the Moderns*, ed. Ralph C. Wood (Notre Dame, IN: University of Notre Dame Press, 2015), 97.

[53] Jane Chance, *The Lord of the Rings: The Mythology of Power* (New York: Twayne Publishers, 1992), 21.

[54] This is also the main thesis of Tom Shippey's book *J. R. R. Tolkien: Author of the Century*. Shippey demonstrates that Tolkien, for all his medievalism and old-fashioned religious and philosophical views, engaged deeply and seriously with peculiarly twentieth-century questions, problems, and political-philosophical movements in his fiction.

[55] I am thinking here in particular of attempts, pervasive now in academia and in literary criticism, to interpret literary works almost exclusively through the lens of power relations, be they of race, gender, or sexuality. This is not to say these topics are not, in themselves, worthy of serious consideration: Tolkien himself talks surprisingly frequently in his letters about sex and gender, and we will have occasion to discuss both in the pages that follow. Moreover, ideas about race, ethnicity, and, in particular, racial memory were an important, if previously often

postmodernity's privileging of temporality over eternity as well as of power relationships over seemingly everything else is, for Tolkien, at the heart of the contemporary spiritual malaise and nihilism that his fantasy specifically addresses and combats. In a sense, then, this book brings together two significant streams of contemporary scholarship on Tolkien, showing how, through his fantasy, the great Oxford don used medieval philosophical, theological, and literary ideas and techniques to address thoroughly modern and postmodern problems in a modern and even postmodern way—all while telling a ripping good story.

Finally, most books on Tolkien mention the importance of recovery for understanding Tolkien's work, but few if any note and develop its centrality to Tolkien's work in any detail. Recovery, Tolkien writes, is a "regaining of a clear view. I do not say 'seeing as they are' and involve myself with the philosophers, though I might venture to say 'seeing things as we are (or were) meant to see them'—as things apart from ourselves. We need, in any case, to clear our windows; so that the things seen clearly may be freed from the drab blur of triteness or familiarity—from possessiveness."[56] So, there is a paradoxical sense in which this book is not about Tolkien's work at all but rather about the timeless truths about ourselves, creation, and its Creator that his work reveals and opens up. This is the third reason for reading this book.

Tolkien's fiction works as a sort of phenomenology—a school of philosophy exactly contemporary to Tolkien's own professional career that sought to return human consciousness to the most basic and primal layers of experience by bracketing out the conceptual abstractions that overlay and often obscure these layers. By returning us to the primal givenness of being, the phenomenologists argued, we return to an experience of what things truly are, i.e., being as it primally

---

overlooked, part of Tolkien's worldview. A sober and balanced study of Tolkien's ideas on this subject can be found in Dimitra Fimi, *Tolkien, Race and Cultural History: From Faeries to Hobbits* (London: Palgrave Macmillan, 2010). Where things go wrong, as they often do, in such studies is when they beg the question. In other words, they assume as true an interpretive framework that Tolkien's work itself is trying to demonstrate as false—that we can reduce all natural and social phenomena to mere power relations.

56 *TL*, 58.

and immediately presents itself to us. Phenomenology, therefore, is not philosophy in the usual sense: it seeks to go beyond the analysis of ideas to the primal experience upon which these ideas are founded and from which they derive their truth and meaning. But again, the most profound philosophers who worked well before or outside of phenomenology, from Plato to Pascal to Wittgenstein, all say the same thing: the end of philosophy is to go beyond philosophy and actually to *see* the truth of things and, in particular, to see them as a gift. Is it any accident that Plato's dialogues often end in the recounting of a myth? Tolkien, like Plato, realized that the deepest truths cannot be expressed and certainly cannot be experienced or seen in abstract formulae or syllogisms, but only in story. It is also for this reason we can see why Tolkien cut out, as he mentioned in the letter cited above, any overt references to Christianity or Catholicism in his work. Such references would overlay and thus obscure a recovery whereby the reader may see the world in its primal givenness with fresh eyes and experience the pure gratuitous gift that being is. Thus, as Tolkien himself remarks above, he thought of himself as doing something deeper than philosophy defined merely as the systematic and rigorous examination of concepts and ideas. Tolkien was working his way to a deeper, more comprehensive way of *seeing* the world—to a recovery of things as they are, in other words.[57]

Nevertheless, this book shows that there is an internal logic to recovery in Tolkien's works, one that can almost be termed a "science" (in the medieval sense of a body of knowledge ordered to and by first principles). Thus, the recovery of hope, an explicit goal that Tolkien claims for his writing, presupposes a recovery of eternity; the recovery of eternity presupposes the recovery of virtue; the recovery of virtue, that of fellowship; that of fellowship, a recovery of nature; and the recovery of nature presupposes a recovery of language, the

---

57 "The world and reason are not problematic; rather we say, if one may speak such, that they are mysterious. But this mystery defines them; it is not a question of dissipating it by some 'solution'—it falls short of solutions. True philosophy is relearning how to see the world, and in this sense a story well-told can manifest the world with as much 'depth' as a philosophical treatise." Maurice Merleau-Ponty, *Phénoménologie de la perception* (Paris: Editions Gallimard, 1945), xvi. NB: All translations are the author's unless otherwise noted.

most primal recovery of all, for it is the recovery of the indissoluble unity of meaning and being at the root of all true and fundamental human knowing. To Tolkien, the philologist, language and reality are phenomenologically inseparable.

Among these various "recoveries" the recovery of eternity is for Tolkien the culmination and perfection of any genuine recovery of the world. Tolkien repeatedly asserted that time, death, and immortality were at the center of his work. Reflections on time and intimations of eternity run as a red thread throughout Tolkien's books, because they are the essential basis for the hope and consolation that is the ultimate aim and fulfillment of fantasy. Again, however, little attention has been paid to the central importance of time and eternity in Tolkien's work.[58] As Tom Shippey has pointed out, Tolkien's works (and *The Lord of the Rings* in particular) are, despite their medievalism and the clear influence upon them of the medieval literature that Tolkien loved, profoundly modern in the themes they address and how they address them, which is also to say that they are timeless. This is not a contradiction, for a recovery of the past is a necessary condition for a recovery of the eternal life, the "Secret Fire," latent within our world.

---

58 Verlyn Flieger published some years ago a fascinating and important book on the notion of time in Tolkien's work [Verlyn Flieger, *A Question of Time: J. R. R. Tolkien's Road to Faerie* (Kent: Kent State University Press, 1997)], but her study concentrates almost exclusively on Tolkien's speculations on the possibility of time travel through dreams or ancestral memory and the extensive scientific literature that influenced or may have influenced Tolkien. It does not, curiously, talk about the importance of eternity or the crucial difference for him between time and eternity.

CHAPTER ONE

Creation, Sub-creation, and Recovery

Tolkien's famous essay "On Fairy-Stories," where he introduces the terms "sub-creation" and "recovery," seems to have been the product of a long gestation and shows signs of many rewrites.[1] "On Fairy-Stories," therefore, is long, meandering, and sometimes hard to follow, making a concise yet comprehensive and accurate account of it difficult. Yet, the

---

1   Thomas Honegger, "Academic Writings," in *A Companion to J. R. R. Tolkien*, ed. Stuart Lee (Hoboken, NJ: Wiley-Blackwell Publishing, 2020), 37. Tolkien wrote and delivered this essay just before World War II broke out, precisely at the time when he had just published *The Hobbit* (in 1937) and was working on the first chapters of what would become *The Lord of the Rings*. In other words, he composed it precisely at the time when he had either completed or was just starting his two great masterworks. The essay was later published after the war, in a volume dedicated to Charles Williams; however, this volume quickly went out of print and it seems to have been read by few people prior to the fame generated by *The Lord of the Rings*. Honegger, "Academic Writings," 35.

main ideas are simple enough, and it well rewards the reader with deep insights into Tolkien's fiction and what he was trying to do, especially what he was trying to recover for the reader through sub-creation.

The Nature and Function of Fairy-stories

Tolkien takes the series of anthologies (denoted by the colors of their covers) of fairy-stories published in the late nineteenth century by Andrew Lang as typical of the various errors and misunderstandings that proliferated about fairy-stories in the late Victorian period and which it was one of the goals of his essay to correct.[2] First and foremost, Tolkien objects to the popular notion that fairy-stories are primarily meant for children; that what makes a fairy-story a fairy-story is the presence in it of diminutive supernatural beings (or "fairies"); and that these stories inhabit a sort of primitive dream world that we modern men and women have outgrown (making them again stories really only fit for children).

First and foremost, fairy-stories, Tolkien insists, are for adults: he questions whether children even have any special liking or attraction to fairy-stories. In his own experience, having been, of course, a child himself and also the father of four children in turn, he has found that children do not have a special taste for make-believe, but rather want to know whether what they are reading or hearing is *real* or *true*. Tolkien mentions that as a child he was far more interested in subjects like history, language, astronomy, and botany than in so-called "fairy tales." Children, he asserts, have a far greater desire to know what is real and true than adults—especially modern adults—give them credit for. This indicates that modern adaptations of ancient fairy-stories often miss the mark with children, because they assume that fairy-stories must be about make-believe and not about realty and truth.

---

   2   Of course, the focus on Andrew Lang is most obviously explained by the fact that "On Fairy-stories" was given by Tolkien as part of the Andrew Lang series on folklore at the University of St. Andrews, but that did not, in characteristic Tolkien fashion, prevent him from criticizing the work of the man in whose honor the lectures were named.

The second error Tolkien sees in popular modern adaptations of old fairy-stories and the way they are understood is that previous generations, especially the Victorians, assumed that what makes these stories fairy-stories is the presence of certain kinds of beings (fairies—usually, as was mentioned above, of a diminutive and delicate nature). Tolkien argues, however, that what gives a successful fairy-story its unique charm and power is the entire setting of the story itself—the world in which it takes place. The world of a good or successful fairy-story is a perilous realm in which strange (though not absurd) things can and do happen. In such a setting, therefore, fairies are completely natural, not supernatural,[3] and, indeed, it is even possible to have a genuine fairy-story without any fairies in it at all: "Faerie contains many things besides elves and fays, and besides dwarfs, witches, trolls, giants, or dragons: it holds the seas, the sun, the moon, the sky; and the earth, and all things that are in it: tree and bird, water and stone, wine and bread, and ourselves, mortal men, when we are enchanted."[4] In a good fairy-story, the reader steps into another world that yet has all the reality of this world. That is, what the reader gets is a heightened experience of his own primary world, in the sense that he gains a greater awareness of the primal elements, inanimate, animate, and rational, that make up the world in which we live.

Thus, if there is any magic in fairy-stories, it comes primarily not from a technique used by characters in the story (usually called by us "magic"), but from the character of the world itself that contains the characters: "Faerie itself may perhaps most nearly be translated by Magic—but it is magic of a peculiar mood and power, at the furthest pole from the vulgar devices of the laborious, scientific, magician. There is one proviso: if there is any satire present in the tale, one thing must not be made fun of, the magic itself."[5] Tolkien finds the story of *Sir Gawain and the Green Knight* exemplary in this respect: there is no use of spells and magical effects in the story; instead the story exudes a magical air in which strange things can and do happen and yet which

---

3   *TL*, 4–5.
4   *TL*, 9.
5   *TL*, 10–11.

appear perfectly natural and consistent within the world in which they take place. This is because magic in the realm of Faerie is not simply a plot device or an embellishment of the story, but a way of getting at the fundamental goal of fairy-stories themselves:

> The magic of Faerie is not an end in itself, its virtue is in its operations: among these are the satisfaction of certain primordial human desires. One of these desires is to survey the depths of space and time. Another is (as will be seen) to hold communion with other living things. A story may thus deal with the satisfaction of these desires, with or without the operation of either machine or magic, and in proportion as it succeeds it will approach the quality and have the flavour of fairy-story.[6]

"To survey the depths of space and time" and "to hold communion with other living things" are two of the fundamental purposes of fairy-stories, and, Tolkien adds, these two goals may be accomplished without "the operation of either machine or magic." This latter comment is significant: for Tolkien, what makes a fairy-story a fairy-story is not the presence of discrete mechanisms or events within the story, but the setting and structure of the story itself. Its primary objective is to survey the "depths of space and time," which is to say, to pitch us into a renewed sense of the strangeness and mysteriousness of our world. And deeply connected with this is the desire to commune with other living things: to recover a sense of the world not only as vibrating with life but also as something living or expressive of a deep kinship or fellowship with all beings (and their Creator).

Hence, as we shall see in more detail in the next section, the fairy-story creates a secondary world of mysterious strangeness in order to recover a sense of the primary world—the world we live in day by day—as also, in its essence, mysterious and strange. This explains why Tolkien is not afraid in his essay to criticize not just Victorian misunderstandings of what fairy-stories are about, but the actual fairy-stories that have come down to us from the Middle Ages. Tolkien notes his dissatisfaction with the myths, legend, epics of his native

6 *TL*, 13.

country. In particular, the Arthurian legends are too explicitly Christian, and for him, this is "fatal"[7]: it allows the primary world of history to impinge upon the secondary world of fantasy, which, if it is to stand as a secondary world, must not make any direct or explicit references to the primary world. Tolkien is also critical of the dream mechanism found in some works of medieval literature (such as *The Pearl*), by which the visitor to Faerie finds that it was all only a dream—a mechanism that destroys that sense of reality that a really good fairy-story must create and sustain.[8] Nor is communion with other living things satisfied by beast fables, which are thus not really fairy-stories at all: their setting is all too firmly ensconced in the primary world, with animals simply taking the roles of human characters or agents.

So what makes a fairy-story a fairy-story for Tolkien? For him, it is an act of sub-creation in which the author creates a new and self-standing world that is yet a mirror of our own. As such, we can look into this sub-created world and see our own primary world reflected back to us in all of its mystery and strangeness. What makes sub-creation possible is human language:

> The incarnate mind, the tongue, and the tale are in our world coeval. The human mind, endowed with the powers of generalization and abstraction, sees not only *green-grass*, discriminating it from other things (and finding it fair to look upon), but sees that it is *green* as well as being *grass*. But how powerful, how stimulating to the very faculty that produced it, was the invention of the adjective: no spell or incantation in Faerie is more potent. And that is not surprising: such

---

[7] "Myth and fairy-story must, as all art, reflect and contain in solution elements of moral and religious truth (or error), but not explicit, not in the known form of the primary 'real' world. (I am speaking, of course, of our present situation, not of ancient pagan, pre-Christian days. And I will not repeat what I tried to say in my essay ["On Fairy-stories"], which you read.)" *Letters*, 144.

[8] Though, as we shall see later, Tolkien's attitude toward dreams and the dream mechanism was not as simple and straightforward as simple rejection, since his "The Lost Road" and "The Notion Club Papers," both unpublished during his lifetime, seem to suggest otherwise.

incantations might indeed be said to be only another view of adjectives, a part of speech in a mythical grammar. The mind that thought of *light, heavy, grey, yellow, still, swift*, also conceived of magic that would make heavy things light and able to fly, turn grey lead into yellow gold, and the still rock into swift water.[9]

Our mind is incarnate, Tolkien notes, and therefore it is inseparable from the tongue (not "language"—an abstraction) and the tale. The tongue is inevitably and essentially mixed up with things insofar as it is only through the incarnate mind and the tongue that things are revealed as what they are. Even more so, with this revelation, our incarnate mind has a quasi-magical power to rearrange both words and things into a new creation: "But in such 'fantasy', as it is called, new form is made; Faerie begins; Man becomes a sub-creator."[10] Through the creative use of language, the human mind not only creates a secondary world, but by doing so realizes that this is possible only because the primary world is made according to the same principles as the secondary world. In doing so, it reveals that language is not just incidental to the world but a constituent part of it.

I shall treat of the relation of language to reality and of both to fantasy in much more detail in chapter 3, but for now I would simply draw the reader's attention to Tolkien's strong rejection of the notion, popular among the Victorians, that myths in general and nature myths in particular are just a primitive form of natural science. To assert this, Tolkien argues, is to miss completely what is going on in these stories and why human beings are bothering to tell them. Human beings tell these stories not to explain natural phenomena, as least not primarily; they tell them in order to understand their place in the world and the world's place in human life and action. Personification in old myths is not, Tolkien argues, a primitive projection of human consciousness onto dead and sterile things, but rather an expression of deep sympathy with the inner significance of things not only for human beings but in themselves.[11] Things and the language (or tongue) that reveals them for

9   *TL*, 22.
10 *TL*, 23.
11 "Then these natural objects can only be arrayed with a personal

what they are are all intertwined and inextricable. Thus, in addressing the notion that, say, the god Thor is just the personification of thunder or divinization of an enraged farmer, Tolkien asserts: "It is more reasonable to suppose that the farmer popped up in the very moment when Thunder got a voice and face; that there was a distant growl of thunder in the hills every time a story-teller heard a farmer in a rage."[12] The same goes, *mutatis mutandis*, for the relation of myth to history: myths are not just primitive attempts to explain or memorialize real historical events; rather, Tolkien argues, it would be more accurate to say that historical figures are added to story than that stories are simply mythical history: "History often resembles 'Myth', because they are both ultimately of the same stuff. If indeed Ingeld and Freawaru never lived, or at least never loved, then it is ultimately from nameless man and woman that they get their tale, or rather into whose tale they have entered."[13] Real historical events are as much shaped by the stories by which and within which human beings understand themselves as these stories are shaped by historical events. Again, both myth and history point to a primal unity of world and consciousness that only comes to the fore in the act of sub-creating a world of one's own.

Thus, Tolkien asserts, fairy-stories manifest three faces: the mystical toward the supernatural, the magical toward nature, and the mirror of scorn and pity toward man. "The essential face of Faerie is the middle one, the Magical,"[14] he says. The magical face of Faerie draws the other two, the mystical and the mirror of scorn and pity, together: the magical in nature points to a supernatural source, just as it shows the wretchedness of humanity's fall from any deep or sustained communion with other living things (as exemplified in the medieval *Mirour de l'Omme*). Nevertheless, through the creative imagination,[15] rooted in the nature

---

significance and glory by a gift, the gift of a person, of a man. Personality can only be derived from a person." *TL*, 24.

12 *TL*, 25.
13 *TL*, 30.
14 *TL*, 26.
15 The Romantic doctrine of the creative imagination is thus an important influence on Tolkien's thinking about the truth and power of myth and fairy-stories: "the Fancy is the image-making faculty, what Coleridge called

and power of language, human beings have the power to recover this primal unity of incarnate mind, tongue, and world through the act of sub-creation.

Sub-creation and Recovery

Given what we have seen of Tolkien's argument so far, we can now turn to the final sections of his essay, where he lays out the fundamental goals of fairy-stories. These are recovery, escape, and consolation.

Recovery for Tolkien is the essential precondition in fairy-stories for achieving the other two goals of escape and consolation; therefore, it enjoys a preeminent place in the argument. As we saw in the previous section, most understandings of fairy-stories seemed to miss this point entirely, i.e., that fairy-stories are essentially about recovery of the world, of the one who experiences the world, and, finally, of the world's Creator. Indeed, these misunderstandings seem to assert the opposite: that myths and fairy-stories are really about natural phenomena or historical events; that they recover nothing, but rather overlay the real story of science or history with a patina of mystification and glittery distraction. Tolkien asks, how could it be possible for these stories to have the power that they have over our imagination if they were not recovering truths, indeed, fundamental truths, about the world? As Tolkien notes, "Small wonder that *spell* means both a story told, and a formula of power over living men."[16] The fairy-story, if done right,

---

'a mode of memory emancipated from the order of time and space', while the Imagination is 'the power of giving to ideal creations the inner consistency of reality.'" R. J. Reilly, "Tolkien and the Fairy Story," in *Understanding* The Lord of the Rings: *The Best of Tolkien Criticism*, ed. Rose Zimbardo and Neil Isaacs (New York: Houghton Mifflin, 2004), 97. Nevertheless, as Reilly goes on to remark, Tolkien was also critical of Coleridge. Tolkien did not see the fancy and imagination as two distinct and separate faculties as did Coleridge, but rather the fancy as an integral part of the imagination and not distinct from it. Tolkien uses the term "fantasy" to designate the shaping of the creative imagination by the sub-creative art, and thus designates the organic union of fancy and creative imagination in genuinely sub-creative art.

16 *TL*, 31.

should have a certain power of enchantment, not because of the power in the story itself, but because such a story lends the world a power, significance, and beauty that it has lost. Thus, the recovery of the world we find in fairy-stories is a recovery of the meaning and sense of things apart from human plans and desires; it is therefore also a recovery of the moral sense or reality of the world.[17] Good and evil are not mere projections of the human subject: in the fairy-story we enter into a world where good and evil are woven into the very fabric or natures of things, behaving therefore in ways that we would not expect. In a way, then, Tolkien remarks, children are more insightful than adults in discerning the true purpose of fairy-stories: when reading or listening to such a story, their fundamental question is not "is it real" (in the sense of "is it *contemporary*"), but rather "Was he [the main character] good? Was he wicked?"[18]

But again, as Tolkien emphasizes repeatedly, the goal of fairy-stories is sub-creation: the creation of an alternate world that stands completely and autonomously on its own inner principles, which includes its own mode of temporality: "they [fairy-stories] open a door on Other Time, and if we pass through, though only for a moment, we stand outside our own time, outside Time itself, maybe."[19] Tolkien makes here a key point, which will become more evident in the following chapters: fairy-stories derive their believability—their sense of reality—from their ability to take us out of our time, the time of the primary world, and indeed out of time itself. In the fairy-story, we get a glimpse of things in their timeless and therefore true natures prior to their creation in the mind of the Creator. This is why Tolkien is careful to argue that, in a paradoxical way, the believability of fairy-stories should in no way depend on some "childish 'wish to believe'":

> I had no special childish "wish to believe". I wanted to know. Belief depended on the way in which stories were presented to me, by older people, or by the authors, or on the inherent tone and quality of the tale. But at no time can I remember that the

17 Reilly, "Tolkien and the Fairy Story," 100.
18 *TL*, 39n1.
19 *TL*, 32.

enjoyment of a story was dependent on belief that such things could happen, or had happened, in "real life." Fairy-stories were plainly not primarily concerned with possibility, but with desirability. If they awakened *desire*, satisfying it while often whetting it unbearably, they succeeded.[20]

The power or spell of a good fairy-story should not appeal to a preexisting desire to believe, but rather the opposite should obtain: the good fairy-story should *awaken* a desire that was not already there, or at the very least that was dormant. The power of a good fairy-story lies in its ability to awaken a desire of a reality greater than that of the primary world; in doing so it should reverse our normal, rational view of things, namely, that the primary world is more real than the world of Faerie. Thus, reminiscing about his love and desire for dragons as a child, Tolkien says:

> But the world that contained even the imagination of Fafnir was richer and more beautiful, at whatever cost of peril. The dweller in the quiet and fertile plains may hear of the tormented hills, and the unharvested sea and long for them in his heart. For the heart is hard though the body be soft.[21]

Thus, when children ask, "Is it true?" Tolkien asserts that they really mean something like, "I like this, but is it contemporary?" That is, the strict correspondence of the fairy-story with the primary world is by far secondary to the desire that the story awakens and, by extension, to the reality desired. Indeed, a strict correspondence of the fairy-story to our time is secondary, if not irrelevant (or destructive). This is due to the fact, as we saw Tolkien say above, that fairy-stories open the door to an "Other Time" and, indeed, take us outside of time itself. (The deeper significance of this statement is developed at length in chapter 7 on the recovery of eternity.)

But to construct a secondary world that is convincing as a world in its own right is, as Tolkien remarks, extraordinarily difficult, and requires a sort of "elvish craft":

20 *TL*, 40–41.
21 *TL*, 42.

> To make a Secondary World inside which the green sun will be credible, commanding Secondary Belief, will probably require labour and thought, and will certainly demand a special skill, a kind of elvish craft. Few attempt such difficult tasks. But when they are attempted and in any degree accomplished then we have a rare achievement of art: indeed narrative art, story-making in its primary and most potent mode.[22]

The difficulty of creating a secondary world lies, contrary to what one might think, not in giving free rein to the unbridled imagination, but in restraining it and creating a world that is consistent, cogent, and indeed thoroughly rational. For a secondary world to work it must be as rigorous, rational, and lawful as possible, for it must include literally everything: not just rational characters and agents, but hills, landscape, and forests. Tolkien goes so far as to say:

> Fantasy is a natural human activity. It certainly does not destroy or even insult Reason; and it does not either blunt the appetite for, nor obscure the perception of, scientific verity. On the contrary. The keener and the clearer is the reason, the better fantasy will it make. If men were ever in a state in which they did not want to know or could not perceive truth (facts or evidence), then Fantasy would languish until they were cured. If they ever get into that state (it would not seem at all impossible), Fantasy will perish, and become Morbid Delusion.[23]

The construction of a good and convincing fantasy story requires that the sub-creator respect scrupulously the natures of things and their interconnection; fantasy is not a license to create absurdities or to violate the immutable natures of things. The fundamental reason for this, Tolkien claims, is that sub-creation is simply a reflection of the creative

---

22 *TL*, 49.

23 *TL*, 55. Hence, the fairy-story is a case of, as Thomas Aquinas would put it, grace building upon nature. Just as divine grace does not destroy the natures of things and their capacities but perfects them, so the fairy-story does not negate the primary world, but imbues it with the life and meaning that is already there in it.

act by which our primary world has been made.[24] Sub-creation is done in reverent imitation of God's creation of our world: "Fantasy remains a human right: we make in our measure and in our derivative mode, because we are made: and not only made, but made in the image and likeness of a Maker."[25] The act of sub-creation liberates us from the primary world not so that we can deny it, dominate it, or flee from it, but rather in order that we can understand and therefore love it more deeply.

Hence, as we have seen over and over again, Tolkien emphasizes that what gives the fairy-story an air of enchantment is not the particular characters or types of beings within it; rather it is the story itself—or the realm of Faerie that the story allows us to enter—that makes the characters and types of being within it enchanted. Such stories allow us to look upon our primary world afresh, with a renewed sense of its mysterious meaning: "We should look at green again, and be startled anew (but not blinded) by blue and yellow and red. We should meet the centaur and the dragon, and then perhaps suddenly behold, like the ancient shepherds, sheep, and dogs, and horses—and wolves. This recovery fairy-stories help us to make. In that sense only a taste for them may make us, or keep us, childish."[26] Or, to cite the full context of the passage that we cited earlier in the introduction:

> Recovery (which includes return and renewal of health) is a re-gaining—regaining of a clear view. I do not say "seeing things as they are" and involve myself with the philosophers, though I might venture to say "seeing things as we are (or were)

---

[24] This sort of imaginative exercise in understanding the nature of our world and its creation is actually very ancient, with Plato's *Timaeus* being a preeminent example. Pierre Hadot, *Le voile d'Isis: Essai sur l'historie de l'idée de nature* (Paris: Gallimard, 2004), 79–80, 210–15. Indeed, *The Timaeus* is a particularly good example of how a philosopher like Plato, though formally opposed to myth as lacking the rigor of a proper *logos* or "account," nevertheless must resort to myth in order to give any sort of logical account of the primordial origins of things or of the highest metaphysical truths.

[25] *TL*, 56.

[26] *TL*, 57. As Craig Bernthal puts it, myth and fairy-story help us recover "a true vision of the world by de-familiarizing it. To understand dragons is to see, once again, what a horse or wolf is." Bernthal, *Tolkien's Sacramental Vision*, 64.

meant to see them"—as things apart from ourselves. We need, in any case, to clean our windows; so that the things seen clearly may be freed from the drab blur of triteness or familiarity—from possessiveness. Of all faces those of our *familiares* are the ones both most difficult to play fantastic tricks with, and most difficult really to see with fresh attention, perceiving their likeness and unlikeness: that they are faces, and yet unique faces. This triteness is really the penalty of "appropriation": the things that are trite, or (in a bad sense) familiar, are the things that we have appropriated, legally or mentally. We say we know them. They have become like the things which once attracted us by their glitter, or their colour, or their shape, and we laid hands on them, and then locked them in our hoard, acquired them, and acquiring ceased to look at them."[27]

Here Tolkien mentions a new and very important aspect of recovery: that its main purpose is not so much to recover things "as they are" but to recover them "as they should be," i.e., as things that stand apart from ourselves, without appropriation or possessiveness.[28] Recovery is about experiencing the world (and ourselves) anew as things that have a goodness and intelligibility independent of human projects and valuations; they have what medieval theologians would have called the "transcendental" properties of truth and goodness ("all beings insofar

---

[27] *TL*, 57–58. Hence, a dragon like Smaug, who sits possessively over his horde in the Lonely Mountain without appreciating its value in the least, is a type or figure of consciousness prior to recovery. The modern mind is many ways a "draconic" mind.

[28] Here, Tolkien in his essay makes an aside reference to Chestertonian fantasy, *Mooreeffoc*, which is simply "Coffee Room" spelled backwards. By this word, Chesterton refers to the way a simple rearrangement of letters can render what is very familiar and trite strange and new. *Mooreeffoc* "may cause you suddenly to realise that England is an utterly alien land, lost in either some remote past age glimpsed by history, or in some strange dim future to be reached by a time machine." *TL*, 59. But Tolkien then goes on to remark that this idea of fantasy found in Chesterton is too limited with respect to the kind of fantasy he is talking about: genuine, creative fantasy is about creating a whole new world and not focusing, "as a time-telescope," on one particular aspect or region of our world.

as they exist are inherently intelligible and desirable"[29]). Or to turn things around again, the recovery that fantasy brings about reveals that, in fact, what things *should be* is what they *truly* are:

> Fantasy is made out of the Primary World, but a good craftsman loves his material, and has a knowledge and feeling for clay, stone and wood which only the art of making can give. By the forging of Gram cold iron was revealed; by the making of Pegasus horses were ennobled; in the Trees of the Sun and Moon root and stock, flower and fruit are manifested in glory.[30]

Notice here that Tolkien sees fantasy as being as much a craft as smithing and carpentry are, a craft that is rooted in a deep love of its material and in an intimate, tacit knowledge of it. The only difference is that the material of myth and fairy story is language itself. Of course, this relationship is mutual: the recovery inherent in any craft reveals things in their inherent truth and goodness, while this truth and goodness in things elicits and causes knowledge, skill, and love in the craftsman.[31] And most importantly, the craftsman (or writer of fantasy) does not thereby wish to dominate or control his material but rather desires to let it stand in all its truth and glory.

This brings us, then, to what Tolkien says is the next principal function of fantasy, and this is escape. This is an eminently positive function of fantasy. One of the harshest criticisms leveled against fairy-stories and fantasy, in Tolkien's time and ours, is that fantasy literature is "escapist," a term, of course, which in current use has a negative connotation. Fashionable opinion in Tolkien's time looked down upon fantasy and fairy-stories as modes of escape from the realities or pressing problems of life, usually of a contemporary social or political nature. Tolkien argues, however, that these critiques have things

---

29 See Thomas Aquinas, *De ver.*, I, 1 and XXI, 1.
30 *TL*, 59.
31 As Pierre Hadot and many other scholars have pointed out, the word *sophia*, or "wisdom," in the earliest centuries of Greek civilization was primarily applied to the knowledge associated with crafts such as smithing and weaving. It meant something more akin to a *savoir-faire* than any sort of abstract speculative knowledge. Hadot, *Le voile d'Isis*, 148–49.

precisely backwards and fundamentally misunderstand the importance of recovery in fairy-stories:

> Fairy-stories, at any rate, have many more permanent and fundamental things to talk about. Lightning, for example. The escapist is not so subservient to the whims of evanescent fashion as these opponents. He does not make things (which it may be quite rational to regard as bad) his masters or his gods by worshipping them as inevitable, even "inexorable." And his opponents, so easily contemptuous, have no guarantee that he will stop there: he might rouse men to pull down the street-lamps. Escapism has another and even wickeder face: Reaction.[32]

Only the escapist is free from the tyranny of worshipping the idols of the present as the inevitable products of progress, precisely because he has recovered things as they are, good, intelligible, and valuable in themselves outside of his own time and age—even more, outside of any age. More importantly, he has recovered the world as alive and pulsating with meaning and significance, the very opposite of idolatry.

Indeed, Tolkien in connection to this makes a comment that is seemingly offhand but very telling: "The notion that motor-cars are more 'alive' than, say, centaurs or dragons is curious; that they are more 'real' than, say, horses is pathetically absurd. How real, how startlingly alive is a factory chimney compared with an elm tree: poor thing, insubstantial dream of an escapist!"[33] That the dead mechanisms of modern life are more real for us than the living creations of the human imagination, Tolkien asserts, should give us pause. Certainly automobiles exist in a way that dragons do not, yet dragons and centaurs and other creatures of fantasy reveal the world to us in a way that automobiles

---

[32] *TL*, 62. Tolkien supposedly asked C. S. Lewis rhetorically: "What class of men would you expect to be the most preoccupied with, and most hostile to, the idea of escape? The answer, of course, is jailers." As Curry comments on this exchange: "Now one can reply that what jailers really hate is *escape*, but they love *escapism*; but all turns on whether *escapism* is already a sort of escape." Patrick Curry, "The Critical Response to Tolkien's Fiction," in Lee, *A Companion to J. R. R. Tolkien*, 381.

[33] *TL*, 62–63.

and other machines do not. Machines have only a derivative being; they are extensions of us and therefore, to the degree we become dependent upon them and to the degree that they remake and transform our world, we do not and cannot see things for what they really are, apart from us and our own designs. To reduce reality to these machines is to understand things backwards: it is to understand the greater by the lesser, the living by the dead. Dragons and centaurs, by contrast, throw us into a world that is, to be sure, created by us, but which, paradoxically, we do not control. Like Niggle's leaf, these creatures and the stories and worlds they inhabit open up onto a realm of meaning that is far larger than we can even imagine. They are larger than our primary world and thereby actually better suited to enabling us to understand our primary world more deeply. Bradley Birzer expresses very well what Tolkien is trying to do when he writes:

> For Tolkien, mystery surrounds us. But modernity has deformed our perception of this reality. His mythologizing of the world, Tolkien believed, increased our ability to see the beauty and sacramentality of creation. It also allowed ideas and loves to transcend time and space. In essence, Tolkien's mind remained complexly medieval and oriented toward myth and mystery.[34]

To put it even more provocatively, the medieval conception of the world as inherently true and good and thus charged with potentially sacramental significance is far more real and hard-headed than the modern scientific, technological view of the world, which only understands it insofar as it fits our own (all things considered very limited, even stunted) plans, understanding, and projects. As Stratford Caldecott puts it, "Mythological thinking does not provide an 'escape' from reality so much as an 'intensification' of it."[35]

Tolkien argues that there are desires deeper than these flights of fancy; even deeper than flight from "the noise, stench, ruthlessness, and extravagance of the internal-combustion engine. There are hunger, thirst, poverty, pain, sorrow, injustice, death." And indeed, the last refers

---

34 Birzer, *J. R. R. Tolkien's Sanctifying Myth*, 23.
35 Caldecott, *The Power of the Ring*, 4.

to "the oldest and deepest desire, the Great Escape: the Escape from Death."[36] Of all the events that haunt human existence, our inevitable death is the one that looms the largest, even if most of us choose to ignore it as much as possible. As the most human of creations, fairy-stories are designed to satisfy perhaps human beings' greatest desire: escape from death. Hence, "Fairy-stories are made by men not by fairies." This is a point that it is well to keep in mind in reading Tolkien's work, for he does not always adopt the human point of view, if only to highlight this theme all the more: "Few lessons are taught more clearly in them [the Elves] than the burden of that kind of immortality, or rather endless serial living, to which the 'fugitive' would fly."[37] Thus, as we shall have opportunity to see in later chapters, the importance of the race of Elves in Tolkien's fiction (well beyond that which Tolkien had found in folk tradition), the race that enjoys precisely the sort of immortality which would be a sort of "serial living" (the Ringwraiths are another, though somewhat different, case, as we shall see), underscores this fundamental theme of fairy-stories or fantasy. What fantasy offers us most importantly and primally is an escape from death; whence comes its power and even necessity for human beings. But, and this is the greatest paradox for Tolkien, this escape from Death is based on a recovery that is not a flight *from* reality but precisely a true and fundamental recovery *of* reality. The good news of fantasy is that it says that our desire to escape from death is not vain, but its satisfaction can be found in a recovery of reality itself.

True Myth

It is but a logical progression that from recovery in fairy-stories we go to escape and finally to consolation or, rather, the consolation of the happy ending, for which Tolkien coined the term *eucatastrophe* (*eu-* being the Greek prefix for "good"). This happy ending is not incidental to the fairy-story but essential to it; it is what recovery and escape logically and inevitably lead to:

36 *TL*, 68.
37 *TL*, 68.

> The consolation of fairy-stories, the joy of the happy ending: or more correctly of the good catastrophe, the sudden joyous "turn" (for there is no true end to any fairy-tale): this joy, which is one of the things which fairy-stories can produce supremely well, is not essentially "escapist," nor "fugitive." In its fairy-tale—or otherworld—setting, it is a sudden and miraculous grace: never to be counted on to recur. It does not deny the existence of *dyscatastrophe*, of sorrow and failure: the possibility of these is necessary to the joy of deliverance; it denies (in the face of much evidence, if you will) universal final defeat and in so far is *evangelium*, giving a fleeting glimpse of Joy, Joy beyond the walls of the world, poignant as grief.[38]

The paradox here is that the "eucatastrophe," or the "sudden joyous turn," is the rigorous, logical result of the fairy-story; and yet, it is also a "miraculous grace: never to be counted on to recur." From the purely natural or human point of view, a happy ending seems impossible or at least very unlikely, and yet it is, from the standpoint of the ending of the fairy-story, the only logical outcome that was possible. This is what gives the fairy-story its power and satisfaction, but also its very strong ring of truth: "The peculiar quality of the 'joy' in successful Fantasy can thus be explained as a sudden glimpse of the underlying reality or truth. It is not only a 'consolation' for the sorrow of this world, but a satisfaction, and an answer to that question, 'Is it true?'"[39] And what gives these stories an even stronger ring of truth is that, as Tolkien notes, they do not deny sorrow and failure—in fact, in these stories they are necessary for the eucatastrophic conclusion: "poignant as grief," the happy ending is only such through the very integration and transmutation of grief.

At the end of his essay on fairy-stories, Tolkien is therefore compelled to mention the Gospel, the story of the prophesied birth, life, death and resurrection of Jesus Christ. For in the Gospel, Tolkien argues, "Legend and History have met and fused":

---

38 *TL*, 68–69.
39 *TL*, 71.

> This story [the Gospel] has entered History and the primary world; the desire and aspiration of sub-creation has been raised to the fulfillment of Creation. The Birth of Christ is the eucatastrophe of Man's history. The Resurrection is the eucatastrophe of the story of the Incarnation. This story begins and ends in joy. It has pre-eminently the "inner consistency of reality".... To reject it leads either to sadness or to wrath.[40]

The Gospel is a fairy-story that is true in every sense of the word: true as a fairy-story of a world that is created by God out of joy and love, but also true as a real event in history. As Tolkien always insisted, he never saw his work as fiction in the sense of make-believe: in fact, he mentions in several places that in writing his works of fantasy, he saw himself as writing history more than fiction ("I am historically minded. Middle-earth is not an imaginary world").[41]

But there is another, deeper sense in which the Gospel fairy-story is true according to Tolkien. As Jonathan McIntosh explains:

> The Gospel ... is not merely a real-life story containing a eucatastrophe or happy ending, but precisely in being real it constitutes for Tolkien the eucatastrophe or happy ending of all other fairy-stories, for in it all other fairy-stories have, in a sense, become *true*, have been graced with the special dispensation of real, historical, physical, created being.[42]

Because mythical truth and historical fact converge in the Gospel, it is the key to the meaning of all other fairy-stories, for the Gospel is a universal myth that is grounded in historical time. The truth of all other fairy-stories, pagan or secular, is found in the Christian Gospel, and there it finds its "sanctification."[43] Thus, far from blinding him to the

---

40 *TL*, 72.

41 *Letters*, 239. As *The Histories of Middle-earth* makes clear, Tolkien was obsessed with the relation of myth to history and explored various hypotheses of how the one may turn into the other.

42 McIntosh, *The Flame Imperishable*, 155.

43 "Myth could be dangerous, or 'perilous', as he usually stated it, if it remained pagan. Therefore, Tolkien thought, one must sanctify it, that is, make

truth of things, Tolkien's Catholic faith opened him up to the vision of the inner, sacramental significance of things as creatures and the world as Creation, and therefore to the fundamental truth of things, for a sacrament is a material and efficacious sign of God's grace, and as such, infuses the material with spiritual meaning and real spiritual power.[44]

Tolkien therefore remained completely unmoved by a popular trope of anti-Christian polemic which seeks to imply that Christianity is not true (or at least cannot make any claim to absolute or universal Truth), because the Christian story is just one of many other pagan, Near-Eastern myths of a creation, a universal flood, or a dying and rising savior (such as we find in the *Epic of Gilgamesh* or the myth of Isis and Osiris, etc.). The Christian story is just one fairy-story among others, if not completely derivative from them, so this story goes.

But of course, these sorts of polemics engage in question begging: they assume what they are trying to prove, i.e., that the Christian myth is reducible to or caused by the pagan myths, not the other way around. To the contrary, Tolkien (in line, one might add, with the early Church Fathers, who actually knew these pagan myths extremely well),[45] saw these myths as actually *confirming* the truth of Christian myth: by foreshadowing or pointing to all the major features of the Christian story, they pre-announce their fulfillment, purification, and perfection in the historical account in the gospels. That is, the Christian myth is the truth of all myth insofar as it actually happened in history. And yet its truth is still timeless and thus able, if dimly, to be known and

---

it Christian and put it in God's service." Birzer, *J. R. R. Tolkien's Sanctifying Myth*, xxiii.

44 "Because he [Tolkien] believed in the truth of certain dogmas, these acted for him like torches or crystalline lamps that transmit light into dark places." Caldecott, *The Power of the Ring*, 5.

45 More specifically, this was at least the line of reasoning taken by the Alexandrian school of Patristic theology, represented most forcefully by Clement of Alexandria. As Imbert notes, Clement's position on the relation of pagan myth to Christian revelation was a key influence on the thought of John Henry Newman, the nineteenth-century English cardinal, theologian, and intellectual who was also the founder of the Birmingham Oratory where Tolkien grew up and received his religious formation. Imbert, *From Imagination to Faërie*, 136.

foreshadowed in pagan myth and story. In the Gospel, the timeless truths (properly understood) of pagan myth came to intersect with history, our primary world, and therefore the Gospel recovers and redeems these truths. Indeed, only because the Gospel story really happened in history can pagan myths and fairy-stories be understood in their universal sense and significance, because only the Christian story enacts these truths and meaning in our primary world in real historical time.[46]

Thus, in writing his essay "On Fairy-Stories," Tolkien wished to demonstrate (and, I believe, largely succeeded in doing so) that fairy-stories are not just flights of fancy, primitive science, or garbled history, but are vehicles of profound truth and therefore address fundamental and essential human desires. For Tolkien the most profound truth is that the world is created by a personal Creator and thus his creation is infused with intelligible meaning. To make fairy-stories, then, is to return us and our fellow creatures to our Creator: "Man, Sub-creator, the refracted Light / through whom is splintered from a single White / to many hues, and endlessly combined / in living shapes that move from mind to mind."[47] We, however, have fallen from that making or sub-creation, which is our right as human beings; yet, we still continue to sub-create, however imperfectly, for it is "by the law in which we're made": "'twas our right / (used or misused). That right has not decayed: / we make still by the law in which we're made."[48] As Yannick Imbert remarks, "recording myths for Tolkien was possible because of his conviction that a myth could be a record since it remained a 'splintered light', a veiled truth shining forth out of humankind's creation by God. If myth is a partly mistaken historical account, it nonetheless remains a human endeavor, fruit of the human ability to express something reminiscent of a long-forgotten truth about God and creation."[49] Thus it is to Tolkien's own views of that Fall that we shall now turn.

---

46 In making these last points, I should note that the relationship of the Christian and pagan elements in Tolkien's fantasy will be explored in more detail in the subsequent chapters.
47 *TL*, 54.
48 *TL*, 55.
49 Imbert, *From Imagination to Faërie*, 146.

CHAPTER TWO

"The Fall, Mortality, and the Machine"

We had occasion in the introduction to mention the long letter Tolkien wrote to Milton Waldman in 1951, hoping that the latter would persuade Collins to publish *The Silmarillion* together with *The Lord of the Rings*. In the course of the letter, Tolkien attempts a summary of the main themes of his work, stating:

> Anyway all this stuff is mainly concerned with Fall, Mortality, and the Machine. With Fall inevitably, and that motive occurs in several modes. With Mortality, especially as it affects art and the creative (or as I should say, sub-creative) desire which seems to have no biological function, and to be apart from the satisfactions of plain ordinary biological life, with which, in our world, it is indeed usually at strife. This desire is at once wedded to a passionate love of the real primary world, and hence filled with the sense of mortality, and yet unsatisfied by it. It has

various opportunities of "Fall." It may become possessive, clinging to the things made as "its own," the sub-creator wishes to be the Lord and God of his private creation. He will rebel against the laws of the Creator—especially against mortality. Both of these (alone or together) will lead to the desire for Power, for making the will more quickly effective,—and so to the Machine (or Magic). By the last I intend all use of external plans or devices (apparatus) instead of development of the inherent inner powers or talents—or even the use of these talents with the corrupted motive of dominating: bulldozing the real world, or coercing other wills. The Machine is our more obvious modern form though more closely related to Magic than is usually recognized.[1]

For Tolkien, that human beings are fallen creatures was not a matter of religious dogma, but a basic phenomenon of human existence: human beings constantly aim for a happiness and greatness before which they always fall infinitely short. As Tolkien says in another letter to his son Michael, to be fallen means that we cannot enjoy what is good or know what is true "with free enjoyment" but only with suffering and mortification.[2] We can, that is, no longer freely experience and see the world as it is, free of possessiveness and appropriation. This fact is reflected in all human stories: human stories, Tolkien asserts, universally and without fail are about a fall of some sort: "There cannot be any 'story' without a fall—all stories are ultimately about the fall—at least not for human minds as we known them and have them."[3] There would, therefore, be no need for recovery of the world as creation if not for the Fall, Mortality, and the vain attempts to overcome both through the Machine. To understand fully, therefore, what recovery is and how Tolkien achieves that recovery, we must look at these three themes.

---

1 *Letters*, 145–46.
2 *Letters*, 51.
3 *Letters*, 147.

The Fall

The Fall, as Tolkien sees it, lies in the possessiveness that human beings, as sub-creators, have over their own creations. Hence, Tolkien reveals that sub-creation, which, as we saw in the previous chapter, he describes as a human right and a mode of loving and understanding our Creator and his creatures, has also a negative and sinister possibility. The human sub-creator can become so possessive of his creation that he "rebels against the laws of his Creator" and sets himself up as the lord and god of his own world—the classic sin of pride. The law of the Creator against which the human sub-creator rebels most vehemently and consistently is the law of his own mortality. The fallen human being refuses to accept death as a gift from his Creator, as a letting go of time and finitude, but rather clings to time and finitude. This rebellion then leads to the Machine, to the attempt to fix technologically what nature refuses to human will and pride. This last phenomenon, Tolkien indicates, only comes to full realization in modernity, though he notes that its roots go back to premodern magic and even further.

Interestingly, however, Tolkien explains that he examines the Fall first through the point of view of a nonhuman race of incarnate, rational beings: a race that is immortal (or, more precisely, whose lives last as long as Middle-earth or *Arda* lasts), namely the Elves. All the tales of the First Age as recounted in the *Quenta Silmarillion* are concerned almost solely with the rebellion of the Elves against the Valar, the god- or angel-like beings that rule Middle-earth as regents of the one God and Creator, Ilúvatar. Moreover, these tales not only are about the Elves but also are reportedly told from the elven point of view (hence, the race of Men comes only incidentally into the stories).

Again, though, the Elves are immortal, so what accounts for their Fall? I think that Tolkien suggests that this question puts things backwards: mortality and the fall into time are consequences of the Fall, not their causes. Through the Elves, Tolkien wishes to examine the Fall itself apart from the consequence known to us human beings, that of mortality, which tends to obscure for us the nature of the Fall itself. The Elves fall precisely because, as a race, they are gifted with a high degree of wisdom and of creativity and skill in art; and precisely because they do not die within Middle-earth, they develop a "possessive attitude" toward their works and toward Middle-earth itself.[4] As readers of *The Silmarillion* know, the first Dark Lord, Morgoth, stole the Silmarils of Fëanor. These were jewels in which was encased the light of the two trees of Valinor that provided all the heat and light for Middle-earth prior to the creation of the sun and moon. As a result of this theft, Fëanor and the race of Elves called the Noldor pursued Morgoth from the Undying Lands (Valinor) back to Middle-earth, where they fought a series of long, devastating and ultimately fruitless wars against Morgoth. All of this, Tolkien notes, was due to the possessiveness of Fëanor and his followers toward the Silmarils. Not only did they disobey the Valar in pursing Morgoth back to Middle-earth, but they swore a blasphemous oath to oppose anyone, the Valar and even Ilúvatar himself, who would prevent them from recovering the jewels. The Elves were all the more blinded by the conviction that they were fighting evil in the person of Morgoth. Morgoth, in Tolkien's world, was indeed thoroughly evil, but in opposing him out of possessiveness and pride, the Elves became in some ways like the very Enemy they claimed to oppose.

Over time, as Tolkien explains to Waldman, the Elves came to regret their rebellion, and he remarks on the curious combination of beauty and sadness in the Elves. The Elves "wanted to have their cake without eating it. They wanted the peace and bliss and perfect memory of 'The West', and yet to remain on the ordinary earth where their prestige as the highest people, above wild Elves, dwarves, and Men, was greater than at the bottom of the hierarchy of Valinor."[5] As such, they were, in the Second Age, as prone to fall again as in the First Age, saying of Sauron and his success in convincing the Elves to help in the forging of the Rings of Power: "He [Sauron] was still fair in that early time, and his motives and those of the Elves seemed to go partly together: the healing of the desolate lands. Sauron found their weak point in suggesting that, helping one another, they could make Western Middle-earth as beautiful

---

4 "The fall of the Elves comes about through the possessive attitude of Fëanor and his seven sons to these gems [the Silmarils]." *Letters*, 148.

5 *Letters*, 151.

as Valinor. It was really a veiled attack on the gods, and incitement to try and make a separate independent paradise."[6]

What was the nature of these rings of power, and how do they play a key role in Tolkien's presentation of the Fall as the moving cause of his stories? Tolkien explains their nature, again in his letter to Milton Waldman:

> The chief power (of all the rings alike) was the prevention or slowing of *decay* (i.e., "change" viewed as a regrettable thing), the preservation of what is desired or loved, or its semblance—this is more or less an Elvish motive. But also they enhanced the natural powers of a possessor—thus approaching "magic," a motive easily corruptible into evil, a lust for domination. And finally they had other powers, more directly derived from Sauron ("the Necromancer": so he is called as he casts a fleeting shadow and presage on the pages of *The Hobbit*): such as rendering invisible the material body, and making things of the invisible world visible.[7]

The rings of power have certain powers and effects that may broadly be called "magical." But as Tolkien notes here, their primary power is preventing decay and granting a certain ersatz immortality, and indeed this control—or distortion—of time is the basis of the rings' other magical powers. This power of preventing decay is no doubt a good thing, and the power of the three Elven rings of power turns out, in the end, to have been the main reason why the Elven realms in Middle-earth were havens of beauty, art, lore, and tranquility. It was precisely the power of those Elven rings (forged without the direct help of Sauron and therefore uncorrupted by him) that made these havens possible.[8] Nevertheless, this power is also the occasion for a fall; and if it is an occasion for the Fall of the Elves, it is *a fortiori*, especially so for Men. As Tolkien remarks concerning the part of *The Silmarillion* called

---

6 *Letters*, 152.
7 *Letters*, 152.
8 Elrond, for example, symbolizes ancient wisdom, and his house, Rivendell, is a place of lore and reflection. *Letters*, 153, note.

"The Downfall" (or the *Akallabêth*), describing the Fall of the Men of Númenor in the Second Age:

> *The Downfall* is partly the result of an inner weakness in Man—consequent, if you will, upon the first Fall (unrecorded in these tales), repented but not finally healed. Reward on earth is more dangerous for men than punishment! The Fall is achieved by the cunning of Sauron in exploiting this weakness. Its central theme is (inevitably, I think, in a story of Men) a Ban, or Prohibition.[9]

In reward for helping the Elves defeat Morgoth in the First Age, the Valar created an island in the Western Ocean near to the Blessed Realm of Valinor called Númenor (Tolkien's version of Atlantis), where a race of Men dwelt blessed with a span of life thrice that of other men and with powers of art and knowledge akin to those of the Elves. And yet, as with the Elves, so with the Men of Númenor: "Their long life aids their achievements in art and wisdom, but breeds a possessive attitude to these things, and desire awakes for more *time* for their enjoyment."[10] A condition that was laid upon the Men of Númenor, in return for which they enjoyed a blessedness unknown to all other Men, was that they were banned from traveling west to the Undying Lands beyond sight of Númenor.[11] So, along with the pride and possessiveness that leads to the Fall of the Elves, we have with Men the added element of mortality, even if attenuated by an extraordinarily long life.

In the account of the Second Age in *The Silmarillion*, Tolkien traces the fall from grace of the Númenóreans from acquiescence to the Ban, to unwilling obedience of the Ban, to open rebellion against the Ban.

---

9 *Letters*, 154.
10 *Letters*, 154.
11 "But the Lords of Valinor forbade them to sail so far westward that the coasts of Númenor could no longer be seen; and for long the Dúnedain were content, though they did not fully understand the purpose of this ban. But the design of Manwë was that the Númenóreans should not be tempted to seek for the Blessed Realm, nor desire to overpass the limits set to their bliss, becoming enamoured of the immortality of the Valar and the Eldar and the lands where all things endure." *Akal*, 262.

Eventually, the last of the Númenórean kings, Ar-Pharazôn, moved from unwilling obedience to open rebellion; and in doing so, he was seduced by Sauron, who in turn went from being a conquered enemy of the Men of the West to being the closest advisor and power behind the throne of Ar-Pharazôn. In doing so, Sauron substituted the worship of Morgoth for Eru or Ilúvatar, the true Creator, so that, although taken to Númenor as a hostage of the king, Sauron turned the tables and secretly became the master of his captors. As Tolkien notes in *Morgoth's Ring*: "His [Sauron's] cunning motive is probably best expressed thus. To wean one of the God-fearing from their allegiance it is best to propound ... to him a Lord who will sanction what he desires and not forbid it."[12] Sauron could not propose to the Men of Númenor worship of himself, but only of Morgoth: "worship of Melkor will raise him [Sauron] from hostage to high priest." And the result was that

> ... a shadow fell upon them: in which maybe the will of Morgoth was at work that still moved in the world. And the Númenóreans began to murmur, at first in their hearts, and then in open words, against the doom of Men, and most of all against the Ban which forbade them to sail into the West.[13]

Thus, like with the Elves, we have a "second Fall" of Men (Tolkien hints at the "First Fall," which is clearly the Fall of Adam recounted in Genesis, though Tolkien is careful not to refer to this Fall directly).[14] But unlike the Elves, the Men of Númenor's rebellion was caused by an increasing fear of death and of the order of the world created by Ilúvatar—indeed, it was further fueled by the comparison of their fate to that of the Elves. Tolkien puts the explanation for the different fates

---

12 *MR*, 398.
13 *Akal*, 264.
14 "But when he [Felagund] questioned him concerning the arising of Men and their journeys, Bëor would say little; and indeed he knew little, for the fathers of his people had told few tales of their past and a silence had fallen upon their memory. 'A darkness lies behind us', Bëor said; 'and we have turned our backs upon it, and we do not desire to return thither even in thought. Westwards our hearts have been turned, and we believe that there we shall find Light'." *QS*, xvii, 141.

of Men and Elves into the mouths of emissaries sent by the Valar to dissuade the Númenóreans from their rebellion: "The Eldar, you say, are unpunished, and even those who rebelled do not die. Yet that is to them neither reward nor punishment, but the fulfillment of their being. They cannot escape, and are bound to this world, never to leave it so long as it lasts, for its life is theirs."[15] "For," they continue, "it is not the land of Manwë [chief of the Valar] that makes its people deathless, but the Deathless that dwell therein have hallowed the land; and there you would but wither and grow weary the sooner, as moths in a light too strong and steadfast."[16] There is, in short, no physical or technical solution to mortality: mere occupation of the Undying Lands would not make the Men of Númenor immortal. Rather, as we shall see further on, for mortal Men to inhabit the Undying Lands would be a torment for them. Immortality is a function of the created nature of the inhabitants of that land, and it cannot be wrested by mere external force, ingenuity, or conquest.

Tolkien recounts how this fear of death and rebellion against the created order led to greater and greater heights of power and wealth, achievements in art and science and technology; yet this increase in material, political, military, intellectual, and artistic power only bred more nihilistic despair:

> And the Doom of Men, that they should depart, was at first a gift of Ilúvatar. It became a grief to them only because coming under the shadow of Morgoth it seemed to them that they were surrounded by a great darkness, of which they were afraid; and some grew willful and proud and would not yield, until life was reft from them.[17]

The more that the Númenóreans became possessive of the things of Middle-earth and tried to control and dominate them, the more these things came to lack any inherent value or meaning, and the more they saw themselves as "surrounded by a great darkness." Whereas

---

15 *Akal*, 264–65.
16 *Akal*, 264.
17 *Akal*, 265.

before, the Men of Númenor had a benign influence on the Men of Middle-earth—bringing them the gifts of technology and trade and protecting them, at least to a limited extent, from slavery to Sauron—they now began to act in a manner very much like Sauron and started to tyrannize the inhabitants of Middle-earth.[18]

Thus, the last king of Númenor, Ar-Pharazôn, became ensnared by the lies of Sauron, who played upon the king's now-inordinate fear of death. Indeed, as Tolkien recounts it, the king even allowed Sauron to institute a sort of Satanic cult on the island of Númenor, in whose rites, Tolkien hints, human sacrifices were performed.[19] And at the center of its creed was a species of nihilism, wherein Sauron preached that the origin of all things lay in an "Ancient Darkness" or nothingness whose lord is Melkor-Morgoth. As Tolkien recounts Sauron saying, "And out of it the world was made. For Darkness alone is worshipful, and the Lord thereof may yet make other worlds to be gifts to those that serve him, so that the increase in their power shall find no end."[20] And out of this primal darkness, Sauron claims, comes an unlimited freedom and power: "Melkor, Lord of All, Giver of Freedom ... shall make you stronger than they [the Valar]."[21] But, of course, the freedom that comes from worship of Melkor-Morgoth is really a nihilistic freedom of self-destruction, and its power is one that can only destroy, or at best ape or mock, good things created by Ilúvatar.

Thus the king, Ar-Pharazôn, led Númenor to destruction. Gathering a mighty armada, he invaded the Land of the Valar. All seemed to go well at first, and he was able to land his army on the shores of the Undying Lands. But then a great cataclysm occurred: the mountains rose up and fell on the invading army, and the seas opened up and swallowed not only the Númenórean armada but the entire island of Númenor itself, thus destroying the entire civilization. Furthermore, Tolkien says,

---

18 *Akal*, 266–67.

19 "Thereafter the fire and smoke went up without ceasing; for the power of Sauron daily increased, and in that temple, with spilling of blood and torment and great wickedness, men made sacrifice to Melkor that he should release them from Death." *Akal*, 273.

20 *Akal*, 271.

21 *Akal*, 272.

the seas became bent, meaning that it was now impossible for mortal Men to sail due west and find the Undying Lands of the Valar; now if they sailed west, they would only return to where they started. A straight road remained where one could sail beyond the bounds of Middle-earth to the Blessed Realm, but this way remained open only for the Elves and a few mortals specially rewarded by the Valar. Of the Númenóreans, only a few who remained loyal to the Valar and friends to the Elves survived, fleeing as exiles to Middle-earth and establishing the kingdoms of Arnor and Gondor.

Nevertheless, Tolkien ends his account of the downfall of Númenor with this curious statement:

> For the Dúnedain [the Men of Númenor] held that even mortal Men, if so blessed, might look upon other times than those of their bodies' life; and they longed ever to escape from the shadows of their exile and to see in some fashion the light that dies not; for the sorrow of the thought of death had pursued them over the deeps of the sea.[22]

For Tolkien, as we shall see in some detail later, one of the most important consequences of the Fall was a fall into time and away from the (relative) eternity of the Undying Lands. Not only are mortal Men now bound to the world spatially, but also temporally: not only can they no longer look into other dimensions of spatial existence, but neither can they escape their own time in their fallen and unredeemed state (an escape still possible, in Tolkien's legendarium, so long as the Undying Lands remain accessible). Nevertheless, as we shall also see, Tolkien did think that both space and time not only *could* be redeemed but indeed that they *had been* redeemed.

The Ring and the Machine

What are the main features and effects of the One Ring of Sauron (and by extension, the other rings of power)? And how do these rings exemplify the effects of the Fall? Tolkien takes care to remark that there

[22] *Akal*, 281.

is nothing externally remarkable about it: it is an apparently plain circle of pure gold, perfectly round, but otherwise no different from what today we would recognize as a wedding ring. Nevertheless, it is clear to Bilbo, who first discovers the Ring in the depths of the Misty Mountains where it is jealously guarded by Gollum, and to others that this is no ordinary ring. It turns the wearer invisible, and for a long time this is all that it apparently does. It seems to be a mere device for escaping difficult situations and no more. (When Tolkien first wrote *The Hobbit*, that was indeed all it was—its deeper importance only occurred to Tolkien as he was writing the early chapters of *The Lord of the Rings*.) But as Bilbo continues on with no apparent signs of aging, the Ring takes on a more sinister aspect: it is able to stretch out one's lifespan beyond its natural limits; this quality of the Ring reveals in turn an enormous power over nature and other rational creatures that the wearer is thereby able to wield.

By stretching out life and giving thereby the wearer almost unlimited power, the Ring endows its wearer with a thirst for time that is limitless. This is the case for one of Tolkien's most terrifying and enduring creations, the Ringwraiths: men who took from Sauron the rings of power but in the process became mere shadows of their former selves, slaves to the will of Sauron and objects of terror to those still living. Tolkien, through Aragorn, describes their experience of the world in this way:

> They [the Ringwraiths] themselves do not see the world of light as we do, but our shapes cast shadows in their minds, which only the noon sun destroys; and in the dark they perceive many signs and forms that are hidden from us: then they are most to be feared. And at all times they smell the blood of living things, desiring and hating it. Senses, too, there are other than sight or smell.[23]

Since, under the sway of the Ring, their natural lifespan has been stretched out to almost nothing, the Ringwraiths cannot experience the world as the living do: they can only perceive the world indirectly

---

23 *FR*, I, 11, 189.

through shapes and shadows in the mind in a sort of inversion or parody of angelic apperception (the intuitive knowledge that, according to Scholastic philosophy, purely spiritual beings—angels and demons—have of the world, since they do not have sense organs). Tolkien does say that they "smell the blood of living things," although, by having Aragorn add, "Senses, too, there are other than sight or smell," Tolkien seems to imply that the Wraiths sense—but only in a way analogous to the way living creatures do; and since their desire for living beings is insatiable, they hate what they desire.

So there is very much a sense in which the Ring, by stretching out the creature's nature in time, amplifies both the best and worst qualities of the wearer, although, given the Fall discussed previously, it is inevitably the worst qualities that are amplified the most, and the best are turned to evil. At the same time, as Tom Shippey notes, the Ring seems to have a will and power all its own; its effects are not merely psychological, working by suggestion. Thus, when Frodo and his fellow hobbits are being questioned by the Breelanders at the Prancing Pony, Tolkien writes: "It seemed to him [Frodo], somehow, as if the suggestion [to put on the Ring] came to him from outside, from someone or something in the room."[24] The Ring seems to have a real personality of sorts; it certainly has a will or desire, and its effects, such as stretching out beyond natural limits one's lifespan, are certainly real enough and not just psychological. As Frodo approaches Mordor with Sam and Gollum, he feels this power or agency in the Ring as an extension of the Eye of Sauron:

> But far more he was troubled by the Eye: so he called it to himself. It was that more than the drag of the Ring that made him cower and stoop as he walked. The Eye: that horrible growing sense of a hostile will that strove with great power to pierce all shadows of cloud, and earth, and flesh, and to see you: to pin you under its deadly gaze, naked, immovable. So thin, so frail and thin, the veils were become that still warded it off. Frodo knew just where the present habitation and heart

24 FR, I, 9, 157.

of that will now was: as certainly as a man can tell the direction of the sun with his eyes shut. He was facing it, and its potency beat upon his brow.[25]

It is interesting to note here the contrast between the heavy materiality of the Ring and the naked, immovable gaze of the Eye of Sauron. The Ring itself seems to amplify the will and intellect not of the wearer but of the maker, making all the solid materiality of the world so many veils, "frail and thin," between oneself and that hostile will. This power of the Ring is even perceived, unknowingly, by Sauron's own servants (perhaps precisely because they are his slaves): "He [Sam] was no longer holding the Ring, but it was there, a hidden power, a cowing menace to the slaves of Mordor."[26] Tolkien himself perhaps explains this ambiguity of Sauron's Ring best when he writes, in his letter to Rhona Beare:

> The Ring of Sauron is only one of the various mythical treatments of the placing of one's life, or power, in some external object, which is thus exposed to capture or destruction with disastrous results to oneself. If I were to "philosophize" this myth, or at least the Ring of Sauron, I should say it was a mythical way of representing the truth that *potency* (or perhaps rather *potentiality*) if it is to be exercised, and produce results, has to be externalized and so as it were passes to a greater or

---

25 *TT*, IV, 2, 630.

26 *RK*, VI, 1, 907. Of course, the Ring is not the only such object in Tolkien's fiction. One notes the particularly ominous malice of the Watchers of the Tower of Cirith Ungol, statues that seem to be strangely animated: "They seemed to be carved out of huge blocks of stone, immovable, and yet they were aware: some dreadful spirit of evil vigilance abode in them. They knew an enemy. Visible or invisible none could pass unheeded. They would forbid his entry, or his escape." *RK*, VI, 1, 902. What Tolkien seems to be describing here is a sort of demonic possession or, better, infestation of an inanimate thing or place, which is made possible by the ability of spiritual beings to annex such things to the operations of their various powers. While hard to imagine in our primary world (though their reality is attested to by many accounts), Tolkien uses his creative imagination to render such phenomena more plausible, if not inevitable, given the consistency of his secondary world.

less degree, out of one's direct control. A man who wishes to exert "power" must have subjects, who are not himself. But he then depends on them.[27]

As Tolkien sees it, Sauron is inevitably caught up in a difficulty from which, ultimately, he cannot escape: the exercise of power demands a going out of oneself—an externalization of oneself and thus an opening of oneself to the possibility of being wounded (i.e., a vulnerability). By creating his Ring, Sauron cannot exert supreme control over creation without also becoming dependent on something of his own making and ultimately opening up for himself the possibility of being destroyed by it. Thus, near the end of *The Lord of the Rings*, we find that just as Frodo is about to cast the Ring into the fires of Mount Doom, he discovers that he cannot do it; in fact, it seems that it is no longer his will that is operative but that of the Ring: "'I have come', he said, 'But I do not choose now to do what I came to do. I will not do this deed. The Ring is mine!'"[28] "I do not choose now." But then, just at that moment, "The Dark Lord was suddenly aware of him, and his Eye piercing all shadows looked across the plain to the door that he had made; and the magnitude of his own folly was revealed to him in a blinding flash, and all the devices of his enemies were laid bare."[29] As Tolkien remarks: "In making devices like the Ring to increase our domination of others, we inevitably make ourselves weaker by becoming dependent on them."[30] Devices such as the Ring, Stratford Caldecott explains, "magnify our power but also externalize it, so that we ourselves wither by their use. When they are destroyed, that weakness is exposed. Sauron, when the Ring is destroyed, literally blows away on the wind."[31]

Thus another quality of the Ring is that, though it seems to offer unlimited power, it is deceptive and treacherous, which are two attributes that are closely and even essentially related (to be "true"

27 *Letters*, 279.
28 RK, VI, 3, 945.
29 RK, VI, 3, 946.
30 *Letters*, 211.
31 Caldecott, *The Power of the Ring*, 67.

in its oldest sense of the word, as Tolkien would have well known, is not only a sort of "adequation of thing and intellect," but also to be "faithful" or "reliable"). Frodo knows this well from the experience of carrying it for several months and hundreds of miles, noting, as he approaches Minas Morgul: "But great as the pressure was, he felt no inclination now to yield to it [the Ring]. He knew that the Ring would only betray him, and that he had not, even if he put it on, the power to face the Morgul-king—not yet."[32] (Of course, the last words are ominous, as they indicate that Frodo has not ruled out using the Ring for himself in the future.) But Tolkien describes the experience of wearing the Ring in a little more detail when Sam, thinking his master dead, puts it on:

> The world changed, and a single moment of time was filled with an hour of thought. At once he was aware that hearing was sharpened while sight was dimmed, but otherwise than in Shelob's lair. All things about him now were not dark but vague; while he himself was there in a grey hazy world, alone, like a small black solid rock, and the Ring, weighing down his left hand, was like an orb of hot gold. He did not feel invisible at all, but horribly and uniquely visible; and he knew that somewhere an Eye was searching for him.[33]

As Sam discovers, the Ring effects a great distortion of time, no doubt related to its fundamental power to stretch out one's lifespan; it dims one's vision and yet sharpens one's hearing; all the world becomes "vague" and shrouded in a "grey haze"; and most strikingly, although Sam is invisible to the physical eye, he feels "horribly and uniquely visible," as though an eye is searching for him. Moreover, and perhaps most importantly, "one thing it [the Ring] did not confer, and that was courage."[34] Hence, the paradoxes of the Ring: it confers a limitless time span, invisibility, sharpened hearing, and great power, yet it distorts and obscures the wearer's vision of the world—as Aristotle notes, the sense

---

32 *TT*, IV, 8, 706.
33 *TT*, IV, 10, 734.
34 *TT*, IV, 10, 734–35.

that is most closely related to thought and intelligence[35]—and mires it down in a sort of vague and hazy fog, making its wearer unable to make clear and necessary distinctions, visual, conceptual, or otherwise. This difference between enhanced powers of hearing and diminished powers of sight leads to deception and trickery.[36] Finally, while it renders the wearer invisible, it makes him feel utterly exposed and saps all courage from him, as if his very corporeality has been stripped away and his inner life exposed. Just as the wearer becomes invisible to everyone else, he becomes supremely visible to its disembodied and malevolent creator (all of which are perhaps due to the very stretching out of time that the Ring effects).

The Ring of Sauron, then, is a magic object. But what does it mean for the Ring to be a magic ring (or for any object to be magic for that matter)? In his *Letters*, Tolkien takes great care to define what he means by "magic" and what he does not mean by this word:

> I have not used "magic" consistently, and indeed the Elven-queen Galadriel is obliged to remonstrate with the Hobbits on their confused use of the word both for the devices and operations of the Enemy, and for those of the Elves. I have not, because there is a word for the latter (since all human stories have suffered the same confusion). But the Elves are there (in my tales) to demonstrate the difference. Their "magic" is Art, delivered from many of its human limitations: more effortless, more quick, more complete (product, and vision in unflawed correspondence). And its object is Art not Power, sub-creation not domination and tyrannous re-forming of Creation. The "Elves" are "immortal," at least as far as this world goes: and hence are concerned rather with the griefs and burdens of deathlessness in time and change, than with death.

---

35 *Metaphysics*, A, 1, 980a25.

36 "He [Sam] was glad of the Ring, for here was yet another company of orcs on the march. Or so at first he thought. Then suddenly he realized that it was not so, his hearing had deceived him." *RK*, VI, 1, 898.

> The Enemy in successive forms is always "naturally" concerned with sheer Domination, and so the Lord of magic and machines; but the problem: that this frightful evil can and does arise from an apparently good root, the desire to benefit the world and others—speedily and according to the benefactor's own plans—is a recurrent motive.[37]

Tolkien here draws a sharp distinction between magic as art, "sub-creation and not domination," and magic as "tyrannous re-forming of Creation." If the Elves have magic (and Tolkien notes how the Elves do not understand what others say is magical about their crafts and powers), it comes simply from the fact that their art or craft is much "more effortless, more quick, more complete (product, and vision in unflawed correspondence)." In other words, there is no gap between concept and product as there too often is in merely human production. To put it another way, Elven magic is simply the result of a deep and sympathetic working with the inherent powers or natures of things—of a con-forming with creation and not a re-forming of it. By contrast, too much human art and ingenuity are magic in the sense of re-forming of the world: of devices for dominating nature and making it conform to human desires and wishes contrary to the natural, created order.[38] And those desires that are contrary to the natural, created order have their root in the human desire to go on living indefinitely in an infinite temporal series that is nevertheless finite and thus mortal in its successive parts. Hence, the Elves are not as liable to corruption by the one Ring, since their concern—"deathlessness in time and change," and how to derive meaning from a story whose conclusion recedes indefinitely—is the opposite of Men's.

37 *Letters*, 146.
38 "The words *magia* and *machine* are related etymologically to the same Indo-European root: *mechane/makhana* may be related to the Old Persian *maghush*, from Proto-Indo-European, *magh, 'to have power' (English, 'might')." John R. Holmes, "'Like Heathen Kings': Religion as Palimpsest in Tolkien's Fiction," in *The Ring and the Cross: Christianity and The Lord of the Rings*, ed. Paul E. Kerry, 119–44 (Madison, NJ: Fairleigh Dickinson University Press, 2011), 143.

As powerful as the Ring is, then, it has fatal weaknesses that stem precisely from it being a species of Machine rather than Elven magic.[39] Elven magic comes from a sub-creative desire to recover the goodness, beauty, and truth of creation itself by recovering the natures of things as created and getting and even living inside them; the Machine and, by extension, the Ring, desires to dominate things by twisting and breaking their natures. But it can only do this by externalizing itself in an object that is exposed to destruction and downfall. Thus, one weakness of the Ring is that it can be used by someone else against its maker; but there is another:

> [If] the One Ring was actually *unmade*, annihilated, then his power would be dissolved, Sauron's own being would be diminished to vanishing point, and he would be reduced to a shadow, a mere memory of malicious will. But that he never contemplated nor feared. The Ring was unbreakable by any smithcraft less than his own. It was indissoluble in any fire, save the undying subterranean fire where it was made—and that was unapproachable, in Mordor. Also, so great was the Ring's power of lust, that anyone who used it became mastered by it; it was beyond the strength of any will (even his own) to injure it, cast it away, or neglect it. So he thought. It was in any case on his finger.[40]

By placing all of his will, power, and being into an external object, Sauron greatly enhanced his power—as human power is greatly enhanced by the Machine—and yet, by doing so, he also made his utter annihilation possible. This power bred a supreme self-confidence that turned out to be a supreme self-deception, a self-confidence and self-deception that the Machine has bred in human beings as well, especially in the twilight of modernity.

---

39 The Ring, it should be noted, is *not* an allegory of the Machine: the Ring has in Tolkien's secondary world effects that are *analogous* to the effects that the Machine has on how human beings in our primary world understand themselves and the world about them and also how they interact with that world.

40 *Letters*, 153–54.

The Ring and Neo-Gnostic Modernity

The Machine, therefore, for Tolkien is a response to the Fall and Mortality; it expresses and in turn breeds a distinct theology or religious attitude, and this religion is Gnosticism. This is not an original observation: Bradley Birzer notes the Gnostic nature of the religion brought to Númenor by Sauron, with the latter as a "Gnostic savior."[41] So what is this Gnostic religion of Sauron hinted at in the *Akallabêth* or *Downfall of Númenor* (interestingly, one of the very few explicit references to religion in all of Tolkien's work)?

Gnosticism refers not to one well-defined religious phenomenon but to a constellation of religious movements that first arose in the Mediterranean world of late antiquity (though, of course, with roots stretching back earlier). These Gnostic movements became attached very early on to Jewish and Christian communities such that Gnosticism is often classified or thought of as a Jewish or Christian heresy. What the Gnostics believed is a matter of controversy for several reasons. As already mentioned, there was no unified Gnostic church and no central teaching authority, so there was little uniformity in its teachings; secondly, most of our sources for the beliefs and practices of the Gnostics come from sources hostile to them, which means they must be read critically; thirdly and perhaps most importantly, to the degree that scholars have been able to reconstruct genuine Gnostic teaching, they have found it to be often inconsistent and even contradictory.[42]

---

41 Birzer, *J. R. R. Tolkien's Sanctifying Myth*, 98.
42 Though somewhat dated, a classic work on Gnosticism is Hans Jonas's *The Gnostic Religion: The Message of the Alien God and the Beginnings of Christianity*, 2nd ed. (Boston: Beacon Press, 1958). For the strong parallels between ancient Gnosticism and important trends in twentieth-century philosophy and thought, see also, by the same author, the essay "Gnosticism, Existentialism, and Nihilism" in *The Phenomenon of Life: Towards a Philosophical Biology* (Evanston, IL: Northwestern University Press, 2001), 211–34. For a more recent exposition of Gnostic thought and its significance in the history of ideas, see Remi Brague, *La Sagesse du monde: Histoire de l'expérience humaine de l'univers* (Paris: Fayard, 1999), chapter 6 (where Brague has some criticisms of Jonas's interpretation of the significance of Gnosticism for modernity). The works of Eric Voegelin, which I will cite

Nevertheless, we can with some confidence assert that Gnosticism was (and is) characterized by the following tenets: (1) that escape from this corrupt and wicked world and union with the divine, of which the human soul is a mere particle or spark, can be achieved by means of a "secret knowledge" (in Greek, *gnosis*), known and transmitted only by a select spiritual elite; (2) a radical and extreme dualism between matter and spirit according to which the material or visible world is not just fallen and corrupted (as for Christians by the Fall and original sin), but that all materiality is thoroughly wicked and corrupt and probably the product of a wicked and incompetent demiurge or creator (sub-creator even); and (3) a conception of the human soul as essentially uncorrupt and as united to the divine not by sharing in the suffering, death, and resurrection of Christ (the Incarnation, after all, presupposes the goodness of creation and in particular of materiality and the body), but through a liberation from the confines of the body and escape to the realm of pure spirit.

What does this ancient heresy have to do with modernity? The initiatory nature of Gnosticism (one can only be saved by being secretly initiated in the mysteries of Gnosticism by a master) and its strong supernaturalism and hatred of matter and the body seem distinctly out of place in the modern world. But insofar as modern materialism views the world as a Machine, it asserts a radical dualism, first enunciated and defended by Descartes, between mind and body: the world of value and meaning belongs exclusively to the essentially immaterial thinking subject, while the visible or material world is reduced essentially to "extension"—a mathematical abstraction where things are understood as an agglomeration of mere parts in a machine—and thus devoid of any inherent meaning or value. Indeed, it assumes methodologically that all material things, as mechanisms, are devoid of life: that death, not life, is the default setting of what things really are.[43] Life is a mere epiphenomenon of death—if not a mere illusion generated by highly complex mechanisms. Meaning and intention, therefore, lie in the

---

below, make some fascinating arguments for the strong Gnostic nature of modern political ideologies.

[43] Jonas, *The Phenomenon of Life*, 7–26.

mind alone, which is itself an extensionless, bloodless "I."[44] So, since Descartes Western humanity has viewed nature as a mere mechanical system devoid of any inherent value, purposes, or even intelligibility; all these must be imposed or projected upon it by the isolated, bodyless, immaterial self.[45] Thus only what can be measured and quantified counts for the modern mind as a genuine object of knowledge.

Such a "knowledge" is not really knowledge for Tolkien in at least two senses: it strives to understand things as one tries to understand a machine, by breaking it down into parts, by manipulating and tinkering with them. But as Gandalf remarks concerning the hubris of his fellow wizard Saruman, who strives for such knowledge, "And he that breaks a thing to find out what it is has left the path of wisdom."[46] Knowledge that is truly worthy of the name understands things in their living and unique natures, what they are in their form and function; and as Aristotle argued long ago, the form and function of natures are real and

---

[44] Carl Hostetter, the editor of *The Nature of Middle Earth*, has an appendix on "Metaphysical and Theological Themes" in Tolkien, in which he remarks that Tolkien's Catholic, even Thomist, philosophical anthropology is in direct opposition to the modern, Cartesian view of the human person, which is "in fact a revival of the ancient Platonic/Gnostic/Manichean belief in the superiority of the spiritual to the material; and in their extremes, the belief that the material world, including the body, is inherently evil, a trap for the human soul, whose primary goal is, or ought to be, to free itself from the body and the material world." *NME*, 403–4.

[45] As Patrick Curry notes, modern science was born partly of Descartes's dream to unify all the sciences and with Francis Bacon's project to torture nature to extract her secrets. Patrick Curry, *Defending Middle Earth: Tolkien, Myth and Modernity* (New York: Houghton-Mifflin, 2004), 69. Thus, in the sixth section of his *Discourse on Method*, Descartes boasts that his new philosophy will allow us to become "masters and possessors of nature." René Descartes, *Discours de la Méthode* (Paris: Bordas, 1984), 146. Furthermore, Kant uses a metaphor similar to Bacon's in the preface to his *Critique of Pure Reason*, where he says that reason must relate to nature "not … in the character of a pupil who listens to everything that the teacher chooses to say, but of an appointed judge, who compels the witnesses to answer questions which he himself has formulated." Immanuel Kant, *Critique of Pure Reason*, trans. Norman Kemp Smith (New York: Saint Martin's Press, 1965), B xiii. See also, Hadot, *Le voile d'Isis*, 169ff.

[46] *FR*, II, 2, 259.

distinct realities in a thing precisely because they transcend the natures and functions of the parts. Hence, the creative Imagination, as the Romantics called it, or fantasy, as Tolkien designates it, gives us a more profound and comprehensive knowledge of things than strictly scientific knowledge, for the creative Imagination must pay the utmost attention and respect to the "inner consistency of reality": it, paradoxically, is not free to remake things as it wills; it must respect things as they are in their inherent and true essences.[47]

But in a second sense, modern knowledge is not genuine knowledge insofar as the technological knowledge of modernity is not really about knowing the world and its creatures (including us) on their own terms and for their own value and meaning, but only insofar as they serve the goals and projects of an imperious will: unmoored from any knowledge of what things are, it is only in service to what the will wants. As Tolkien's good friend and fellow Inkling C. S. Lewis explained in his book *The Abolition of Man*, while for premodern men, the problem had been how to make our minds conform to reality, in our modern technological age the problem is how to make reality conform to our desires. Underlying the premodern understanding of knowledge is the presupposition that the world and the things in it are fundamentally good and desirable and that it is good for our intellect to be conformed to them in knowledge.[48]

It is, by contrast, a fundamental assertion of Gnosticism that reality must conform to our will, to our desires, for reality is a prison, a trap, something inherently evil. It is either the product of a malevolent deity (ancient Gnosticism) or, much worse, a brute, random, and indifferent surd, devoid of any inherent meaning or value (modern Gnosticism). The dualism of the ancient Gnostics was strongly supernatural in outlook, with the goal being the liberation of the soul (the eschaton or last judgment) from the world of matter through a secret knowledge.

---

47 "Just because Fantasy deals with things which do not exist in the Primary World, Tolkien holds, it is 'not a lower but a higher form of Art, indeed the most nearly pure form, and so (when achieved) the most potent'. It is relatively easy to achieve the 'inner consistency of reality' in realistic material. But good Fantasy is very difficult to write." Reilly, "Tolkien and the Fairy Story," 98.

48 Kreeft, *The Philosophy of Tolkien*, 92–93.

This knowledge consisted of a sort of realization or awareness of oneself as pure spirit, uncontaminated by the body or matter, and therefore beyond all moral and social obligations and human history. The goal of the modern Gnostic, however, is to employ the secret knowledge of technology to immanentize the heavenly paradise or *pleroma* of the Gnostics, to realize here in this world and in history the eradication of all evil through science and technocratic domination and control. Like in ancient Gnosticism, this immanentization will be effected through a select elite, characterized by their secret, superior knowledge or *gnosis*.

For the modern Gnostic, a utopian dream world can and must be realized in this world. The problem, however, is threefold: for one, reality is ironically (since the modern Gnostic views reality as inert and devoid of all inherent value) indifferent to or resistant to the Gnostic dream world. But rather than see this as the falsification of their dream world, the Gnostic doubles down: "In Gnosticism the nonrecognition of reality is a matter of principle."[49] He or she takes this resistance as proof of the malign nature of reality and the goodness and purity of the Gnostic's intentions. Second, the dream world of the Gnostic, since it is divorced from any connection to reality, can only have the consistency of reality by forcing, by violence if necessary, everyone without exception to dream the dream. Finally, since Gnosticism is founded in principle on the nonrecognition of reality and therefore denies in principle any metaphysical foundation in what is real, its goals and ideals are constantly shifting and unstable. What was considered enlightened and progressive twenty years ago is now seen as irredeemably backward and even evil.[50] Even if the Gnostic *could* compel universal assent to his dream world, that world is highly unstable and always on the point of crumbling. As such, the Gnostic dream world is the categorical opposite or inversion (rather, *perversion*)

49 Eric Voegelin, *The New Science of Politics: An Introduction* (Chicago: University of Chicago Press, 1987), 168.
50 In his essay "On Fairy-stories," Tolkien cites the remark of G. K. Chesterton that when people claimed that some novelty was here to stay, it was as good as saying that it would be seen as dated and shabby only a few years later. See G. K. Chesterton, *Orthodoxy* (San Francisco: Ignatius Press, 1995), 40; *TL*, 61.

of the fairy-story or fantasy in its true sense insofar as the latter, as we saw Tolkien argue in the last chapter, must be founded on a scrupulous love and respect for the reality of the primary world and its inherent purposes and natures. The fairy-story must always have the inner consistency of reality. Thus, the preeminent instance of the fairy-story is the Gospel, for it is the fairy-story that intrudes into history and time, and is thus the complete antithesis of the Gnostic dream world, which is, in turn, a sort of anti-Gospel, being in the end a desperate and futile attempt to realize the eschaton in time.[51]

In direct opposition to Gnosticism, Tolkien explicitly claims that he does not deal with absolute evil; the world is neither the thoroughly evil product of a thoroughly evil demiurge nor a mere Machine, completely indifferent to meaning and value:

> In my story I do not deal in Absolute Evil. I do not think there is such a thing, since that is Zero. I do not think that at any rate any "rational being" is wholly evil. Satan fell. In my myth Morgoth fell before Creation of the physical world. In my story Sauron represents as near an approach to the wholly evil will as is possible. He had gone the way of all tyrants: beginning well, at least on the level that while desiring to order all things according to his own wisdom he still at first considered the (economic) well-being of other inhabitants of the Earth. But he went further than human tyrants in pride and the lust for domination, being in origin an immortal (angelic) spirit [note: of the same kind as Gandalf and Saruman, but of a far higher order]. In *The Lord of the Rings* the conflict is not basically about "freedom," though that is naturally involved. It is about God, and His sole right to divine honour. The Eldar and the Númenóreans believed in The One, the true God, and held worship of any other person an abomination. Sauron desired to be a God-King, and was held to be this by his servants; if he

---

[51] Which fact explains why, for Voeglin, modern neo-Gnostic political ideologies like fascism, communism, socialism, progressivism, etc., are ferociously anti-Christian: they are based on a creed that is defined by a *negation* or inversion of the Christian story. See Voeglin, *The New Science of Politics*, chapter 6.

had been victorious he would have demanded divine honour from all rational creatures and absolute temporal power over the whole world.[52]

As Augustine argued long ago, evil necessarily presupposes goodness. A realty in which you would have a subsistent, equally real and powerful principle of evil is a metaphysical impossibility. Evil by its very nature is a privation or taking away of some good in a thing, as blindness is not any thing in itself but is the privation of sight. As Aquinas points out, this logic applies to rational beings as well: no rational being is purely evil, or at least no rational being starts out as purely evil, but often begins their descent into evil with good intentions, for as rational beings we can only will things *sub speciei boni*.[53] Insofar as pride and the lust for domination come to predominate in a rational being, however, to that degree it suffers a privation of a rightly ordered love toward other creatures and in particular to its Creator. In the end, a rational creature becomes thoroughly evil when it desires to replace God Himself with itself. Only in this sense is the Ring "altogether evil"[54]: it precisely brings about a privation of one's own thought and will through their enslavement to another: "as long as it is in the world it will be danger even to the Wise. For nothing is evil in the beginning. Even Sauron was not so. I fear to take the Ring to hide it. I will not take the Ring to wield it."[55] So says even Gandalf, one of the mighty Maiar.

Among the more interesting and peculiar features of the passage cited above are the very modern reasons for wielding the Ring that Tolkien mentions: the technocratic reordering of the world for the economic wellbeing of its inhabitants. These very modern goals and preoccupations presuppose a form of Gnosticism. Modernity's worldview is based upon a dualism, where creation disappears and is replaced by the Machine (which, in turn, is but a short step from viewing man as machine). What was once called "creation" has now become dead and devoid of any inherent purpose or meaning except

---

52 *Letters*, 243–44.
53 *S.Th.* I-II, 8, 1. See also, *De ver.*, 16, 6, and *Conf.*, II, 5.13.
54 *FR*, II, 2, 267.
55 *FR*, II, 2, 267.

whatever purpose or meaning is put there by human agency. As for the human being, he or she is reduced to a sort of "ghost in the machine" (as aptly described by Gilbert Ryle), with only a tenuous, mysterious, or even hostile relationship to his or her body. Thus, it is remarkable that one of the effects of the Ring is that it turns its wearer invisible: "it is precisely one's material or physical appearance which is suppressed in wearing the Ring, a point leading Alison Milbank to suggest a certain Manicheanism behind the domination of Sauron and Melkor."[56] McIntosh goes on to say:

> Like the modern conception of the subject, Sauron's Ring, in making its wearer invisible to others and thus detaching him from his rootedness and participation in the world, in principle denies the claim that other beings have on him by virtue of their otherness. Invisible to all others while all others remain visible to him, the Ring-wearer assumes a quasi-transcendence in which their being effectively becomes an extension of his own.[57]

Nothing exemplifies the aloof and detached Cartesian subject better than the rational being who wears the Ring of Sauron. This "quasi-transcendence" gives the wearer the illusion of power that may make him or her a "master and possessor of nature." This illusion of power, however, has real consequences in the natural world. As Galdor states during the Council of Elrond, "And yet we see that Sauron can torture and destroy the very hills."[58] This evil of Sauron's goes, for Tolkien, even deeper than its effects on the wearer or other rational beings.

In *Morgoth's Ring*, Tolkien explores the relation between Sauron and his master, the first "Dark Lord," Melkor, known to the Elves as Morgoth (the Black Enemy). In many ways, Morgoth sets the precedents for Sauron's own actions. So what is "Morgoth's Ring" in the title? Tolkien proposes that the whole of Middle-earth is Morgoth's ring, insofar as he, as one of the Valar, had an original and primal role, along with all the other Valar or "Powers," in the making and shaping

---

56 McIntosh, *The Flame Imperishable*, 237.
57 McIntosh, *The Flame Imperishable*, 236.
58 FR, II, 2, 266.

of Middle-earth. In the case of Morgoth, however, his was rather an unmaking and deforming of that creation. Thus, Tolkien notes that, for Manwë, the chief of the Valar, the "task and problem was much more difficult than Gandalf's. Sauron's relatively smaller power was *concentrated*; Morgoth's vast power was *disseminated*. The whole of 'Middle-earth' was Morgoth's Ring."[59] Morgoth, Tolkien writes, did not merely desire to dominate or control Middle-earth, like his servant Sauron, but rather he had a mad desire to destroy the world if he could not completely dominate it:

> Sauron had never reached this stage of nihilistic madness. He did not object to the existence of the world, so long as he could do what he liked with it. He still had the relics of positive purposes, that descended from the good of the nature in which he began: it had been his virtue (and therefore also the cause of his fall, and of his relapse) that he loved order and coordination, and disliked all confusion and wasteful friction. (It was the apparent will and power of Melkor to effect his designs quickly and masterfully that had first attracted Sauron to him.) Sauron had, in fact, been very much like Saruman, and so still understood him quickly and could guess what he would be likely to think, even without the aid of *palantíri* or of spies; whereas Gandalf eluded and puzzled him.[60]

Tolkien suggests here (and as we shall see in other places) that there is an evil that goes far deeper than Sauron or his Ring. Evil pervades Middle-earth far more widely and deeply than what is brought about specifically and explicitly by Sauron and his servants. Just as the industrial-scale killing that he witnessed during World War I, everywhere and yet nowhere, unseen and constantly threatening, so Morgoth's evil dominates Middle-earth.[61] Compared to the evil of Morgoth's Ring, the

---

59 *MR*, 400.
60 *MR*, 396.
61 Janet Croft suggests that Tolkien's experiences of World War I shaped his concept of evil, especially in the case of Frodo's quest, where the evil is both everywhere and unseen, and where courage consists in quiet endurance, since flight is impossible. Frodo's experience is more like the unrelieved stress of modern

Ring of Sauron is relatively comprehensible and straightforward in its evil, for it was designed to bring about "order and coordination" and eliminate all "confusion and wasteful friction." In that sense, the Ring of Sauron is but a modern outgrowth of a more ancient evil, just as modernity and the Machine are but outgrowths of a far more ancient heresy and, ultimately, of the Fall.

But if evil pervades Middle-earth as "Morgoth's Ring," does that mean that Tolkien has fallen into the sort of Gnosticism that he condemns? Is Tolkien questioning the Augustinian view of evil as privation? Or is Tolkien grudgingly admitting that there is some truth to the Manichean (or Gnostic) view that evil can be an independently existing, malevolent force in its own right?[62] Certainly the Ring's power tempts the wearer to inner rebellion against the created order, but insofar as it renders the wearer invisible and, so to speak, "de-natures" him or her, stripping the wearer of any connection to the world around them, even to the body, it acts as an external force. For that reason, "Sauron is only seen once, indirectly—through the Palantir—otherwise his presence is felt through a disembodied eye or his agents."[63] In the end, the problem of whether the Ring manifests a "Augustinian" or "Manichean" view of evil is ultimately a pseudo-problem[64]: for evil to be

---

warfare than anything found in ancient or medieval literature. Janet Croft, "War," in *A Companion to J. R. R. Tolkien*, ed. Stuart Lee (Hoboken, NJ: Wiley-Blackwell Publishing, 2020), 467.

62 Shippey, *Author of the Century*, 135. Thus, Shippey goes on to say, if the Ring were only a "psychic amplifier," then they could simply give it to Tom Bombadil, who seems immune to the Ring's power to corrupt; if it were, by contrast, a purely external malevolent force, then anyone of great enough power—Gandalf or Galadriel—could take it to Orodruin and destroy it. But neither is the case. Shippey, *Author of the Century*, 142.

63 "Thus an essential plane of the conflict between good and evil is internal: either internal to the hero or his community." Christopher Garbowski, "Evil," in Lee, *A Companion to J. R. R. Tolkien*, 423. It should be noted here that contrary to what one might think if one only watched the film adaptations of *The Lord of the Rings*, Tolkien only speaks of the eye of Sauron as something encountered in the mind of the wearer or in the palantir. In the book, Barad-dûr, except for brief moments, is continually shrouded in dark clouds. When Frodo and Sam do glimpse it in those brief moments, no mention is made of a great eye perched on top of it.

64 Which Shippey himself concedes. Shippey, *Author of the Century*, 141. It

privation of what is good is not to deny that evil is in a sense real or that it exerts a force of its own. A will deformed by a lust for domination and hatred of its Creator suffers the greatest privation that there is: possession of the highest good through love of that highest good. Yet that privation is always rooted in a rational being created good and thus can warp the very real effects of that being's very real actions.

Thus even Frodo, the chief hero of the story, undergoes a change, subtle and perceivable only to someone like Gandalf, yet real. Being stabbed by the blade of the Ringwraith, the hold that Frodo's spirit has on his body cannot but be made more tenuous as the Quest plays out:

> [To] the wizard's eye there was a faint change, just a hint as it were of transparency, about him, and especially about the left hand that lay outside the coverlet. "Still that must be expected," said Gandalf to himself. "He is not half through yet, and to what he will come in the end not even Elrond can foretell. Not to evil, I think. He may become like a glass filled with a clear light for eyes to see that can."[65]

Tolkien hints that this evil, this denaturing and privation of his natural being as a result of his wounding by the Morgul blade, may be turned to a far greater good, for Frodo "may become like a glass filled with a clear light for eyes to see that can." In the end, even the evil of Morgoth that so pervades Middle-earth can be redeemed and turned to a greater good. The privation that the evil caused in Frodo can be the occasion for him to be filled with light and his being thereby not only restored but raised to a higher ontological reality. To recover our primary world through fantasy, therefore, is to recover the possibility of the redemption of all evil in the world. It is thus the antithesis of the magic ring of the Gnostic, who does not see the world as redeemed or even redeemable, but as something to be broken and destroyed in order to conform it

---

should be noted here that Shippey refers to the "Boethian" view of evil rather than to the "Augustinian" view, referring to the late Roman philosopher's views on evil in his *Consolation of Philosophy*. But Boethius was heavily influenced by Augustine, and his view of evil is therefore essentially the same as Augustine's.

65 *FR*, II, 1, 223.

to his or her dream world. Good or true fantasy does the opposite: it grounds us in the inherent goodness and meaningfulness of being; it allows us to see that goodness and meaningfulness as it emerges out of evil and suffering. Thus it is no accident that Gandalf, the paragon of wisdom in Tolkien's legendarium, is the only one who is able to see this slow transformation in Frodo.

CHAPTER THREE

The Recovery of Language

Tolkien was a philologist whose lifelong professional interest and personal passion was languages—especially ancient and medieval languages. From a very young age, not only was Tolkien learning classical and modern languages formally at school, but he was teaching himself languages off the curriculum such as Gothic and Welsh. Most importantly, he was creating his own languages, which would be the seeds for his languages of Middle-earth. The most important fact about his own created languages, however, is that Tolkien was not content to invent a language with no temporal dimension (like Esperanto)[1]; rather

---

[1] Actually, Tolkien's estimation of Esperanto was not entirely negative: he studied it and it was, at least partially, an inspiration for creating his own languages. He even says of Esperanto in the opening paragraph of his essay "A Secret Vice": "I particularly like Esperanto, not least because it is the creation ultimately of one man, not a philologist, and is therefore something like a 'human language bereft of the inconvenience due to too many successive cooks'"—which is as good a

he created a whole history and culture for these languages, devising and then tracing syntactical and morphological changes from primal language roots, much like the way in which comparative philologists traced how the various languages of Eurasia evolved from a primal Indo-European language. His created languages were meant to be anything but artificial (again, like Esperanto), but living entities rooted in a distinct world.[2]

In other words, Tolkien's interest in language and its importance was not just a result of a personal passion. For him language was part and parcel of reality itself and a fundamental and constituent principle of what we might call the "fabric of being" ("To ask what is the origin of stories (however qualified) is to ask what is the origin of language and of the mind."[3]). To put it another way, language is the sea in which we, as rational incarnate beings, swim: the world is world only insofar as it is made present to us, or revealed to us, in and through language. At the most fundamental level of human experience, world and language, thing and word, cannot be separated without doing violence to the original givenness of the world and of the multifarious beings in it. Insofar as language becomes corrupted, i.e., becomes worn, trite, abstract, and riddled with jargon or propaganda slogans, to that degree it can become a barrier to the world and not our primary means of access to it (because it is a constitutive element of that experience itself). Hence, the most vital need of modern humanity is a recovery of the power, weight, beauty, and deep, lived meaning of language in general and of words in particular, for to recover language is to recover reality.

---

description of the ideal artificial language (in a particular sense) as I can give." *MC*, 198. Of course, Tolkien's praise of Esperanto here is qualified: it is as good an *artificial* language as one could invent. But Tolkien was not aiming at creating artificial languages but living ones. Thus, he says of Esperanto in one of his letters, "Volapük, Esperanto, Ido, Novial, etc. etc. are dead, far deader than ancient unused languages, because their authors never invented any Esperanto legends." *Letters*, 231.

2 As Tolkien says of his love of creating languages, "It is not a 'hobby', in the sense of something quite different from one's work, taken up as relief-outlet. The invention of languages is the foundation. The 'stories' were made rather to provide a world for the languages than the reverse. To me a name comes first and the story follows." *Letters*, 219.

3 *TL*, 17.

Recovery of Language, Recovery of Reality

As John Holmes remarks: "Tolkien's skill at creating names is universally stipulated, even by critics who otherwise dislike *The Lord of the Rings*. Like Tolkien's invented languages his invented names precede the plot. 'To me ... a name comes first and the story follows' (*Letters*, 219)."[4] The names of places, people, and things in Tolkien's fiction have an authenticity and weight that, it can be argued, almost no fantasy writer since Tolkien has been able to replicate (most names for places and peoples in contemporary fantasy have a contrived, artificial feel).[5] As Tolkien mentioned to an interviewer:

> The seed [of the myth] is linguistic, of course. I'm a linguist and everything is linguistic—that's why I take such pains with

---

[4] John R. Holmes, "*The Lord of the Rings*," in *A Companion to J. R. R. Tolkien*, ed. Stuart Lee (Hoboken, NJ: Wiley-Blackwell Publishing, 2020), 139.

[5] For example, Tolkien gives the reader a sense of moving into a more ancient world as the hobbits leave the Shire for Bree by switching from names with roots in Old English to names with distinctly Celtic roots: "Since the survival of traces of the older language of the Stoors and the Bree-men resembled the survival of Celtic elements in England, I have sometimes imitated the latter in my translation. Thus Bree, Combe (Coomb), Archet, and Chetwood are modelled on relics of British nomenclature, chosen according to sense: *bree* 'hill' *chet* 'wood'." *RK*, Appendix F, 1135. What is remarkable is that the reader feels this effect, even when he or she knows nothing of the linguistic foundation, which remains purposely hidden. We also find Tolkien saying this of names of both people and places in the appendices of *The Lord of the Rings*: "Of these things in the time of Frodo there were still some traces left in local words and names, many of which closely resembled those found in Dale or in Rohan. Most notable were the names of days, months, and seasons; several other words of the same sort (such as *mathom* and *smial*) were also still in common use, while more were preserved in the place-names of Bree and the Shire. The personal names of the Hobbits were also peculiar and many had come down from the ancient days." *RK*, Appendix F, 1130. Thus, Tom Shippey remarks: "This was Tolkien's major linguistic heresy. He thought that people could feel history in words, could recognize language 'styles', could extract sense (of sorts) from sound alone, could moreover make aesthetic judgements based on phonology. He said the sound of 'cellar door' was more beautiful than the sound of 'beautiful'. He clearly believed that *untranslated* elvish would do a job that English could not." Shippey, *The Road to Middle-earth*, 114.

names. The real seed was starting when I was quite a child by inventing languages, largely to try to capture the esthetic mode of the languages I was learning, and I eventually made the discovery that language can't exist in a void and if you invent a language yourself you can't cut it in half. It has to come alive—so really the languages came first and the country after.[6]

Here we have a clue to the authenticity of Tolkien's names: Tolkien took great pains to situate them in a coherent language and the language itself in a coherent linguistic world, with history, life, and depth. Precisely because words open up or reveal a world, they have power and efficacy (the doors of Moria are, after all, governed by words).[7] World and language arise together, as Tolkien sees it, and the recovery of one is the recovery of the other.[8] Even more, as primeval with the things they reveal, words play a necessary part in the making of the world they reveal, as Flieger notes: "The writer's tools of sub-creation are words… This being the case, words are not merely for describing or reporting but for actual making, for real-izing in the literal sense of the word the writer's imaginary world."[9]

What are the roots of Tolkien's views on language? Many of his views were, of course, the fruits of what he learned in his long career as a philologist.[10] But particularly influential for Tolkien's view of language and reality was the work of his friend and fellow Inkling, Owen Barfield.[11]

    6   Resnick, "An Interview with Tolkien," 41, cited in Birzer, *J. R. R. Tolkien's Sanctifying Myth*, 28.

    7   FR, II, 4, 306.

    8   This is why, as Dimitra Fimi warns, we must not take completely at face value Tolkien's claims that his myths arose from his languages (after all, the earliest poem of his legendarium took its inspiration from an Old English poem, *Christ*). "What seems to be closer to the truth, therefore, is that language invention and myth-making did not begin independently, but became interconnected very early in Tolkien's career as a writer." Fimi, *Tolkien, Race and Cultural History*, 66.

    9   Flieger, *Splintered Light*, 41.

    10   For an extensive and deeper exploration of the academic and intellectual background to Tolkien's views on language and myth, see Imbert, *From Imagination to Faërie*, chapter 3.

    11   For the influence of Barfield on Tolkien, see Flieger, *Splintered Light*, 35; and Birzer, *J. R. R. Tolkien's Sanctifying Myth*, 30.

As is evident from his essay "On Fairy-Stories" as well as from his letters, Barfield's thought, as expressed in his book *Poetic Diction*, had a particularly strong impact on Tolkien's mind, since it expressed many of the insights that he himself had come to as a philologist. We shall look in some detail on Barfield's argument presently. But I want to propose that Tolkien's as well as Barfield's views on language and its relation to reality go back much further—to the Middle Ages, in fact, which is only appropriate for a medievalist like Tolkien.

Tolkien's and Barfield's views on the relation of language and reality are related to what modern scholars of medieval philosophy call "The Problem of Universals." Stated briefly, the problem is this: in what sense can I predicate universal terms ("tree," "dog," "triangle") of particular things (trees, dogs, triangles in ink, wood, bronze, etc.)? Do these universal terms refer to something real beyond the particular things about which we use them, or are they somehow in the things they refer to? If the latter, in what sense does the universal exist in the thing? If these terms do not refer to anything real in things, then in what sense can our use of these terms—or of language in general—be said to give us any knowledge of things in the world or even refer to anything in the world at all? We cannot get around this problem, because without these universal terms human language and therefore any conceptual thought (or, really, any thought at all) and by extension any knowledge of the world would be impossible.

Now medieval scholastics suggested three possible solutions to this problem.[12] One solution was proposed by those whom modern scholars call "realists." They argued that, if these universal terms are to have any sense at all, they must refer to something real in the same mode as the particular itself. In other words, the universal "tree" must refer to a really existing universal "thing" or, better, "form," that exists as a universal

---

12 What follows is an *extremely* simplified and condensed account of the medieval problem of universals, the subject for over three hundred years of complex and highly technical debates. Early nominalists, for example, still argued that there was a "natural supposit" (*suppositio naturalis*) for terms that was "pre-propositional," i.e., had a meaning independent of its place in discourse—a position that later, "radical" nominalists would drop, and so forth. See Alain de Libera, *La philosophie médiévale* (Paris: Presses Universitaires de France, 2021), 40–42.

in itself apart from all particular, material trees. Plato's doctrine of the existence of separate, immaterial, subsistent Forms is the philosophical precedent for this position. Nevertheless, as distinguished as its philosophical pedigree was, this "hard" or "radical realism" found few defenders: if all that language refers to is the separate universal Form of a thing, then how can it be said to give us any knowledge of particular things in the world? The relation between the Form and the particular thing that imitates it becomes mysterious. Moreover, the ontological status of these separate universal Forms is unclear and problematic: they neither belong to the material world, nor do they exist in individual minds. Most troubling, they seem to exist separately from and even above the divine Mind.

Opposed to the realists were the nominalists. As their name indicates, they argued that a universal term was a mere name (or *nomen* in Latin) that simply stood or supposited for particular things within human language. That is to say, the universal "tree" was simply a word that served as a marker or placeholder in human language for particular things with a certain set of shared features, but which refers to nothing in or beyond the thing itself. The meaning of the universal is simply determined by its utility within human language. There are no universal forms in things themselves to which these terms refer. The foremost and perhaps most radical exponent of this view was the English Franciscan friar and theologian, William of Ockham (c. 1287–1347)—and he had many followers.[13]

But, like hard or extreme realism, this position has severe problems: first, in what sense can a term stand or supposit for a set of particular things without referring to something real, inherent in the things themselves, that they have in common? Even more importantly, on this account of language and its relation to things, how can the human mind distinguish between the essential and inessential properties of a thing, if language refers to nothing real in the thing? How can my use of the term "tree" make any sense or even be, per the nominalists, useful, if, theoretically, it can refer to any number of things or properties, since there is nothing in the things themselves to ground the use of the term?

13 Cf. Libera, *La philosophie médiévale*, 118–20.

What this really means is that language actually gives us no knowledge of the world; it allows us to manipulate our perceptions of and language about the world in ways that may produce predictive results (such as in mathematical models), but language does not reveal anything about things themselves or the world of which they are a constituent part.

Despite these problems, the influence of this school of thought only grew as the Middle Ages wore on and, as many argue, became the basis for the modern understanding of the relation of language or meaning to reality.[14] Once Descartes persuaded modern men and women to view the mind or soul as something completely separate from the body, and the body and all of material reality as simply a lifeless machine without any inherent forms (and, it follows, purpose, meaning, or value), then a nominalist view of language becomes, in a sense, the default understanding of language and reality. If there is no inherent form, meaning, or value in the world, then language becomes understood as a tool for manipulating the world, and language itself refers primarily to ideas in our minds and not to things themselves. We see nominalism reflected and carried forward later into the twentieth century in structuralism (such as that found in the work of the Swiss linguist Ferdinand Saussure) for which meaning in language comes solely from its use within the language itself (i.e., its "structure").[15] From structuralism it is but a short step to poststructuralism and postmodern deconstruction, where this view is taken to the extreme and language is understood as a purely self-referential yet unstable (read: neo-Gnostic)

---

14 Edward Feser, *Aristotle's Revenge: The Metaphysical Foundations of Physical and Biological Science* (Neukirchen-Seelscheid: Editiones Scholasticae, 2019), 170; see also James Hannam, *God's Philosophers: How the Medieval World Laid the Foundations of Modern Science* (London: Icon Books, 2009). Nominalism was attractive to many medieval theologians in that, by eliminating supposedly superfluous metaphysical entities (think of "Ockham's Razor") like real universals, it seems to affirm more clearly the absolute transcendence and power of God over creatures and the absolute necessity of revelation, since, it claims, natural theology, based as it is on the knowledge of the real natures of things, is empty and vain. Of course, nominalism does this at the very high price of making any natural or rational knowledge of God exceedingly difficult, if not impossible.

15 Ferdinand de Saussure, *Cours de linguistique générale*, ed. Charles Bally et al. (Paris: Payot, 1964), 155–69.

system of competing discourses. Language is thus treated as a fetish, as something that has a quasi-magical power over the world and society to disrupt oppression and the conceptual binaries that are assumed to structure language and thus reality. Perhaps the best representative of this sort of linguistic nominalism in Tolkien's fiction is the corrupt and treacherous wizard Saruman. As Tom Shippey remarks, Saruman is the most contemporary figure in Middle-earth, both politically and linguistically. He is "on the road to 'doublethink'"[16]; this is because for Saruman, language is just a tool for technocratic manipulation and for asserting power.[17]

In contrast to these two views of universals and their relations to things, we find a third position, found most fully developed and powerfully argued in the works of Thomas Aquinas, which modern scholars call "moderate realism." It is this view, I propose, that Tolkien's fantasy is designed to help us recover, not through philosophical argumentation, but directly and fundamentally through a recovery of the primal experience of language that founds this view.[18] To explain moderate realism, it is best to take the two terms separately. This position is a species of realism insofar as it argues that the universal terms we apply to things refer to something

---

16 Shippey, *Author of the Century*, 76.

17 "We may join with that Power. It would be wise, Gandalf. There is hope that way. Its victory is at hand; and there will be rich reward for those that aided it. As the power grows, its proved friends will also grow; and the Wise, such as you and I, may with patience come at last to direct its courses, to control it. We can bide our time, we can keep our thoughts in our hearts, deploring maybe the evils done by the way, but approving the high and ultimate purpose: Knowledge, Rule, Order; all the things that we have so far striven in vain to accomplish, hindered rather than helped by our weak or idle friends. There need not be, there would not be, any real change in our designs, only in our means." *FR* II, 2, 259.

18 Halsall remarks that, for Tolkien, "created being—or being coming into reality—is not a lapse from an idea, but an extension of the creative affections of the One." Halsall, *Creation and Beauty in Tolkien's Catholic Vision*, 80. As Alison Milbank notes in relation to this fundamental principle, "In Thomas this leads to a rejection of nominalism, and promotion of a moderate and participatory realism. For Tolkien the element I would stress is the objectivity of things. Only through the reality of the world can the mind, according to Thomas, reach out to otherness and become the object." Alison Milbank, *Chesterton and Tolkien as Theologians: The Fantasy of the Real* (London: T. and T. Clark, 2007), 17.

real in the things referred to: when I say that those objects over there are trees, the term "tree" refers to something really "in" and common to those objects that justifies me calling them by that term. The particular trees have a common nature or essence that makes them what they are, independently of any mind knowing it. In knowing trees, Aquinas argues, the mind simply isolates through abstraction the common nature already to be found in trees, much as one can, by abstraction, separate out "green" from "green apple": the green is really there in the apple, but the mind isolates the concept "green" from the other properties of the apple and indeed from the apple itself, considering the apple's "greenness" (or its shape, scent, species variety, etc.) apart from the apple, all the while understanding that such qualities cannot be really separate from the apple itself.[19] But the position is "moderate" insofar as Aquinas argues that the universal term does not refer to a reality or thing apart from particulars. No universal "tree" exists apart from particular, material trees. The universal as universal exists only in the mind as a concept, expressed through a term. This term is itself expressed in many different languages using different words, which change from language to language and from age to age. Nevertheless, human knowledge is possible because it is based on this primal unity of intellect and thing: the formal reality of the thing, in Aquinas's account is identical to its formal reality in the mind insofar as the mind knows or is *con-formed* to ("formed with") the thing. Thus, on the moderate realist account and only on that account can we give a plausible explanation of how genuine human knowledge of the world is possible.

The significance of this account of the relation of language to world becomes clear when we turn to a source that, as was mentioned above, Tolkien read, knew, and appreciated highly: Owen Barfield's *Poetic Diction: A Study in Meaning*. This work is crucially important in that it

19 In his essay "On Fairy-stories," Tolkien uses an example very similar to that of Aquinas in discussing the power of language to sub-create: we can separate, he says, "green" from the givenness of "green-grass" and think of a world in which it makes sense to have a "green-sun" *TL*, 22–23. In a similar way, Aquinas argues, we can know both "green" and "apple" by abstraction—mentally separating or distinguishing the apple from its accident or color green, but nevertheless knowing, in the process, that the color "green," while it does not exist as such apart from the apple, is all the same really *in* the apple. *S.Th.*, I, 85, 1, ad 1.

illuminates in more explicit and theoretical form the philosophy of language underlying Tolkien's work. As we also mentioned above, what we can see in Barfield's work—and what probably attracted Tolkien to it—is that is not only argues for a moderate realist view of language and meaning, but it claims even further (beyond what any of the medievals would have claimed) that myth and fantasy demonstrate, in a sort of phenomenological showing, the truth of this position. As Colin Duriez puts it, "All of them [the Inklings] seemed convinced that myth had the ability to generalize without losing contact with the individual character of natural things."[20] To put it in another way, in a world dominated by the Machine and a nominalist view of language and reality, myth and fantasy become the privileged, if not the only, access to a recovery of a genuine experience of the world where thought is not separated from things.[21]

In short, just as Aquinas and other medieval moderate realists argued that the universal as universal is really there in the thing *in potentiality*, so Barfield argues that although human culture has come to abstract the metaphorical meaning from the literal meaning in language, it still necessarily remains the case that the metaphorical or poetic meaning is really there in the things themselves, *at least in potentiality*, and that these meanings (literal and metaphorical) are an essential element in the givenness of things themselves to our experience.

In examining the nature of language, myth, and meaning, Barfield's main target is the great nineteenth-century Anglo-German scholar of Indo-European myth and language, Max Müller—a target also

[20] Colin Duriez, "Where Two or Three Are Gathered: Tolkien and the Inklings," in *Light Beyond All Shadow: Religious Experience in Tolkien's Work*, ed. Paul E. Kerry and Sandra Miesel (Madison, NJ: Fairleigh Dickinson University Press, 2011), 160.

[21] Verlyn Flieger gives a good summary of Barfield's thought in *Splintered Light*, 38–39, which has been the basis of my own (with, of course, a very different emphasis). I have, in particular, supplemented my summary with insights from another of Barfield's books, *Saving the Appearances: A Study in Idolatry* (Middletown, CT: Wesleyan University Press, 1988). This latter book was first published much later, in 1957, and thus after *The Lord of the Rings*, but it develops more clearly and in more detail the main theses of Barfield's earlier book and is helpful for a fuller understanding of Barfield's argument.

of Tolkien in his essay "On Fairy-stories." For Müller, the primitive myths of the Indo-Europeans were basically thinly disguised solar, lunar, and stellar myths meant to explain to a primitive people the causes of various celestial and natural phenomena. In short, early myths are simply primitive and therefore crude, inaccurate, and incomplete attempts at doing natural science. According to Barfield, however, Müller commits a basic fallacy: he projects back onto the past—onto the primitive mind—the abstract thinking and intellectual preoccupations of a much later stage in human development.[22] Müller assumes that there was already a literal, non-metaphorical meaning to terms for primitive humanity, to which primitive men added metaphorical or mythical meanings in vain attempts at quasi-scientific, natural explanations. Thus, to use Barfield's example of the Latin word *spiritus*, or its Greek equivalent, *pneuma*, the base or root meaning for the primitive Latins and Greeks was "breath"; but they then added on, Müller argued, metaphorical or abstract meanings cognate with the various meanings of the English word "spiritual" in an attempt to explain the origin, nature, and effects of life and the soul.[23]

But Barfield argues that Müller had things precisely backwards. As he puts the problem concisely in his later book *Saving the Appearances*: "If we find language growing more and more metaphorical, the further back we go into the past, what possible justification can there be for assuming a still earlier time when it was not metaphorical at all?"[24] As for the problem of linguistic roots mentioned by Müller:

> "Roots," far from being the germs of speech, are the product of ages of intellectual abstraction carried on, first instinctively by ordinary speakers, and afterwards deliberately by the grammarians and the philologists.... They [19th century philologists] mistook elements for seeds—and called them roots.[25]

---

22 Owen Barfield, *Poetic Diction: A Study in Meaning* (Middletown, CT: Wesleyan University Press, 1973), 74–75.
23 Barfield, *Poetic Diction*, 80–81.
24 Barfield, *Saving the Appearances*, 119.
25 Barfield, *Poetic Diction*, 81–82.

There is no literal layer to language in its most primitive forms; rather, "these poetic, and *apparently* 'metaphorical' values were latent in meaning from the beginning."[26] When the ancient Greeks and Latins spoke of *pneuma* or *spiritus*, they meant both what we in English would call "breath" and "spirit"—the material thing and its mental or spiritual counterpart—as one unbroken meaning. Only after centuries of philosophical argumentation and conceptual refinement, starting with the Presocratics and working through Plato and Aristotle, did the ancients succeed in separating these meanings. Even then and on through the Middle Ages, however, the primal force of the original meanings of these words was still felt and perceived. This force continues to be felt today, even if faintly and remotely, in poetry and myth, fantasy and fairy-story:

> And the poesy felt by us to reside in ancient language consists just in this, that, out of our later, analytic, "subjective" consciousness, a consciousness which has been brought about along with, and partly because of, this splitting up of meaning, we are led back to experience the original unity.[27]

Here we come to the crux of Barfield's argument: that poetic diction points to a primal unity of word and thing out of which all meaning emerges, a primal unity whose footsteps the imagination can recover for the modern mind.[28] In myth and fantasy, the modern mind can burst out of its nominalist shell, where language is a closed system detached from things and only arbitrarily related to them, to a world of meaning in which language and things are coeval:

> Mythology is the ghost of concrete meaning. Connections between discrete phenomena, connections which are now apprehended as metaphor, were once perceived as immediate

---

26 Barfield, *Poetic Diction*, 85.
27 Barfield, *Poetic Diction*, 85–86.
28 "It is these 'footsteps of nature' whose noise we hear alike in primitive language and in the finest metaphors of poets. Men do not *invent* those mysterious relations between separate external objects, and between objects and feelings or ideas, which is the function of poetry to reveal. These relations exist independently, not indeed of Thought, but of any individual thinker." Barfield, *Poetic Diction*, 86.

realities. As such the poet strives, by his own efforts, to see them, and to make others see them, again.[29]

As Barfield puts it in *Saving the Appearances*, through mythical language modern men and women can come to partake in what he calls an "original participation" of thing and word, world and language. By contrast, words, images, and concepts for the modern mind have become idols, since they have become detached from the world of living things and people that give them their original meaning: "To the extent therefore that the phenomena are experienced as machine, they are believed to exist independently of man, not to be participated and therefore not to be in the nature of representations."[30]

For premodern humanity, the situation was quite different, which Barfield explains, again in *Saving the Appearances*:

> The background picture then was of man as a microcosm within the macrocosm. It is clear that he did not feel himself isolated by his skin from the world outside him to quite the same extent as we do. He was integrated or mortised into it, each different part of him being united to a different part of it by some invisible thread. In his relation to his environment, the man of the middle ages was rather less like an island, rather more like an embryo, than we are.[31]

It is significant that Barfield brings in Thomas Aquinas to support this point. For a moderate realist like Aquinas, word and thing are but two aspects of one actuality from out which word and thing emerge as distinct but nevertheless constitutive components of one act, the givenness of the being of the beings themselves:

> On the one hand "the word conceived in the mind is representative of the whole of that which is realized in thought" (*verbum igitur mente conceptum est repraesentativum omnis eius quod actu intelligitur*) [*S.Th.*, I, 34, 3]. But on the other hand the phenomenon itself

29 Barfield, *Poetic Diction*, 92.
30 Barfield, *Saving the Appearances*, 51.
31 Barfield, *Saving the Appearances*, 78.

only achieves full reality (*actus*) in the moment of being "named" by man; that is, when that in nature which it represents is united with that in man which the name represents.[32]

Things, of course, exist independently of the human mind for Aquinas, and always remain what they are without human beings knowing or naming them. And yet, "Speech did not arise as the attempt of man to imitate, to master or explain 'nature'; for speech and nature came into being along with one another."[33] There is a potential for meaning in the things themselves prior to any human cognition of them, and there is a unity in our primal experience of the world that is prior to all abstract and discursive thinking about things, "for thinking in act *is* the thing thought, in act; just as the sense in act, are the things sensed, in act (*Intellectus in actu est intelligibile in actu; sicut sensus in actu est sensibile in actu*)[34]"—a unity that has, as its presupposition, a primal unity of thing and a creative and eternal Mind.[35]

According to Barfield, then, poetic or mythical language helps the modern mind recover a primal layer of meaning where the separation between word and thing, mind and world has disappeared. Thus, I think that Verlyn Flieger, as astute a commentator on Tolkien as one can find, seriously misses the mark when she asserts that "Myths embody the quest for meaning in an otherwise random universe. The great mythologies of the world, through the stories of their gods and heroes, create order (not necessarily benevolent but accessible to human understanding) out of what would otherwise be chaos."[36] That the universe is inherently random and meaningless and that myth is simply a construct that human beings lay over the phenomena to give them meaning and purpose represents precisely the modern, nominalist view of language and its relation to reality that both Barfield and Tolkien strenuously challenge.

32 Barfield, *Saving the Appearances*, 85.
33 Barfield, *Saving the Appearances*, 123.
34 *S.Th.*, I, 12, 2, ad 3.
35 Barfield, *Saving the Appearances*, 85–86.
36 Verlyn Flieger, *Interrupted Music: The Making of Tolkien's Mythology* (Kent: Kent State University Press, 2005), 11.

As we have seen so far (and will discuss further in the next chapter, "The Recovery of Nature"), however, language for Tolkien is part of the very fabric of reality, both mental and extra-mental. We therefore find a common theme in Tolkien's stories, especially in *The Silmarillion*, where one sure sign of the growing folly and pride of a culture or people is their abandonment of Elvish and other ancient tongues, tongues, that is, in which there is or was a felt unity between word and thing.[37] Thus, as the Númenóreans hasten to the downfall of their kingdom, the Elven speech is at first discouraged and then banned outright—a development that is also closely linked to their mortality and shortened lifespans. The forgetting of ancient languages in the name of utility or progress is a forgetting of the primal unity of thing and meaning that is caught up in the history of a word and language.[38] As Treebeard says to Merry and Pippin, "You call *yourselves* hobbits? But you should not go telling just anybody. You'll be letting out your own right names if you're not careful." Language is not arbitrary; there are "right" names for things: "[So] *my* name is like a story. Real names tell you the story of the things they belong to in my language, in the Old Entish as you might say."[39] Words all by themselves tell a story, because they have a history that goes back to that primal unity of sense and thing and thus to an entire world. That is why the Ents, along with Elves, are so keen to preserve their ancient languages: "For Ents are more like Elves: less interested in themselves than Men are, and better at getting inside other things."[40] Knowing the roots of words in their earliest and most ancient forms is to get inside not only the word but the reality of the thing it refers to and the lifeworld in which the thing has meaning and intelligibility. Thus, Tolkien takes great pains in his works to show the deep connection between the names of the days and the months and the seasons of

37 Michael N. Stanton, *Hobbits, Elves and Wizards: Exploring the Wonders and Worlds of J. R. R. Tolkien's* The Lord of the Rings (New York: Palgrave-Macmillan, 2002), 150.

38 The speech of the Valar does not change because the Valar do not die. Thus, linguistic decay is linked to mortality. Fimi, *Tolkien, Race, and Cultural History*, 103. See also *Lost Road (and Other Writings)*, edited by Christopher Tolkien (New York: Houghton-Mifflin-Harcourt, 1987), 172.

39 *TT*, III, 4, 465.
40 *TT*, III, 4, 468.

the year in the various calendars of Middle-earth (see Appendix D of *The Lord of the Rings*), and he makes sure that the distinction between modern and ancient languages is felt in his translation of the original languages in which *The Lord of the Rings* was supposedly written.[41]

Tolkien is not arguing that there is some original ur-language with magical properties (like the "original language of Adam," which earlier ages sought and believed to have magical power over things). Nevertheless, ancient languages reveal a layer of sense that is so concrete and so entwined with the inner reality of the things they refer to that they do have a privileged place in human thought and even have a quasi-magical power. It is a power rooted in life and a loving unity with the world the language reveals. By contrast, the modern, materialist and nominalist view of language fetishizes language, viewing it as a mere machine for domination and control, without any inherent relation to the things it describes. Language, in fact, is seen as creating reality itself; it becomes a mere tool of propaganda and manipulation, divorced from the real and inherent natures and purposes of things. Thus, language is reduced to a quasi-magical fetish, which has an effect very much like the voice of Saruman:

> Those who listened unwarily to that voice could seldom report the words that they heard; and if they did, they wondered, for little power remained in them. Mostly they remembered only that it was a delight to hear the voice speaking, all that it said seemed wise and reasonable, and desire awoke in them by swift agreement to seem wise themselves.[42]

[41] "It seemed to me that to present all the names in their original forms would obscure an essential feature of the times as perceived by the Hobbits (whose point of view I was mainly concerned to preserve): the contrast between a wide-spread language, to them as ordinary and habitual as English is to us, and the living remains of far older and more reverend tongues. All names if merely transcribed would seem to modern readers equally remote: for instance, if the Elvish name *Imladris* and the Westron translation *Karningul* had both been left unchanged. But to refer to Rivendell as Imladris was as if one now was to speak of Winchester as Camelot, except that the identity was certain, while in Rivendell there still dwelt a lord of renown far older than Arthur would be, were he still king at Winchester today." *RK*, Appendix F, 1134.

[42] *TT*, III, 10, 578.

Thus detached from the inner reality of things, modern discourse becomes like the cloak of Saruman, "the colour of which was not easy to tell, for it changed if they moved their eyes or if he stirred."[43] All stable meanings melt into the air, leaving only for tyrants to determine—and enforce—their meaning (until it changes again).

Mythos, Logos, and the Logos

In essence, the argument that Barfield makes and that Tolkien seeks to show in his fiction is neatly expressed by the twentieth-century Czech phenomenologist Erazim Kohak: "*Meaningful* being, not pure meaning or sheer being, is reality." Being or reality most primally and originally as given to us is shot through with meaning. There are no meanings floating free of the world of beings, but neither is there a realm of raw being, devoid of inherent meaning and intelligibility, at least *in potentia*. Kohak continues: "Philosophy can claim to be the *scientia generalis* because it seeks to see and articulate the sense of being as it presents itself primordially, prior to the imposition of any special perspective or purpose."[44] Tolkien's fiction is doing very much the work of philosophy in this original and primal sense of showing the sense of the world. What is that sense? That we are inside a very great story. Being at its most fundamental level is no different from art or story; in a sense, literature righty done goes deeper than philosophy insofar as it, to use again Kreeft's words, "incarnates philosophy."[45] Thus, far from engaging in abstract allegory, good literature and especially good fantasy allow us to see the world not just in a different way, but in its primordial sense and meaning, i.e., as it was *meant* to be read and understood. It is the mark of a good sub-creation when it is the case that things in the primary world remind us of the sub-creation rather than the sub-creation reminding us of things in our primary world.[46] In

---

43 *TT*, III, 10, 578.

44 Erazim Kohak, *The Embers and the Stars: A Philosophical Inquiry into the Moral Sense of Nature* (Chicago: University of Chicago Press, 1984), 49.

45 Kreeft, *The Philosophy of Tolkien*, 22.

46 I think Kreeft speaks for many readers of Tolkien when he says, "I know *The Lord of the Rings* is not an allegory because I don't find myself saying,

good fantasy, we do not have the sense that we are imposing meaning upon the world, but rather that language and its words are revealing the meaning and sense of the world: "The words are not mere labels for concepts. Rather, it is *in* the words that things live and move and have their being; and *in* the words they come to us."[47]

Thus, if being in its most fundamental, which is to say primordially given, sense is "meaningful being," then being in its most basic and concrete sense is a story or *logos*, "(rational) account," "word," or "discourse." The word is not extraneous to being or reality but inherent in or essential to it. Since any finite word or story spoken by human beings is always contingent and accidental (for things can exist with no human beings present, and languages and the cultures arise, change, and die), primitive being points to a Word or Author of things prior to any particular, historical human language. Verlyn Flieger notes how what Tolkien is trying to do with fantasy and sub-creation is very reminiscent of Plato's doctrine of recollection:

> Tolkien's concept of Recovery is not unlike the Platonic concept of recollection, the idea—as expressed in the *Timaeus*—that knowledge is recollection of things already learned, that we constantly rediscover and repossess what we have formerly known. Sub-creation thus has a purpose beyond itself. The making of a Secondary World is not simply the production of enchantment as its end result. The Secondary World can and should redirect our attention to the Primary World and through that World to its Maker. It should enable us to regain, to recollect what we have always known but have forgotten how to see. Through imitation of God, man has the opportunity to recover His works.[48]

---

of anything in it, 'That reminds me of this or that', but I constantly find myself saying, of this or that, 'That reminds me of something in *The Lord of the Rings*.'" Kreeft, *The Philosophy of Tolkien*, 25.

   47   Kreeft, *The Philosophy of Tolkien*, 156.

   48   Flieger, *Splintered Light*, 25. I think that the relevant dialogue of Plato that Flieger here is thinking of is the *Phaedo* or the *Meno*, not the *Timaeus*.

Through his creation of a secondary world with its own languages, Tolkien attempts to recover how meaning is discovered and made in our own primary world. Indeed, discovering meaning and making are, Barfield argues, the same in poetry (or fantasy) ("Really there is no distinction between Poetry and Science, as kinds of knowing at all. There is only a distinction between bad poetry and bad science"[49]). Thus, to reveal the being of things in their primal sense is to reveal them as created, but this is done through sub-creation, which is often the only way in which the modern mind can perceive this inner sense of things in the primary world.

In sum, the primal givenness of being as meaningful being presupposes a Maker of that meaning, for if the word (*logos*) arises primordially and coevally with being *in potentia*, then all meaning and all words presuppose the Word (ὁ Λόγος), who always and already realizes this meaning *in actuality*. This *Logos* is, as the opening of the Gospel of John proclaims, Christ. Now, as we saw in the chapter on creation and sub-creation, Tolkien saw Christ already present in the pagan myths, particularly the Northern myths that he loved. Of course, the full meaning of the *Logos* of the universe, that of a Person of creative and self-sacrificial love, was obscured by many errors. Nevertheless, like the Christian poet of Beowulf, Tolkien's work attempts to manifest a real solidarity of the Christian message with the pagan past. I shall have much more to say on the relation of paganism to Christianity in Tolkien's fiction in the next chapter, but suffice it to say here that the pagan past, for Tolkien, is like a palimpsest to the Christian present. This is manifested in words like *dryhten*, which, while used by Anglo-Saxon Christians to refer to God as "Lord," still retains its old pagan military associations. This is actually a linguistic analogue to the theological *praeparatio evangelii*.[50] Tolkien applies this same principle to language as used by modern men and women. Hence, one of the more notable and impressive aspects of Tolkien's fantasy is the degree to which it avoids using modern language—particularly modern jargon—and yet

---

49 Barfield, *Poetic Diction*, 138–39.
50 Holmes, "Like Heathen Kings," 137.

is still perfectly accessible to contemporary readers. Again, the intimate connection between thought and language means that any sub-creation that will recover the world for us must avoid language, especially modern jargon, that covers it over and makes it trite and familiar (or reminds us too much of our primary world).[51] As Stratford Caldecott remarks:

> Tolkien saw natural things freighted with the depth of meaning that all things possess, being rooted in the mind of God. God does not create things simply to fill up space. God creates for a reason, and the ultimate reason for his creation is love. Each thing, and especially each living thing, is a word, a symbol, a revelation. Each is a note, or a theme, in some great music. At any rate, it is more than itself: that is, more than the thing most people see when they look at it.[52]

Thus, as we shall see in a later chapter, to uncover and recover the inner sense or meaning of things is also to recover fellowship with things, for what the things themselves reveal if seen without prejudice is that they have an inherent fellowship with one another and with the human mind (*ens et verum convertuntur*) that can only be rooted in a fellowship with a Mind and Will that created them from nothing out of love. It is a Word that is not heard audibly by the human ear, precisely because it permeates all of the created world as a great music.[53]

---

[51] The intimate connection between thought and language means that one cannot use modern language to express ancient thoughts or vice versa. "[T]here would be an insincerity of thought, a disunion of word and meaning. For a King who spoke in a modern style would not really think in such terms ... Like some non-Christian making a reference to some Christian belief which did not in fact move him at all." *Letters*, 225–26. See, Shippey, *Author of the Century*, 225.

[52] Caldecott, *The Power of the Ring*, 31.

[53] Thus, Tolkien writes this curious passage near the end of *The Lord of the Rings*, where he says concerning an intimate conference between Gandalf, Elrond, Galadriel, and Celeborn before they are to part: "If any wanderer had chanced to pass, little would he have seen or heard, and it would have seemed to him only that he saw grey figures, carved in stone, memorials of forgotten things now lost in unpeopled lands. For they did not move or speak with mouth, looking from mind to mind; and only their shining eyes stirred and kindled as their thoughts went to and fro." *RK*, VI, 6, 985. It is almost as if, now that the tale is almost at an end,

We are now in the position to understand more clearly why readers of Tolkien such as Peter Kreeft and Craig Bernthal have seen in Tolkien's work a sacramental vision of the world: "The mythopoetic world is a fully sacramental world, in which matter and spirit have not been divorced."[54] By that they mean that Tolkien sees our experience of the world at its most primordial level as shot through, not just with meaning, but with an efficacious meaning that bestows grace, if we are but open and receptive to this grace. In this sacramental vision, water is not just dihydrogen oxide and fire is not just the exothermic oxidation of a combustible substance, but rather they are physical phenomena that have inherent spiritual meanings as well, such as purification, zeal, and rebirth. Just as Barfield argued that, at its primal level of language and experience, the material and the spiritual are not separate things (*à la* Descartes) but one reality, so the sacraments of the Catholic Church are not mere human constructs but ways of revealing an already underlying primal reality. This is no less true of the water of baptism and the oil of confirmation than it is of *lembas*, the "waybread" (or *viaticum*) of the Elves, which is, of course, a material substance (bread), but also sustenance for the spirit (as is the Eucharist).[55] This is also true of the sacrament of marriage: the bodies of the married couple are not mere machines whose parts are interchangeable and can be changed at will, like rebuilding an automobile, but contain within themselves a meaningful and inherent telos naturally

---

a hint must be given of an even higher, wordless form of communication that is at the root of all audible human communication, much like the way in which the autobiographical books of Augustine's *Confessions* end in a wordless vision of divine realities by Augustine and his mother, Monica, at Ostia. See *Conf.* IX, 10.23–26.

54 Bernthal, *Tolkien's Sacramental Vision*, 59; Kreeft, *The Philosophy of Tolkien*, 159.

55 "The *lembas* has a virtue without which they would long ago have lain down to die. It did not satisfy desire, and at times Sam's mind was filled with memories of food, and the longing for simple bread and meats. And yet this waybread of the Elves had a potency that increased as travelers relied on it alone and did not mingle it with other foods. It fed the will, and it gave strength to endure, and to master sinew and limb beyond the measure of mortal kind." *RK*, VI, 3, 936. *Lembas*, Birzer remarks, is the most specific Christian symbol or reference in the entire *Lord of the Rings*: "For Tolkien, nothing represented a greater gift from God than the actual Body and Blood of Christ." Birzer, *J. R. R. Tolkien's Sanctifying Myth*, 63. See also *Letters*, 53.

oriented toward (pro)creation and the knitting together of generations in an incarnate, spiritual fellowship. As such, the male and female bodies are sacramental realities, and it is one of the more notable qualities of the Ring that, as noted in the previous chapter, it makes the body disappear and de-sexes it. Thus, as Bernthal remarks, "By recontextualizing the sacraments in a romantic quest, Tolkien helps to *recover* their meaning, recovery being one of the functions of fairy-story."[56]

By contrast with the knowledge of the poet, knowledge as represented by Sauron and Saruman (i.e., the technological mastery of the Machine) is not to be trusted, for they do not reveal the inherent nature of things. Thus the miracles of technology wrought by Sauron and Saruman are only pale copies and even mockeries of true magic: "[M]agic, as practiced by Gandalf … seems to consist of using language as a tool to gather and concentrate and focus the ambient energies of nature … Thus what seems to be magic may be only (only!) a powerful sympathy with nature."[57] True magic is thus what is eminently real and natural, a primal sympathy between word and thing, while the marvels of technology, which may appear magical to the uninitiated, are ultimately destructive assertions of raw power over a recalcitrant nature. Shippey sums up this understanding of the essential relation between word and thing in Tolkien well when he says (with perhaps some hyperbole at the end), "Like a goldfish in a weedy pool, the theme that flashes from much of Tolkien's work is that of the identity of man and nature, of namer and named. It was probably his strongest belief, stronger even than his Catholicism (though of course he hoped the two were at some level reconciled)."[58]

Myth and History

What Barfield's views on myth and, more comprehensively, a Thomistic moderate realist view of language and reality fundamentally assert and reveal is that our experience, at its most fundamental level is one of

---

56 Bernthal, *Tolkien's Sacramental Vision*, 33.
57 Stanton, *Hobbits, Elves and Wizards*, 47.
58 Shippey, *The Road to Middle-earth*, 131–32.

primal unity between thing and word, meaning and being. What Barfield adds to the Thomistic account is an historical dimension: to recover the meaning of words is to recover the meaning of things, and to effect such a recovery is to recover the history of words and thus the history of things. What things really are is bound up inextricably with the history of how human beings have experienced them. This does not mean that the meanings are arbitrary and changing: quite the opposite, their meaning derives from a primal unity of word and thing that founds or roots all subsequent historical meanings. Paradoxically, then, we can truly trust only old stories, as Sam says to Ted Sandyman.[59]

Thus, Tolkien was long fascinated by a question that he made explicit in his *Notion Club Papers*, a series of dialogues written in the late 1940s (just as he was finishing *The Lord of the Rings*) that supposedly take place during the 1980s among members of a group very much like Tolkien's own Inklings, in which time travel is a predominant preoccupation. As one of his characters asks:

> If you went back would you find myth dissolving into history or history into myth? Somebody once said, I forget who, that the distinction between history and myth might be meaningless outside the Earth. I think it might at least get a great deal less sharp on the Earth, further back. Perhaps the Atlantis catastrophe was the dividing line?[60]

This question is crucial for Tolkien, because, as we saw in the chapter on sub-creation, the key proof of the truth of Christianity is that it is myth become historical reality. Now Tolkien can be easily misunderstood here: contemporary readers will likely reduce one term to the other. A reader of a typically nineteenth-century rationalist turn of mind will read Tolkien as saying that myth is really just bad history (*à la* Max Müller); a postmodern, post-Marxist reader will read Tolkien as saying that history is really just a myth that reflects and justifies

---

[59] Walter Scheps, "The Fairy-tale Morality of *The Lord of the Rings*," in *A Tolkien Compass*, rev. ed., ed. Jared Lobdell (Chicago: Open Court Publishing, 2003), 45.
[60] *SD*, 249.

a self-interested ruling class. In contrast to these misunderstandings, Tolkien is arguing that true myth, which the Gospel is and which good fantasy replicates or at least points to, is both *fully myth* and *fully history*, without compromise or comingling. This is because such stories reveal the timeless meanings inherent in things, whose movement and development are, nevertheless, essentially oriented toward a fulfillment within history.

Thus, as Lionel Basney argues, key to the structure of *The Lord of the Rings* is the growth of history and legend (or myth) into each other. Throughout the epic, action and lore interpenetrate each other.[61] As Joe Kraus notes, "the heroes of *The Lord of the Rings* often rescue themselves because they remember something important that their enemies have forgotten."[62] Thus, a genuine knowledge of the past ("genuine" meaning bound up with a knowledge of the languages in which this past was experienced and transmitted to us) constantly reveals that what was thought to be mere myth is actually true history. As Celeborn says to the Fellowship in Lothlorien, "do not despise the lore that has come down from distant years; for oft it may chance that old wives keep in memory word of things that once were needful for the wise to know."[63] Thus we read in *The Lord of the Rings* about the importance of ancient lore for Faramir and for his country, Gondor, written in languages that few now can read.[64] Scholarly research can save the world: Gandalf's researches in the archives of Gondor concerning the Ring (and Denethor's own disdain for it out of purely political considerations) end up making a decisive difference in defeating Sauron.[65]

There is, in other words, a pattern of the incarnation of myths into history or real life (e.g., the Hobbits to the Rohirrim):

---

[61] Lionel Basney, "Myth, History, and Time in *The Lord of the Rings*," in *Understanding* The Lord of the Rings: *The Best of Tolkien Criticism*, ed. Rose Zimbardo and Neil Isaacs (New York: Houghton-Mifflin, 2004), 186–87.

[62] Joe Kraus, "Tolkien, Modernism, and the Importance of Tradition," in The Lord of the Rings *and Philosophy: One Book to Rule Them All*, ed. Gregory Bassham and Eric Bronson (Chicago: Open Court Publishing, 2003), 137.

[63] *FR*, II, 8, 374.

[64] Cf. *TT*, IV, 5, 670.

[65] Cf. *FR*, II, 2, 252.

"Halflings!" laughed a Rider that stood beside Éomer. "Halflings! But they are only a little people in old songs and children's tales out of the North. Do we walk in legends or on the green earth in the daylight?"

"A man may do both," said Aragorn. "For not we but those who come after will make the legends of our time. The green earth, say you? That is a mighty matter of legend, though you tread it under the light of day!"[66]

The last comment, by Aragorn, is very Chestertonian: you talk of marvels and legends as if they were something extraordinary; and yet the green earth, and the trees and the sun and the moon and all creation, i.e., reality itself, is a marvel, a matter of myth and legend! That there is something rather than nothing is a miracle—a gift—and thus much more properly a matter of myth and legend than of scientific discourse.[67] Hence, when Éomer meets Aragorn, Legolas, and Gimli, in his wonder he says:

"It is hard to be sure of anything among so many marvels. The world is all grown strange. Elf and Dwarf in company walk in our daily fields; and folk speak with the Lady of the Wood and yet live; and the Sword comes back to war that was broken in the long ages ere the fathers of our fathers rode into the Mark! How shall a man judge what to do in such times?"

"As he has ever judged," said Aragorn. "Good and ill have not changed since yesteryear; nor are they one thing among Elves and Dwarves and another among Men. It is a man's part to discern them, as much in the Golden Wood as in his own house."[68]

So language and the stories that it gives rise to are rich with history, and that means with meaning and purpose. As Aragorn reminds Éomer, however, that meaning and purpose are not arbitrary. Quite to the contrary, the primal meanings of things and words reveal "good and ill," which themselves do not change, nor are they different for different peoples, but their meaning flows from the inherent natures of things themselves:

66 *TT*, III, 2, 434.
67 Chesterton, *Orthodoxy*, 65–67.
68 *TT*, III, 2, 438.

> You have seen Ents, O King, Ents out of Fangorn Forest, which in your tongue you call the Entwood. Did you think that the name was given only in idle fancy? Nay, Théoden, it is otherwise: to them you are but the passing tale; all the years from Eorl the Young to Théoden the Old are of little count to them; and all the deeds of your house but a small matter.[69]

Ancient tales are not bad science, nor is history myth mystified as science; true myth and true history are one: "And now the songs have come down among us out of strange places, and walk visible under the Sun."[70] Thus, as Blasney aptly puts it: "For Middle-earth's inhabitants, myth becomes history by way of experience. For us, myth becomes experience only by way of Tolkien's history."[71]

In fact, one of the remarkable features of Tolkien's fiction is that he writes it in the mode of history. One of the features of his work that lends it the depth and fascination it has are the quasi-historical appendices that he added at the end of *The Return of the King*. Normally, such a scholarly apparatus in a work of fiction would mean commercial death, but the appendices in fact not only enhance the authenticity of Tolkien's secondary world, but also allow the modern reader to enter the world of true myth through, paradoxically, a fake history. Tolkien also heightens this effect with his pseudo-encyclopedic prologue "Concerning Hobbits" and the elaborate care he takes to establish a textual history of the work, for which he is only the supposed translator.[72]

In this treatment of myth and history, Basney sees an attempt by Tolkien to reconcile cyclical pagan time and linear Judeo-Christian time (which revolves around the notion of the fullness of time).[73] Although the pagan Greeks and Romans produced historians of outstanding

---

69 *TT*, III, 8, 549.
70 *TT*, III, 8, 550.
71 Basney, "Myth, History, and Time," 193.
72 "It is evident that Tolkien more and more emphatically thought of his works *as texts within the fictional world*, and that he regarded this 'duplication of texts' as centrally important to the effect he wished to achieve." Gergely Nagy, "The Silmarillion: Tolkien's Theory of Myth, Text, and Culture," in Lee, *A Companion to J. R. R. Tolkien*, 112.
73 Basney, "Myth, History, and Time," 190.

quality, the pagans of Greece and Rome (as well as of Northern Europe) had no historical consciousness, no notion of history as having an inner purpose or *telos* of development; to be sure, for ancient historians history revealed intelligible patterns, but for the most part they saw history as a mere cycle of the ascent and descent of various polities. Only with Christianity comes the notion of history being linear, i.e., having a beginning and developing to an end or consummation, which transcends history, time, and this very world (and which, as we will see later, gets bastardized in the modern notion of progress). In the Christian story, as Tolkien reminds us in his essay "On Fairy-stories," the cyclical, mythical history of the pagans meets and fuses with the linear history of the Gospel, such that the Gospel actualizes in time and makes real the true elements of historical pagan myth. In such a fusion, history becomes laden with timeless mythical meaning, while myth acquires historical reality.

This fusion (but not confusion) of history and myth, however, has come apart with modernity, and they are now seen as opposed or, alternately, attempts are made to reduce one to the other. History becomes either an antiquarian fetish,[74] or it becomes a mere tool of social engineering and propaganda. Saruman and Denethor are very much types of this latter view of history, "because they dream of using evil's power to accomplish the good." By contrast, as Kraus explains:

> Frodo, Aragorn, and Gandalf defeat Sauron by making him irrelevant, by finding a way of making him impotent rather than confronting him directly. As a metaphor, that suggests [that] ... [r]eaders can escape the dilemma of modernism ... in the same way that Tolkien's heroes can: by turning to a mythical past and finding themselves in a history that keeps unfolding.[75]

If history is nothing but an unending playing out of oppressive power structures, then the end result can only be despair, for if one is trapped

---

74 That Tolkien was no mere reactionary consumed by a sentimental nostalgia for the past is evidenced by his satire of antiquarianism in the person of the lore master of the Houses of Healing: "'Go find some old man of less lore and more wisdom who keeps some in his house!' cried Gandalf." *RK*, V, 8, 865.

75 Kraus, "Tolkien, Modernism, and the Importance of Tradition," 146.

in such an understanding of history, then one cannot imagine escaping the Ring's power. Modern men and women, Tolkien suggests, can only find hope in real history, which is a Story, that of the Gospel, where history and myth come together in such a way as to take us out our time altogether, giving our own temporal existence eternal and universal significance. In a sense, then, Tolkien returns us to an Augustinian conception of history, in which faith in progress toward some constantly shifting goal is demonstrated to be illusory, while real history—that of the city of God—is the providential ordering of human events toward God's final revelation of himself, which is in history and yet transcends it. Tolkien does not cite Augustine directly, but he does cite favorably the English Catholic historian Christopher Dawson, whose philosophy of history is very close to that of Augustine: "'The rawness and ugliness of modern European life'—that real life whose contact we should welcome—'is the sign of biological inferiority, of an insufficient or false reaction to environment'. The maddest castle that ever came out of a giant's bag in a wild Gaelic story is not only much less ugly than a robot-factory, it is also (to use a very modern phrase) 'in a very real sense' a great deal more real."[76] We live, Tolkien continues, "in an age of 'improved means to deteriorated ends'. It is part of the essential malady of such days—producing the desire to escape, not indeed from life, but from our present time and self-made misery—that we are acutely conscious both of the ugliness of our works, and of their evil."[77] Thus the irony of living in an age which praises itself as the culmination of human enlightenment and progress and yet is one from which so many of its denizens want to escape.

---

[76] *TL*, 64. Yannick Imbert discusses extensively the influence of Dawson on Tolkien, notably the idea that, contrary to the dominant thinking of their day (and ours), religion is not a secondary phenomenon to man's earliest attitude to reality, which is by default an empirical materialism. Rather, in understanding culture and even reality itself, religion is a primary and fundamental phenomenon. See Imbert, *From Imagination to Faërie*, 34–41.

[77] *TL*, 65.

CHAPTER FOUR

The Recovery of Nature

It is truly curious that modernity, for all of its sentimentalization of nature and its exaltation of the natural sciences as the privileged (if not only) route to truth, presents us with no clear definition or even idea of what "nature" means. This is in marked contrast to ancient Greek philosophers, culminating in Aristotle, who thought long, hard, deeply, and very precisely about what nature is. Aristotle himself concludes that what is natural must be defined in contrast to what is "artificial." A natural being is one that has an inherent or inner principle of growth and development that makes the thing what it is.[1] Fire has a nature whereby it burns or oxidizes and brings about certain determined effects; trees have a nature that determines their structure, growth, and reproduction; human beings have a certain nature whereby they have an inherent

---

[1] This definition of "nature" comes from the second book of Aristotle's *Physics* (B, 1, 192a10–35).

tendency to know what is true and desire what is good. An artificial substance, by contrast, has no such inner *telos* or principle of change and development; any purpose or function in an artificial substance such as a machine is imposed from without.[2] What this means is that all natural things or natures have an inherent goal, purpose, or tendency; natural things therefore have an inherent good or value in insofar as the actualization and fulfillment of the nature's inherent tendencies is its perfection or good. Modern ideas of nature, such as they are, usually reduce nature to a sort of mechanism. In other words, they understand nature as something purely artificial (and thus, from the Aristotelian point of view, "nature" is not properly understood as nature).[3] Ever since Descartes, modern men and women have understood the natural world as if it were a big Machine; by doing so, they have lost not only nature, but also all meaning and purpose, since ultimate meaning and purpose are found, if not in, then through nature properly understood. Hence, a recovery of the true sense of nature is crucial for a recovery of any genuine wellbeing and happiness, and it is this recovery of nature that is one of the principal aims of Tolkien's creative work.

The Creation Myth of Middle-earth

As Verlyn Flieger claims, "The chief function of any mythology, real or feigned, is to mirror a culture to itself, giving it a history and identity as well as a connection to the supernatural or transcendent."[4] The problem is that the modern myth of nature as Machine is notable in lacking

---

2 Thus, in the second book of his *Physics*, Aristotle uses the image of a wooden bed to illustrate the difference between natural and artificial substances: if you were to bury the wooden bed in the ground, the result would not be a crop of beds; rather the wood from which the bed was made would reassert itself and sprout forth a tree of whatever kind the wood came from; the form of the bed, being artificial, does not and cannot reproduce itself. What is natural in the substance always reasserts itself. *Physics*, B, 1, 193a10–15.

3 Hadot, *Le voile d'Isis*, chapter 11.

4 Flieger, *Interrupted Music*, 139. See also Leslie A. Donovan, "Middle-earth Mythology: An Overview," in *A Companion to J. R. R. Tolkien*, ed. Stuart Lee (Hoboken, NJ: Wiley-Blackwell Publishing, 2020), 97.

any supernatural or transcendent referent—a Story, even—which, as we will see, Tolkien saw as essential to a complete and true account of nature. Tolkien saw that if his secondary world was to stand on its own, it needed a creation story: "For Tolkien, not only was it the case that all human sub-creation must presuppose and is made possible and meaningful by a prior, divine act of creation, but ... it was his express purpose to foreground this relationship within his own mythology by making it one of the central themes of his fiction."[5]

We can read this creation story in a text Tolkien titled *The Ainulindalë* (the "Song of the Ainur"), which his son, Christopher, placed at the beginning of *The Silmarillion*. This decision was, of course, not Tolkien's, but Christopher thought it important to begin the collection of Tolkien's myths and legends with a general account of the world that encompasses *The Hobbit* and *The Lord of the Rings*. We can see that Christopher's choice was appropriate in two ways: first, because it makes clear the fundamental principles upon which Tolkien's secondary world was created and thus gives meaning and form to all that happens in that world. Second, in giving us his creation myth, Tolkien is also laying out the principles by which we and our primary world were created; this is because "we make in our measure and in our derivative mode, because we are made: and not only made, but made in the image and likeness of a Maker."[6] By unfolding the inner logic of language and fairy-story, Tolkien's creation story is meant to unfold the logic of the *Logos* Itself in and through whom we and our primary world were and are made.

Tolkien's creation myth is a clear statement of monotheism and, as such, it echoes the biblical account in Genesis. Thus, *The Silmarillion* begins with the stark, biblical phrase, "There was Eru, the One, who in Arda is called Ilúvatar."[7] Tolkien makes it quite clear that all of Arda, his

5 McIntosh, *The Flame Imperishable*, 7.
6 Gregory Bassham, "Tolkien's Six Keys to Happiness," in The Lord of the Rings *and Philosophy: One Book to Rule Them All*, ed. Gregory Bassham and Eric Bronson (Chicago: Open Court Publishing, 2003), 57.
7 *Ainu*, 15. Tolkien toyed and agonized throughout his writing career with introducing his collection of myths, later published by his son as *The Silmarillion*, with some sort of "framing device" in which the myth is introduced through the words of some sage or bard, which is then, depending on the time at which Tolkien

entire secondary world that includes Middle-earth, has its origin in one all-powerful and all-knowing creative being. So far, this does not differ much from the biblical account (though the epithet of Eru, "Ilúvatar," or "All-Father," looks ahead to the New Testament). Where Tolkien develops or expands on the account in Genesis is in his notion of creation being the result of a "Great Music": that the world is an order or cosmos precisely insofar as it is a reflection of a harmony or music that governs the All.[8] Eru creates the *Ainur*, who are beings analogous to the angels in the Bible: they are fully spiritual, yet finite, created beings. What is interesting in Tolkien's account is that these angelic beings share in Eru's creation of Arda by participating in the Great Music. Eru only proposes the theme; the Ainur are then invited to participate in this theme and develop it as sub-creators themselves; in other words,

---

was writing, recounted to an Anglo-Saxon visitor to the realm of Faerie, etc. Many of these "framing devices" also involved forms of "time travel" through dreams or "ancestral memory" and so forth. Ultimately, Tolkien never settled on any one "framing device" and seemed to find all of them unsatisfactory in one way or another. Whittingham notes, referring to the many early drafts of Tolkien's creation story in *The Cottage of Lost Play*: "Although removing the framework of Eriol's visit to the Cottage of Lost Play reduces the story's depth of history, Tolkien establishes the story's primacy, making creation rather than Eriol's travels the first tale of the legendarium and providing an 'In the beginning' quality." Whittingham, *The Evolution of Tolkien's Mythology*, 63.

8 This notion of the world being a "Great Music" or created by something analogous to music is, as Brad Eden demonstrates, not original to Tolkien, but was a common trope in ancient and medieval philosophy and theology, particularly neo-Pythagorean and Neoplatonic thought. See Brad Eden, "'The Music of the Spheres': Relationships between Tolkien's *The Silmarillion* and Medieval Cosmological and Religious Theory," in *Tolkien the Medievalist*, ed. Jane Chance (London: Routledge, 2008), 183–93. Isidore of Seville writes: "Nothing exists without music; for the universe itself is said to be framed by a kind of harmony of sounds, and the heaven itself resolves under the tones of that harmony" (*Etymologiarum sive originum libri*, cited in Bernthal, *Tolkien's Sacramental Vision*, 90n22). This notion of the "Great Music" of creation was also a popular trope in the late nineteenth to early twentieth century among artists as different as Richard Wagner and Alexandr Blok, and thus was an idea that the young Tolkien would probably have been familiar with. See Rémi Brague, *Le propre de l'homme: Sur une légitimité menacée* (Paris: Flammarion, 2015), chapter 5.

the divine creation of the world is a genuine creation only insofar as it involves participation among its intelligent or rational creatures:

> But for a long while they sang only each alone, or but few together, while the rest hearkened; for each comprehended only that part of the mind of Ilúvatar from which he came, and in the understanding of their brethren they grew but slowly. Yet ever as they listened they came to deeper understanding, and increased in unison and harmony.[9]

It is, then, through singing this Great Music and participating in it, by sub-creating and making myth and song, that the rational creatures of Eru come to know more fully his creation and increase "in unison and harmony" in fellowship with their fellow spiritual beings.

However, according to the *Ainulindalë*, there is not just one theme but three: in the "first music," the Ainu, Melkor, began "to interweave matters of his own imagining that were not in accord with the theme of Ilúvatar." He, Melkor,

> had gone often alone into the void places seeking the Imperishable Flame; for desire grew hot within him to bring into Being things of his own, and it seemed to him that Ilúvatar took no thought for the Void, and he was impatient of its emptiness. Yet he found not the Fire, for it is with Ilúvatar. But being alone he began to conceive thoughts of his own unlike those of his brethren.[10]

Melkor, later known as Morgoth, was not content to participate as a sub-creator in the Great Music of Ilúvatar; Melkor sought the "Secret Fire" or "Flame Imperishable" due to his impatience and his desire for the "Void" and to usurp Ilúvatar himself, since only the latter can give the Secret Fire to creatures. What is this Secret Fire? Tolkien mentions it very early on in his account:

> Never since have the Ainur made any music like to this music, though it has been said that a greater still shall be made before Ilúvatar by the choirs of the Ainur and the Children of Ilúvatar

---

9 *Ainu*, 15.
10 *Ainu*, 16.

after the end of days. Then the themes of Ilúvatar shall be played aright, and take Being in the moment of their utterance, for all shall then understand fully his intent in their part, and each shall know the comprehension of each, and Ilúvatar shall give their thoughts the secret fire, being well pleased.[11]

Ilúvatar is the author of all creation who both remains outside of it as its creator and yet also dwells in it insofar as all that occurs in that creation is but the product of his thought and imagination, which, in effect, gives life, thought, and imagination to creatures.[12] It follows that, to the degree that the Ainur and all rational creatures participate in the Great Music of creation, to that degree they come to participate in the Secret Fire (which is, in a sense, the spirit of Ilúvatar) that gives life and reality to Eru's creation. Just as Niggle's Tree becomes a reality—becomes enkindled with a sort of secret fire—at the end of the story, so do the themes sung by the Ainur become a living reality (and it is indeed no accident that, as Stratford Caldecott points out, the angels in the Patristic tradition are themselves understood as the "living thoughts" of God).[13] Dickerson adds, "Thus, each of the Ainur has 'his own thoughts'. Even more, Illúvatar gives each the choice of whether or not even to participate in this Music of the Ainur. Each may do so, not under compulsion, but '*if* he will' (emphasis added)."[14]

Still, Melkor refuses to participate truly in the Great Music, but desires to dominate it with his own music. In response, Ilúvatar proposes a second theme which incorporates Melkor's attempts at his own music, and in a wondrous fashion, the Music that comes from Iluvatar's incorporation of Melkor's brazen and monotonous attempt at music is even deeper, richer, and more beautiful. As Ilúvatar says to Melkor, "And thou, Melkor, shalt see that no theme may be played that hath not its uttermost source in me, nor can any alter the music in my despite. For he that attempteth this shall prove but mine instrument in the devising of things more wonderful, which he himself hath

---

11 *Ainu*, 15–16.
12 *MR*, 345.
13 Caldecott, *The Power of the Ring*, 191.
14 Dickerson, *A Hobbit Journey*, 116.

not imagined."¹⁵ There is thus no disharmony that Ilúvatar cannot incorporate, absorb, and transform into an even greater harmony. By introducing this disharmony into the very origins of the Great Music, Tolkien acknowledges that he is developing an idea that is not found, at least not directly, in the biblical account:

> I suppose a difference between this Myth and what may be perhaps called Christian mythology is this. In the latter the Fall of Man is subsequent to and a consequence (though not a necessary consequence) of the "Fall of the Angels": a rebellion of created free-will at a higher level than Man; but it is not clearly held (and in many versions is not held at all) that this affected the "World" in its nature: evil was brought in from outside, by Satan. In this Myth the rebellion of created free-will precedes creation of the World (*Eä*); and *Eä* has in it, subcreatively introduced, evil, rebellions, discordant elements of its own nature already when the *Let it Be* was spoken. The Fall or corruption, therefore, of all things in it and all inhabitants of it, was a possibility if not inevitable. Trees may "go bad" as in the Old Forest; Elves may turn into Orcs, and if this required the special perversive malice of Morgoth, still Elves themselves could do evil deeds.¹⁶

Nature or, better, "natures" participate in the Fall in the sense that there is rebellion and disharmony already in the natures of things. This does not mar their basic goodness and beauty for, after all, Ilúvatar triumphs in his final theme over the discord of Melkor, but, nevertheless, things can now fail to fulfill or perfect their natures.

As a result of this marring of the Great Music by Melkor, Ilúvatar proposes a third theme in which there are elements not found in the first and which belong to Ilúvatar alone, namely, the "Children of Ilúvatar," who have a mysterious role to play in the repairing and redemption of Arda:

---

15 *Ainu*, 17.
16 *Letters*, 286–87.

> For the Children of Ilúvatar were conceived by him alone; and they came with the third theme, and were not in the theme which Ilúvatar propounded at the beginning, and none of the Ainur had part in their making. Therefore when they beheld them, the more did they love them, being things other than themselves, strange and free, wherein he saw the mind of Ilúvatar reflected anew, and learned yet a little more of his wisdom, which otherwise had been hidden even from the Ainur.[17]

In this third theme is found the creative principle by which the "Children of Ilúvatar," Elves and Men, come into being. Tolkien takes pains to note that they are, in a sense, direct creations of Ilúvatar and thus specially loved by the Ainur precisely because they are beings "other than themselves, strange and free" and manifesting the mysterious wisdom of Ilúvatar. These creatures conclude the original Great Music, but they also look forward to an even greater Great Music in which all things will be created anew and given their own Secret Fire.

That Tolkien conceives of creation as a Great Music is consonant with his notion that, as we saw in the last chapter, all of reality is shot through with meaning, with "word" (*logos*) and, ultimately, with the Word (the *Logos*, Christ). Meaning is thus preeminently a matter of hearing. But without vision or sight, sound or hearing would be incomplete, for, Tolkien recounts, once the Great Music is over, the Ainur then receive sight when they only had hearing.[18] Eru shows them a vision of Arda, which the Great Music of the Ainur had helped fashion. Arda, of course, is the home of Middle-earth. Some of the Ainur fall in love with this vision and enter Arda, where they become known as the "Valar" or "powers" of the world and further assist Eru in shaping his creation. As a condition for entering Arda, the powers of the Valar are bound up with and contained by the created world. Thus they are called the "Powers of the World."[19] While exercising great power within Arda, they are not omnipotent; they are finite beings, even if enormously powerful and beautiful. As spiritual or angelic beings, they have great wisdom

---

17 *Ainu*, 18.
18 *Ainu*, 17.
19 *Ainu*, 20.

and knowledge, but again, they do not see the end of all things ("the Valar have not seen as with sight the Later Ages or the ending of the World"[20]). These Valar exercise a "delegated authority" "of rule and government, not creation, making or re-making." They are divine insofar as they were "originally 'outside' and existed 'before' the making of the world."[21] Their power and wisdom are derived from their knowledge of the cosmological drama that they perceived first as drama and then as reality. What makes Arda fully real and not just a creative idea is the Secret Fire or Flame Imperishable that Eru places at the heart of Arda: "And I will send forth into the Void the Flame Imperishable, and it shall be at the heart of the World, and World shall Be; and those of you that will may go down into it."[22]

After the Great Music, central to the creative efforts of the Valar in the shaping of Arda and Middle-earth is the role of light: only much later in the history of Middle-earth do what we call the sun and moon become the lamps by which the earth is lit. Rather, in a mythological account strongly reminiscent of Northern mythologies, Arda is originally lit by two lamps on either end of a flat earth; later, after their destruction by Melkor, Arda is lit by two Trees, Laurelin and Telperion, which illuminate the world by an alternating waxing and waning light. Most important in this image for Tolkien is the symbolism of this light:

> As far as all this has symbolical or allegorical significance, Light is such a primeval symbol in the nature of the Universe, that it can hardly be analyzed. The Light of Valinor (derived from the light before any fall) is the light of art undivorced from reason, that sees things both scientifically (or philosophically) and imaginatively (or subcreatively) and says that "they are good"—as beautiful. The Light of Sun (or Moon) is derived from the Trees only after they were sullied by Evil.[23]

Light, as Tolkien here observes, is a phenomenon that "can hardly be analyzed" precisely because it is the precondition for all analysis, all

---

20 *Ainu*, 20.
21 *Letters*, 146.
22 *Ainu*, 20.
23 *Letters*, 148, note.

reasoning: much like the physical light of the sun is the precondition for all seeing, so is an intelligible light a precondition for all thinking or intellectual seeing.[24] The Light of Valinor (the blessed and undying Land of the Valar in the West of Arda) represents the primal unity and perfect synthesis of art and reason, of sub-creation and real, primary creation. Such a unity is also very good and beautiful; it represents the primal synthesis of being and meaning that we saw as the essence of a primal experience of the world and origin of mythic language.

As the Valar shape Arda in this primeval Light, they also take on material or bodily forms in complete harmony with their character. Out of love for the Children of Ilúvatar[25] they therefore take on the form of the Children, and they further take on the forms of male or female in accordance with their character as well: "for that difference of temper they had even from their beginning, and it is but bodied forth in the choice of each, not made by choice, even as with us male and female may be shown by the raiment but is not made thereby."[26] That is, the male or female nature of the Valar follows from their roles as guardians and preservers of natural things. As Liam Campbell points out, "In *The Silmarillion* for example, the creation of the Valar is, by definition, a binding of character and nature.... In Tolkien's cosmological design the Valar create, sustain, and are sourced in aspects of nature. Nature in Tolkien's legendarium, in other words, is connected to the divine and is the province of angels."[27] Tolkien here also introduces a further rank of angelic powers, the Maiar, who assist the Valar in the shaping and sustaining of Arda. Though of lesser rank than the Valar, the Maiar are

---

24 This image comes, of course, from Plato's *Republic*, books 6 and 7, where Plato identifies the source of this intelligible light with the transcendent Good, that ultimate form of being that is ultimate precisely because it is absolutely good, i.e., it is fully, perfectly, and always what it is.

25 The Children of God—Elves and Men—were the two chief secrets of Ilúvatar, unknown to the Valar: "Since also they are something wholly 'other' to the gods, in the making of which the gods played no part, they are the object of the special desire and love of the gods." *Letters*, 147.

26 *Ainu*, 21.

27 Liam Campbell, "Nature," in Lee, *A Companion to J. R. R. Tolkien*, 435.

still far more powerful than the Children of Ilúvatar (Sauron, Gandalf, and Saruman are, for example, all Maiar).

There is thus a ranking or hierarchy of beings in Tolkien's mythology. As Leslie Donovan observes, "Such rankings imply a moral hierarchy organized according to a being's closeness in nature and spirit to Ilúvatar." "Yet," Donovan continues:

> Tolkien takes great care to counterbalance the vertical, hierarchical structure of his mythos with an equally important, horizontal cosmic order based on the cooperative union of differing forces. Each Vala is generally paired with another who is equally ranked and who has taken the shape of the opposite gender.[28]

That is, to the extent that we recover the natures of things, to that extent we recover both a vertical order in things—their relation to a creative cause from which they derive their intelligibility and meaning—and a horizontal order in things—how the ends and goals of natures interlock, complement, and complete one another (as male and female do in living things). Hence, there is in Valinor, the home of the Valar, a deep sympathy and oneness between the various Valar or Powers and the natural elements they manifest. There is, first, an almost perfect complementarity among the Valar between male and female, which models and perhaps even causes (mediately) the inherent fruitfulness and (pro)creativity of living creatures. (It is worth noting here that the only Valar who stand outside this binary are Melkor and Ulmo, lord of the seas.) Also, in much the same way as the Valar, the various peoples of Middle-earth are bound intimately to a particular land or aspect of nature: Dwarves to the mountains, Hobbits to the pastoral countryside, Elves to the woods and trees, and even Orcs to the desolate places where nature is under siege.[29]

This deep connection or fellowship with the land in which the various peoples of Middle-earth dwell (and which I will have much

---

28 Donovan, "Middle-earth Mythology: An Overview," in Lee, *A Companion to J. R. R. Tolkien*, 97.

29 Campbell, "Nature," 436.

more to say in the next chapter) is particularly poignant for the elder Children of Ilúvatar, the Elves:

> It is one with this gift of freedom that the children of Men dwell only a short space in the world alive, and are not bound to it, and depart soon whither the Elves know not. Whereas the Elves remain until the end of days, and their love of the Earth and all the world is more single and more poignant therefore, and as the years lengthen ever more sorrowful. For the Elves die not till the world dies, unless they are slain or waste in grief (and to both these seeming deaths they are subject) ... But the sons of Men die indeed, and leave the world; wherefore they are called the Guests, or the Strangers. Death is their fate, the gift of Ilúvatar, which as Time wears even the Powers shall envy. But Melkor has cast his shadow upon it, and confounded it with darkness, and brought forth evil out of good, and fear out of hope.[30]

Like the Valar and Maiar, the Children of Ilúvatar—Elves and Men—are deeply entwined with nature and the fate of Middle-earth, though the effects of the Fall (for the Elves, their rebellion against the Valar over the Silmarils and their theft by Morgoth; for Men, an undisclosed rebellion deep in their past) mar this relationship in contrasting ways. Since the Elves are immortal in the sense that they live as long as Arda lasts, they develop a deep love of Arda, even as exiles in Middle-earth, and develop arts in marvelous sympathy with the powers of various natures. And yet this profound sympathy with Middle-earth and the natures within it is also bound up in sorrow, since they are condemned to see all that they love and cherish pass away and die. Due to the rebellion of Melkor-Morgoth, all natures hasten to decay and death, except for the Elves: "In that time [the coming of the Sun and Moon] the air of Middle-earth became heavy with the breath of growth and mortality, and the changing and ageing of all things was hastened exceedingly."[31] Indeed, the coming of the Sun and Moon occurs only

30 *QS*, i, 42.
31 *QS*, xii, 103.

after a long story of the decline and destruction of the original lights of Arda (the two Lamps and two Trees). By contrast, because of the Fall, Men share in the decay and death of the things of nature; paradoxically, the more they fear this decay and death, the more they hasten it. As the Fall from the Light of Valinor progresses, so death and decay accelerate.

Ultimately, what we find in Tolkien's creation stories is a gradated creation from the harmony of the Great Music through the Light of Valinor to the splintering of that Light; from the disruption of the Great Music through the Fall of Melkor and, through him, the Fall of the Maiar, Elves and Men.[32] The process of creation is expressed mythically through personal powers—divine or angelic, depending on whether one's referent is pagan or Christian. Here, I would argue, Tolkien sees again the perfect confluence of history and myth that one finds in the Gospels, which, of course, begin with the Creation account in Genesis (and which is echoed in the opening of the Gospel of John, "In the beginning was the Word"). Following upon what we saw in his essay "On Fairy-stories," and again in the chapter "The Recovery of Language," Tolkien clearly does not conceive the Valar as mere personifications of natural phenomena. As we saw, Tolkien thinks that, at the primal level, the names for these phenomena are as primal and basic to reality as the things themselves. There are no such things as mere natural phenomena, because such phenomena are mere abstractions. Rather, insofar as they express and manifest aspects of the mind of the Creator of the primary world, the Valar are, in relation to that mind, *real persons*. Tolkien explains this idea in a letter to his son, Christopher, in which he relates a realization he had concerning the nature and reality of the guardian angels while meditating on the Blessed Sacrament:

> I perceived or thought of the Light of God and in it suspended one small mote (or millions of motes to only one of which was my small mind directed), glittering white because of the individual ray from the Light which both held and lit it. (Not

---

[32] A complex process that Verlyn Flieger demonstrates is central to Tolkien's cosmology and mythology. See, Flieger, *Splintered Light*.

that there were individual rays issuing from the Light, but the mere existence of the mote and its position in relation to the Light was in itself a line, and the line was Light.) And the ray was the Guardian Angel of the mote: not a thing interposed between God and the creature, but God's very attention itself, personalized. And I do not mean "personified," by a mere figure of speech according to the tendencies of human language, but a real (finite) person.... As the love of the Father and Son (who are infinite and equal) is a Person, so the love and attention of the Light to the Mote is a person (that is both with us and in Heaven): finite but divine: i.e., angelic.[33]

Since the divine substance is a full, perfect, and absolute substance, all relations within God become themselves substantive—more explicitly, the relations of God to himself become substantive as Persons of the Holy Trinity (for as Tolkien asserts in this letter, the love of the Father for the Son in the Holy Trinity becomes a substantive relation, i.e., a Person, the Holy Spirit). Tolkien reasons that this is also true for the relation of the divine creative Mind to his finite creatures, only the person that results is finite, yet very real and, in a sense, divine. Within God, the relation of the divine attention to the finite creature (unlike the infinite attention of God to His infinite being) becomes itself a substantive relation, i.e., a person, though in this case a finite, created person.[34] Hence, Tolkien took the existence within his mythology of the Valar and Maiar as real persons or entities very seriously, insofar as they were his subcreative analogues to the gods of the pagans or the guardian angels of the Christians.[35]

33 *Letters*, 99.
34 See Aquinas, *S.Th.* I, 13, 7.
35 "Tolkien vacillates between 'gods' and 'angels' [in describing the Valar] because both terms are close but neither is exactly right." Whittingham, *The Evolution of Tolkien's Mythology*, 70. Whittingham notes that as Tolkien revised his creation myth, it came closer and closer to the biblical one (99). See also Marjorie J. Burns, "Norse and Christian Gods: The Integrative Theology of J. R. R. Tolkien," in *Tolkien and the Invention of Myth: A Reader*, ed. Jane Chance (Lexington, KY: University Press of Kentucky, 2004), 163–79. For Tolkien, even the Ents manifest a natural power and become "substantive" as persons: the personal characters of

Far from being opposed to the Gospel, then, the gods and myths of the pagans point, Tolkien claims, to the Christian story as True Myth. Not only is Tolkien's universe clearly a monotheistic one, but, unlike in the various pagan myths, the gods or angelic powers of Tolkien's world work in fellowship with one another, something that is clearly Christian rather than pagan. In any case, debates over the pagan or Christian character of Tolkien's mythology in general or of his Valar in particular tend to overlook the degree to which Tolkien imbues the natural world itself with a sacred character, thus making the distinction moot.[36] As Sandra Miesel observes, "Instead of

---

Ents each reflect the uniqueness of the species that they embody. Holly Ordway, *Tolkien's Modern Reading*, 96.

36 Ronald Hutton argues that Tolkien's legendarium was formed in its most important stage during a relatively pagan period in Tolkien's life (the 1920s) and that, therefore, Tolkien's work is basically pagan in inspiration and content, not Christian. Hutton cites a letter to his son Michael, where Tolkien claims that during that period in his life he "almost ceased going to mass." Hutton argues that the so-called Christian elements—be they providence or showing mercy to evildoers—are not really Christian at all, for the first can be construed as the pagan concept of fate, while the second never works in real life. Now Hutton does make some prudent remarks about the pitfalls of using Tolkien's letters as sources for understanding his work. There seems to have been a conscious effort by the elderly Tolkien to make more Christian his younger, relatively pagan material. Hutton, however, seems to ignore his own good advice by reading the letter cited above rather tendentiously: Tolkien was clearly trying to bolster the flagging faith of his son and probably exaggerated the degree to which he himself may have lapsed from the faith. (In any case, what would a lapse from the faith mean to a man who in later life was a daily communicant at mass and prayed the rosary daily?) Moreover, that we can isolate a particular period in an author's life—and an atypical one at that—as the source of the true meaning of the author's work is rather absurd. See his "The Pagan Tolkien," in *The Ring and the Cross: Christianity and The Lord of the Rings*, ed. Paul E. Kerry (Madison, NJ: Fairleigh Dickinson University Press, 2011), 57–70. As Nils Avar Agøy remarks in his response to Hutton, in Tolkien's mythology Eru creates out of nothing; there is a sharp distinction between Creator and creature; the created world is not eternal, and there is a linear concept of history—all distinctively Christian ideas. Moreover, he notes that Hutton's assertions that Christianity rejects the existence of any created or incarnate beings higher than humans is simply false and that his claim that "magic" as such is anti-Christian is very strange given the copious evidence to the contrary.

inventing a religion for Middle-earth, Tolkien uses Cosmos, Height, and Center as subliminal religious symbols."[37] Therefore, "a tree makes the truest axis mundi, whether this be the Valar's Trees of Silver and Gold, Elven Trees, the royal White Trees of Númenor and Gondor, or the Party Tree at the center of the hobbit's Shire" or Sam's Tree at the end of *The Lord of the Rings*.[38] Thus, religion in Tolkien's secondary world does not necessarily include the worship of God or gods, but it does include a plethora of sacred places or objects. In Tolkien's universe, there is a plenitude of sacred objects: the Two Trees (as mentioned) and sacred places—Lothlorien and Rivendell, for example. There is thus, as Walter Scheps so concisely puts it, a sort of "moral geography" in *The Lord of the Rings*.[39] This sense of "moral geography" (more about which below) is all the more potent in *The Lord of the Rings* to the degree that the creation story found in *The Silmarillion* is firmly hidden in the background; it is thus felt or, better, intuited through the natural world or landscape of Middle-earth itself.[40] The reason Tolkien can achieve this effect is because, as we saw earlier, he was able to imbue his world with a sacramental character, which is the

---

As for Hutton's remarks on the nature and role of providence in Tolkien's work, we shall have ample space to refute his assertions in chapter 8. See "The Christian Tolkien: A Response to Ronald Hutton," in *The Ring and the Cross*. Ordway takes a whole chapter to examine in much detail Tolkien's letter to his son Michael, and the period in Tolkien's spiritual life that this letter refers to, and comes to the same conclusions that I have come to above. See Ordway, *Tolkien's Faith*, chapter 18.

37 Sandra A. Miesel, "Life-giving Ladies: Women in the Writings of J. R. R. Tolkien," in *Light Beyond All Shadow: Religious Experience in Tolkien's Work*, ed. Paul E. Kerry and Sandra Miesel (Madison, NJ: Fairleigh Dickinson University Press, 2011), 8.

38 Jared Lobdell, "*Ymagynatyf* and J. R. R. Tolkien's Roman Catholicism, Catholic Theology, and Religion in *The Lord of the Rings*," in Kerry and Miesel, *Light beyond All Shadow*, 92–93.

39 Scheps, "The Fairy-tale Morality of *The Lord of the Rings*," 43.

40 To the question "Why are the cosmological details so essential to *The Silmarillion* so inessential to *The Lord of the Rings*?" Madsen answers: "*The Lord of the Rings* offers religion obliquely and thus without impediment; it offers religion's effects and not its anxieties." Catherine Madsen, "Eru Erased: The Minimalist Cosmology of *The Lord of the Rings*," in Kerry, *The Ring and the Cross*, 164.

Christian sanctification of the material order (and thus also of the pagan veneration of nature): "In the sacramental understanding of the cosmos, there can be no division between a secular world and a holy, spirit-filled world, between the natural and supernatural—reality is *all* a spiritual production."[41]

We thus find initially in Tolkien's mythology no clear separation between the world of the Valar, their realm, Valinor, and Middle-earth. More accurately and more interestingly, we see as the stories progress their gradual separation from an original unity: whereas in the First Age, there is relatively easy communication between the world of the Valar and that of Middle-earth and the Children of Ilúvatar, in the Second Age, there is the Ban on the Númenóreans on their coming to Valinor, and in the Third Age, after the Downfall of Númenor, the seas become bent and any direct access to Valinor is cut off except for a select few. We therefore see in the progression of Tolkien's own story the gradual separation of finite rational creatures from the Mind that creates and gives meaning to all natural things; from a truly hierarchical (in the literal sense of the Greek, "rule by divine or holy realities") and vertical ordering of the cosmos, which is therefore full of value and meaning, to a flat, mechanistic view of the universe, devoid of inherent meaning and value but full of exertions of domination and control. From there we can see the gradual separation of word from thing, meaning from being, and, ultimately, the rational being from his or her Creator.

Landscape as a Character in Middle-earth

With regard to the role of Middle-earth itself in Tolkien's fiction, Patrick Curry puts it perfectly when he says, "It wouldn't be stretching a point to say that Middle-earth itself appears as a character in its own right."[42] Indeed, probably the one quality of Tolkien's fiction that first enchants and holds many of his first-time readers is the strange and numinous quality of the landscape of Middle-earth—from the menacing strangeness of the Old Forest and the Barrow Downs to the lights of

---

41 Bernthal, *Tolkien's Sacramental Vision*, 88–89.
42 Patrick Curry, *Defending Middle Earth*, 50.

the Dead Marshes (which, moreover, cannot be touched and thus seem to be of more than natural origin). One can easily multiply examples:

> In Tolkien's fiction, especially perhaps in his tales of Middle-earth, nature is an animate presence. Middle-earth is much more than a backdrop against which a plot is played out: it is awake and sentient. Natural elements and features are given character, agency, and even personality: Fangorn Forest is described as a "brooding presence, full of secret purpose."[43]

Thus, when the Fellowship is trying to cross over the Misty Mountains by using the Redhorn Pass, Gimli remarks concerning the mountain, Caradhras (the "Redhorn"): "It is no ordinary storm. It is the ill will of Caradhras. He does not love Elves and Dwarves."[44] Caradhras is "Cruel." Members of the Fellowship hear in the falling stones and in the wind "voices." Tolkien imbues the landscapes of Middle-earth with a "weirdness," which refers back to the Anglo-Saxon concept of the *wyrd* or "fate," whereby things in the natural world pursue their own goals and ends quite independently of rational creatures.[45] When Gimli shouts at the Mountain, "Enough, enough!" what happens? "And indeed with that last stroke the malice of the mountain seemed to be expended, as if Caradhras was satisfied that the invaders had been beaten off and would not dare to return."[46] Thus, in Middle-earth, we find both sameness and strangeness[47]: enough elements that are familiar from our primary world (forests, downs, mountains, marshes, etc.), but suffused with an eerie uncanniness and agency that arrests the reader and forces him or her to look at forests, downs, mountains and marshes as if for the first time, in all their weirdness.

43 Campbell, "Nature," 440, quoting *TT*, III, 2, 574–75.
44 *FR*, II, 3, 381.
45 Ralph C. Wood, "Confronting the World's Weirdness: J. R. R. Tolkien's *The Children of Húrin*," in Kerry, *The Ring and the Cross*, 146.
46 *FR*, II, 3, 293.
47 In Tolkien's work we find rich descriptions of the natural world, but unique to them is the intermingling of recognizable elements from our primary world and elements from his secondary world (athelas, niphredil, the Ents and Huorns, Mearas steeds or the Crebain crows as spies of Saruman). Campbell, "Nature," 433.

The numinous and enchanted landscapes of Tolkien's fiction are imbued with meaning, purpose, and hence, with moral value that also calls for a moral response: "Each landscape presents a moral choice and actualizes a spiritual condition. Tolkien's most lyric descriptions of the world his characters pass through are founded in a deep gratitude for creation, the foundation of his spiritual and ethical vision."[48] Quoting a letter Tolkien wrote to his friend, the poet W. H. Auden, Stratford Caldecott writes:

> "Each of us is an allegory, embodying in a particular tale and clothed in the garments of time and place, universal truth and everlasting life" (*Letters*, 163). In this sense the entire natural world is what we call "sacramental"—not a sacrament in the strict theological sense, but nevertheless a symbolic system apt for the communication of spiritual realities.[49]

The concept of a morally neutral or valueless landscape upon which the moral and value-laden actions of human characters are imposed is utterly foreign to Tolkien's Middle-earth. Rational actors participate in the landscape in a way that is deeply moral and value-laden, and vice-versa: the landscape participates in the action of its rational inhabitants.[50]

This moral quality can be for good or for ill. One of the first truly animated and haunted landscapes the reader encounters is the Old Forest, which the four hobbits, Frodo, Sam, Merry, and Pippin, decide to cross in an attempt to throw the Black Riders off their trail. Since Merry is a Bucklander who had grown up on the eves of the forest, he has an intimate knowledge of it and describes it to his fellow hobbits thusly: "But the Forest *is* queer. Everything in it is very much more

---

48 Bernthal, *Tolkien's Sacramental Vision*, 6.
49 Caldecott, *The Power of the Ring*, 85.
50 Tolkien describes the Third Age in *The Silmarillion*: "Those were the Fading Years.... Many things of beauty and wonder remained on earth in that time, and many things also of evil and dread: Orcs there were and trolls and dragons and fell beasts, and strange creatures old and wise in the woods whose names are forgotten; Dwarves still laboured in the hills and wrought with patient craft works of metal and stone that none now can rival. But the Dominion of Men was preparing and all things were changing, until at last the Dark Lord arose in Mirkwood again." *RP*, 299.

alive, more aware of what is going on, so to speak, than things are in the Shire. And the trees do not like strangers. They watch you."[51] Not only is the Old Forest alive (for any forest, in fantasy or the primary world, is, technically speaking, "alive"), but it is also sentient in a way that the forests of our primary world or even in the Shire are not. A clue to this distinction can be found in the name itself: "Old." In entering the Old Forest, the hobbits are not only going beyond the bounds of our ordinary, comfortable world as represented in the story by the Shire, but they are also going back in time to an age when meaning and thing, sentient and non-sentient, were not separated: "For the moment there was no whispering or movement among the branches; but they all got an uncomfortable feeling that they were being watched with disapproval, deepening to dislike and even enmity. The feeling steadily grew, until they found themselves looking up quickly, or glancing back over their shoulders, as if they expected a sudden blow."[52] It is therefore significant that Tolkien mentions that "They [the hobbits] began to feel that all this country was unreal, and that they were stumbling through an ominous dream that led to no awakening."[53] The Old Forest seems unreal insofar as it is a step back to an earlier time in the relationship of consciousness to the world, in which the boundaries between thought and thing are far more permeable.

What the hobbits discover in the Old Forest is that the forest and the trees in it have purposes, ends, and a rhythm all their own, apart from any interaction with rational creatures. In other words, Tolkien is not committing the pathetic fallacy, which is a more or less arbitrary and evidently subjective projection of human emotions onto non-human entities: in fact, the reason why Tolkien's landscapes haunt the reader so powerfully is that Tolkien is describing purposes and powers that are quite independent of human thought or agency.[54] Things have a music

51   FR, I, 6, 110.
52   FR, I, 6, 111.
53   FR, I, 6, 121.
54   Halsall adverts in this matter to Alfred Siewers's notion of the Celtic "Otherworld," which "denotes a dimension of life and being beyond the immediate confines of time and space; a sense of the overlapping landscapes of the immanent (from the perspective of our senses) and the immaterial (from the

all their own, which is a reflection of the Great Music of Creation. Thus, when the hobbits are rescued from Old Man Willow by Tom Bombadil (about whom I will have more to say in the next chapter), he sings a tune to the tree to get the hobbits out.[55] Although Tom is very much at home in the Old Forest (Tom Bombadil is, as Tom Shippey notes, "from his first conception a *genius loci*, a 'spirit of the place'"[56]), he is, when later talking to the hobbits in the safety of his house on the edge of the forest, quite unsentimental about the Forest and its inhabitants:

> He [Tom Bombadil] told them tales of bees and flowers, the ways of trees, and the strange creatures of the Forest, about the evil things and good things, things friendly and unfriendly, cruel things and kind things, and secrets hidden under the brambles. As they listened, they began to understand the lives of the Forest.[57]

It is significant that Tom mentions cruel and unfriendly creatures here, "evil things and good things."[58] In other words, Tom—and Tolkien—are here hinting at a moral universe that goes deeper and well beyond the intentions, plans, and projects of human beings or other rational creatures. There is certainly here no Rousseauian sentimentalization of nature as the repository of all that is pure and good.

Now Tom Bombadil is, of course, a benign being and a great friend to the hobbits. But Tolkien purposely does not make clear what sort of being Tom is: he is not a Hobbit, nor a Man, Elf, or Dwarf; perhaps he is a Maia, but that, again, is not stated. Perhaps this is precisely the point: the reader need not know what Tom is in order that the natures of things may, as it were, speak through him. As R. J. Reilly puts it, "when Tom Bombadil speaks, it is as if Nature itself—nonrational,

---

perspective of eternity)." Halsall, *Creation and Beauty in Tolkien's Catholic Vision*, 196. Halsall goes on to explain how the early medieval Irish philosopher John Scotus Eriugena attempted to give a philosophical grounding to this Otherworld, showing how the visible world is an unfolding manifestation of divine ideas or realities (theophanies).

55 *FR*, I, 6, 120.
56 Shippey, *Author of the Century*, 63.
57 *FR*, I, 7, 129.
58 Campbell, "Nature," 436.

interested only in life and in growing things—were speaking."⁵⁹ Hence, as the hobbits listen to Tom talk about the Old Forest and its trees and animals, "they [begin] to understand the lives of the Forest, apart from themselves, indeed, to feel themselves as the strangers where all other things [are] at home."⁶⁰ Listening to Tom, the hobbits come to a deeper awareness of the world around them, which paradoxically they had to leave the Shire to recover. What we discover in Tolkien's descriptions of the Old Forest—and of the forests of Lothlorien and Fangorn and of all his landscapes in general—is an echo of the Great Music that Tolkien perceives as the harmony and order that knits all creatures together.

I will here note two other examples of landscapes containing echoes of the Great Music. when the Fellowship crosses the border into Lothlórien, they can hear music in the water of Nimrodel: "Frodo fancied that he could hear a voice singing, mingled with the sound of the water."⁶¹ As the Fellowship marches blindfolded to meet the rulers of Lothlórien, Celeborn and Galadriel, Frodo also can hear various notes in the rustle of the leaves overhead, in the running water, and in the "thin, clear voices of birds high in the sky."⁶² Going farther into that enchanted land, Frodo experiences even more strongly what he experienced with Tom Bombadil and in his journey through the Old Forest—a profound sense of a *recovery* of the inherent sense and meaning of things in the world, which also involves, as in the Old Forest, a stepping back in time:

> It seemed to him [Frodo] that he had stepped through a high window that looked on a vanished world. A light was upon it for which his language had no name. All that he saw was shapely, but the shapes seemed at once clear cut, as if they had been first conceived and drawn at the uncovering of his eyes, and ancient as if they had endured for ever. He saw no colour but those he knew, gold and white and blue and green, but they were fresh and poignant, as if he had at that moment *first perceived them and made for them names new and wonderful*. In winter here no heart

59 Reilly, "Tolkien and the Fairy Story," 95.
60 *FR*, I, 7, 130.
61 *FR*, II, 6, 339.
62 *FR*, II, 6, 349.

could mourn for summer or for spring. No blemish or sickness or deformity could be seen in anything that grew upon the earth. On the land of Lórien there was no stain."[63]

"A light was upon it for which his language had no name": Tolkien here describes a sort of intelligible light that suffuses the whole land of Lothlórien: a light that does not blind the mind or obscure things but makes them shine forth as even more than what they already are; it makes blue bluer and trees more tree-like (if one may so speak). Like in the Great Music, there is a play between hearing music and seeing light, in which the two senses and their objects become fused without confusion. As Sam says to Frodo upon staying for some time in the Elven land, "It's sunlight and bright day, right enough.... I thought that Elves were all for moon and stars: but this is more Elvish than anything I ever heard tell of. I feel as if I was *inside* a song, if you take my meaning."[64] Everything exists in such fullness that it is as if their Platonic Forms, the eternal, intelligible species of things in all their fullness, had become a visible reality: "Frodo felt that he was in a timeless land that did not fade or change or fall into forgetfulness."[65] There is here a sort of regression in time back to the primal unity of word and thing, viz., when things where "first perceived" and when Elves "made for them names new and wonderful." By contrast, when members of the Fellowship look out beyond Lórien to Mirkwood and Sauron's forest fortress of Dol Guldur, they notice that even the trees take part in the strife between the two woods on behalf of their inhabitants: "'There lies the fastness of Southern Mirkwood', said Haldir. 'It is clad in a forest of dark fir, where the trees strive one against another and their branches rot and wither. In the midst upon a stony height stands Dol Guldur, where long the hidden Enemy had his dwelling'."[66]

Thus, when Frodo first enters Lothlórien and must ascend to a platform in a tree to spend the night with the land's elven border guards, he realizes that in this land perception is both heightened and deepened:

63 *FR*, II, 6, 350–51. Emphasis added.
64 *FR*, II, 6, 351.
65 *FR*, II, 6, 351.
66 *FR*, II, 6, 352.

> As Frodo prepared to follow him [Haldir], he laid his hand upon the tree beside the ladder: never before had he been so suddenly and so keenly aware of the feel and texture of a tree's skin and of the life within it. He felt a delight in wood and the touch of it, neither as forester nor as carpenter; it was the delight of the living tree itself.[67]

In recovering the inherent sense of things and their natures, one becomes aware of a paradox: at the most fundamental level of the givenness of the being of things, we realize that there is no real separation between word and thing, consciousness and world, yet in this primal givenness of things we perceive that these things have a life, meaning, and value quite independent of our thinking and valuation.

This is the case also for the other place in Middle-earth mentioned above, Fangorn Forest. Tolkien describes it thusly as Merry and Pippin first enter it: "There was a silence, for suddenly the dark and unknown forest, so near at hand, made itself felt as a great brooding presence, full of secret purpose."[68] As such, all the landscapes in *The Lord of the Rings* (except, perhaps, within the Shire and other cultivated lands) are, in a sense dangerous. In responding to Gimli's assertion that Fangorn Forest is dangerous, Gandalf responds:

> Dangerous! ... And so am I, very dangerous: more dangerous than anything you will ever meet, unless you are brought alive before the seat of the Dark Lord. And Aragorn is dangerous, and Legolas is dangerous. You are beset with dangers, Gimli son of Glóin; for you are dangerous yourself, in your own fashion. Certainly the forest of Fangorn is perilous—not least to those that are too ready with their axes; and Fangorn himself, he is perilous too; yet he is wise and kindly nonetheless. But now his long slow wrath is brimming over, and all the forest is filled with it.[69]

67   *FR*, II, 6, 351.
68   *TT*, III, 2, 442.
69   *TT*, III, 5, 499–500.

The land of Faerie is the "perilous realm" and, thus, by definition, full of danger. But as Tolkien asks in this passage, what is it that we mean by "danger"? As Gandalf reveals to Gimli in this passage, we are all dangerous to a degree, because we live in a moral universe, where all things, not just rational ones, move with ends and purposes of their own—for good, if those ends are consonant with their created natures, for evil if not. What we emphatically do not live in is a bland, flat, morally neutral and valueless mechanistic world. Thus, we are perilous because our choices have real, even cosmic, consequences for good or evil.

Tolkien's Monsters

Nothing shows the perilous nature of the Faërie realm of Middle-earth more than the monsters with which it teems. These monsters are, significantly, not limited to the servants of Sauron, whether Orcs, Trolls, or other beasts: "There are older and fouler things than Orcs in the deep places of the world,"[70] as Gandalf warns the Fellowship upon entering Moria. Hence, Aragorn says as the Fellowship makes its way south: "There are many evil and unfriendly things in the world that have little love for those that go on two legs, and yet are not in league with Sauron, but have purposes of their own. Some have been in this world longer than he."[71] A whole catalog of evil creatures further besets the Fellowship on their journey south: the crebain, Mount Caradhas, the wargs, the Watcher in the water, and of course, the Balrog (all of whom seem to target Gandalf or Frodo). In fact, what is particularly uncanny and disturbing is that in Middle-earth, the line between perfectly natural beings and monsters is often blurry. As Aragorn warns the hobbits in their flight to the ford while marching through what was the ancient, evil kingdom of Rhudaur, "Not all the birds are to be trusted, and there are other spies more evil than they are."[72] One should add, however, that not all the monsters in Tolkien's fiction are evil (taking "monster" in the sense of the Latin word from which it is derived, a *monstrum*, an uncanny

---

70 *FR*, II, 4, 309.
71 *FR*, II, 3, 289.
72 *FR*, I, 11, 183.

thing or event that reveals something of the purposes of the gods and is thus not necessarily evil or good). For example, we encounter many times in Tolkien's fiction the Eagles as messengers and emissaries of the chief Vala, Manwë, and who enter into the story at crucial points as allies of the good and as emissaries of grace.[73]

The ubiquity of monsters in Tolkien's fiction is well known, but why does Tolkien include them? First, as Stratford Caldecott remarks, dragons and by extension monsters in general are for Tolkien not significant in and of themselves but as portals to Faerie.[74] That is, monsters, as manifestations of the uncanny, give the reader a sense that our primary world is like a small island in a vast sea of realms beyond human sensible or even intellectual perception. They intimate a vast sea of being and meaning that is yet unknowable in purely rational terms. This is especially the case when the monster is a harbinger of evil, as evil is unknowable in itself (since it is the pure negation of being, goodness, and intelligibility). As Christopher Garbowski observes, one of the functions of Tolkien's monsters is to evoke a sense of wonder and to dramatize the unknowability of Middle-earth's universe: "Monsters in Tolkien's fantasy are symbolic of the ultimate unknowability of evil in rational terms."[75] What makes Tolkien's fiction such gripping reading is that there is always a sense of an all-encompassing evil or darkness surrounding an island of light, life, and goodness.[76] Elsewhere, Aragorn talks about how Barliman Butterbur, the innkeeper in Bree, has no idea of the evils that lurk around his little land; there are creatures within a day's walk of his homely inn that would freeze his heart with fear.

As Tolkien remarks upon another famous monster in literature, Beowulf's Grendel, monsters indicate that there is both an evil and a goodness beyond the actions, goals, and merely political struggles of human beings:

> Grendel is an enemy who has attacked the centre of the realm, and brought into the royal hall the outer darkness, so that only

---

73 Caldecott, *The Power of the Ring*, 44–45.
74 Caldecott, *The Power of the Ring*, 39.
75 Garbowski, "Evil," 421.
76 Birzer, *J. R. R. Tolkien's Sanctifying Myth*, 91.

in daylight can the king sit upon the throne. This is something quite different and more horrible than a "political" invasion of equals—men of another similar realm, such as Ingeld's later assault upon Heorot.[77]

There are powers at work in the world quite independent of human action or plans, which is why Tolkien takes great pains to mention that there are many creatures—the Balrog, Shelob—that were not created by Sauron nor even under his control.[78] If the Ring represents the Machine, then what Tolkien is trying to show is that evil goes deeper than and even beyond the Machine. In the end, evil cannot simply be defeated by destroying the Machine. Doing so helps, and the destruction of the Ring liberates Middle-earth from a great menace, but its destruction does not eliminate all evil once and for all. Beowulf is powerful as a poem precisely because it presents us with a world whose significance goes beyond mere human interactions and power politics, for Beowulf is in the end slain by the dragon.[79] As Gandalf reminds the Witch-king of Angmar, the chief of the Nazgul, at the gates of Minas Tirith, "Go back to the abyss prepared for you! Go back! Fall into the nothingness that awaits you and your Master!"[80] As this scene demonstrates, the monster has a cosmic or metaphysical function: the hero must be tested against monsters, not just other men, precisely because only in the encounter with and overcoming of monsters is evil

---

[77] *Letters*, 242.

[78] Besides the monster Grendel in *Beowulf*, another inspiration for the nature and function of the monster in fairy-stories is no doubt the Green Knight of *Sir Gawain and the Green Knight*. Notably, he is not necessarily evil, but certainly morally ambiguous: "He [the Green Knight] is a manifestation of a power within living things that cannot be possessed, appropriated, or controlled by human beings, but which nevertheless can act in reciprocity with us." John J. Davenport, "Happy Endings and Religious Hope: *The Lord of the Rings* as an Epic Fairy Tale," in Bassham and Bronson, The Lord of the Rings *and Philosophy*, 211.

[79] "It is the monstrosity and fairy-tale quality of Grendel that really makes the tale important, surviving still when the politics have become dim and the healing of Danish-Geatish relations in an 'entente cordiale' between two ruling houses a minor matter of obscure history." *Letters*, 242.

[80] *RK*, V, 4, 1085.

overcome and the inherently moral reality of the universe affirmed. That is why the genius of the Beowulf poet, Tolkien argued, was to focus on the cosmic dimension of evil and not on the limited (and limiting) dimension of human power politics.

For Tolkien, the monster points to a reality prior to and much deeper than the Machine and the mechanistic view of the universe. Thus, concerning the strange forest before Helm's Deep, Gandalf says: "It is not wizardry, but a power far older ... a power that walked the earth, ere elf sang or hammer rang."[81] In fact, magic in Tolkien is quite rare, precisely because, as David Bratman notes, it is imbued in the landscape and thus escapes "mechanistic use."[82] In sum, the whole purpose of monsters and magic (since both are, in a sense, *monstra*), is to serve as portals to the realm of Faërie, whose whole purpose is, in turn, to put into question the primary world as self-sufficient in meaning. By contrast, the modern mind, in trying to naturalize so-called monsters (as mere misunderstandings of strange or rare creatures), begs the question by assuming that our primary world is metaphysically self-sufficient in both being and intelligibility and that, therefore, all phenomena must fit into a naturalistic, mechanistic framework.

A world without monsters is a metaphysically and morally flat world in which not only is nothing significant, but it thereby becomes impossible to distinguish true goodness and virtue from its counterfeits. As Tolkien remarks in his letters, "Treebeard does not say that the Dark Lord 'created' Trolls and Orcs. He says he 'made' them in *counterfeit* of certain creatures pre-existing."[83] As Treebeard himself says to Merry and Pippin in *The Lord of the Rings*, "Maybe you have heard of Trolls? They are mighty strong. But Trolls are only counterfeits, made by the Enemy in the Great Darkness, in mockery of Ents, as Orcs were of

---

81 *TT*, III, 8, 544.

82 "As for sorcery, in Tolkien, magic is largely imbued into the landscape. That his spells are rare and do not work in a rigid engineering manner, and that both spells and prophecies are prepared for and not pulled out of a hat to escape from plot holes, differentiates Tolkien from some subsequent High Fantasy writers as much as from anyone else." David Bratman, "The Inklings and Others: Tolkien and His Contemporaries," in Lee, *A Companion to J. R. R. Tolkien*, 328.

83 *Letters*, 190.

Elves. We are stronger than Trolls. We are made of the bones of the earth."[84] As Augustine argued long ago, and as Tolkien well knew, evil always counterfeits or puts on the face of the good, precisely because reality as such is good and contains a gradation of degrees of goodness or perfection; and the human mind and will are oriented by nature, by their inherent *telos*, toward what is truly real and therefore what is truly good.[85] Evil, then, must put on some semblance of what is good. As Frodo says to Sam, "The Shadow that bred them [the orcs] can only mock, it cannot make: not real new things of its own. I don't think it gave life to the orcs, it only ruined them and twisted them and if they are to live at all, they have to live like other living creatures."[86] Thus, in Tolkien's universe, every creature has its evil negative: the Ainur and Valar have Melkor; the Maiar, Sauron; the Wizards, Saruman; the Elves, the Orcs; Men, their Wormtongues and Denethors; the Ents, Old Man Willow; and the Hobbits, Gollum. However, far from indicating a Manichean dualism, Tolkien's fiction shows us that evil owes its diversity and variety to the rich diversity of goodness in things alone.[87] If evil is essentially a counterfeit of the good, then there must be real natures to counterfeit and, through them, an objectively real and perfect Good to counterfeit, a Good that can only be known and counterfeited by a rational being. (Paradoxically, this truth shines through in Tolkien's work primarily through its monsters.) Tolkien's view of nature is therefore not sentimental; he does not contrast it with civilization.[88] He does contrast it with the Machine, but the Machine is not synonymous with civilization, even if the two sometimes overlap. Even the Machine for

84 *TT*, III, 4, 486.
85 *Conf.*, II, 6, 13.
86 *RK*, VI, 1, 914.
87 McIntosh, *The Flame Imperishable*, 216.
88 As Meredith Veldman has shown, Tolkien's dislike of anthropocentrism and his privileging of the pastoral over industrial civilization made him an early and perhaps unlikely representative of eco-activism in the Romantic vein. Veldman notes, however, that Tolkien is also very much anti-Romantic in that he vehemently opposed the notion of the unlimited potential and basic goodness of the individual. Meredeth Veldman, *Fantasy, the Bomb, and the Greening of Britain: Romantic Protest, 1945–1980* (Cambridge: Cambridge University Press, 1994), 89.

Tolkien is only a manifestation of a deeper evil in a universe that is fundamentally good and meaningful and therefore moral. It is an evil will that mocks and counterfeits the goodness of that universe, with the Machine being only one of the many ways in which it does that. The solution to this evil, therefore, is not merely defeating the Machine by tinkering with it: the solution to evil is not political or systemic, but rather lies in recovering and renewing a bond of fellowship that we as human beings had and can have with natural beings, one another, and their and our Creator.

CHAPTER FIVE

The Recovery of Fellowship

As we saw in the previous chapter, fellowship, according to Tolkien, is built into the very act of creation of his secondary world; it follows that it is also built, by implication, into the process by which our primary world was and still is created and thus is essential to experiencing and even knowing the world and the things in as they truly are, viz., the gift of a Creator who seeks fellowship with his creatures. To recover, then, the true meaning of fellowship is to recover the true sense of things, and to recover the true sense of things is to recover their embeddedness in a web of creative fellowship. Perhaps the most important fellowship that is the foundation for all genuine human fellowships is a proper fellowship with nature, since it is in fellowship with nature that we also recover a sense of the world as creation and, through creation, reestablish fellowship (or "restore ties"—the literal sense of the Latin *religio*) with our Creator.

Fellowship with Nature

From Tolkien's fiction, it is evident that all genuine fellowship begins with or is rooted in a deep fellowship with natural things and the natural world of which they are a part. This is particularly clear in the numerous interactions between characters of a rational nature and the various beasts of Middle-earth. Thus, Gandalf does not "use" the horse, Shadowfax, nor even "ride" him. Rather, Shadowfax *allows* Gandalf to ride him because there is a bond of fellowship between them.[1] The characters in Tolkien's fantasy that are closest to the earth are also able to communicate with the beasts and even the trees.

As was mentioned above, the very creation of the world is accomplished through fellowship: this fellowship is specifically and purposely created by Ilúvatar, who invites the Ainur to share in the development of his theme that becomes the basis of all creation. The Valar are the "divine ideas" of Ilúvatar, who are personal beings[2] in fellowship with one another and with the Arda they helped fashion.[3] What makes Melkor evil is his breaking of this fellowship (indeed, any fellowship) and trying to create, not only on his own, but in such a way as to dominate the other Ainur. Thus, for Tolkien, fellowship is what underlies and perfects the Great Music; evil is the breaking up of fellowship and the atomization of individuals as interchangeable parts of a cosmic machine.

This cosmic fellowship extends down from the Great Music into Arda and Middle-earth in a sort of "Great Chain of Being." As Rose Zimbardo argues, "Good is the cooperation of all levels of being, a harmony but not an interpenetration of kinds, for each kind of being has its particular excellence and consequently its peculiar contribution

---

[1] As Stanton remarks, "The love between horse and wizard is a concrete example of moral worth as measured by closeness to, or distance from, the world of nature. Men and others can be judged by the horses they keep and how well they keep them." Stanton, *Hobbits, Elves and Wizards*, 37.

[2] See the previous chapter for a discussion about how these divine ideas are, at least in some cases, personal beings insofar as they relate the divine nature to a personal, rational creature.

[3] McIntosh, *The Flame Imperishable*, 91.

to make to the order of the whole."⁴ Thus we have, again, one of the many striking and fascinating features of Tolkien's secondary world: the existence of multiple rational species or races, each of which manifest and highlight some peculiar feature of the created cosmos. The wizards, for example, are angelic beings, Maiar in human form, and thus form a direct connection to the Valar and through them to the Great Music of the Ainur.⁵ They are able to communicate with the beasts and even trees and are thus able to "survey the depths of time and space."⁶ Elves transform the Great Music of creation into a poetry that celebrates and reveals the inner essence or meaning of material things, while Men engage in acts of heroic courage and statecraft. The Hobbits represent the common man, bound to the earth, whose

---

4 Rose Zimbardo, "Moral Vision in *The Lord of the Rings*," in *Understanding The Lord of the Rings: The Best of Tolkien Criticism*, ed. Rose Zimbardo and Neil Isaacs (New York: Houghton-Mifflin, 2004), 69.

5 "Nowhere is the place or nature of 'the Wizards' made fully explicit. Their name, as related to Wise, is an Englishing of their own Elvish name, and is used throughout as utterly distinct from Sorcerer or Magician. It appears finally that they were as one might say the near equivalent in the mode of these tales of Angels, guardian Angels. Their powers are directed primarily to the encouragement of the enemies of evil, to cause them to use their own wits and valour, to unite and endure. They appear always as old men and sages, and though (sent by the powers of the True West) in the world they suffer themselves, their age and grey hairs increase only slowly. Gandalf whose function is especially to watch human affairs (Men and Hobbits) goes on through all the tales." *Letters*, 159, note.

6 "Long they [the Istari] journeyed far and wide among Elves and Men, and held converse also with beasts and with birds; and the peoples of Middle-earth gave to them many names, for their true names they did not reveal. Chief among them were those whom the Elves called Mithrandir and Curunír, but Men in the north named Gandalf and Saruman. Of these Curunír was the eldest and came first, and after him came Mithrandir and Radagast, and others of the Istari who went into the east of Middle-earth, and do not come into these tales. Radagast was the friend of all beasts and birds; but Curunír went most among Men, and he was subtle in speech and skilled in all the devices of smithcraft. Mithrandir was closest in counsel with Elrond and the Elves. He wandered far in the North and West and made never in any land any lasting abode; but Curunír journeyed into the East, and when he returned he dwelt at Orthanc in the Ring of Isengard, which the Númenóreans made in the days of their power." *RP*, 300.

excellence is found in love rather than honor, while the Dwarves, being heavy of substance, transform elemental forces into beautiful things.[7] So each species or race of rational beings in Middle-earth has a special (in the root sense of the word, meaning "pertaining to the species") "fellowship" with an elemental aspect of Middle-earth and Arda as well as to all the specific perfections of different races, peoples, and individuals. Thus, the Fellowship of the Ring is more than a mere bonding among friends or even races, but a reflection of both the inner harmony of the created world as well as its healing and perfection (witness the friendship of Legolas and Gimli, which not only heals the ancient rift between their races, but brings together the ethereal poetry of the Elf with the solid, elemental force of the Dwarf). As we see in the case of Tom Bombadil, and as we later see in the Elves of Lothlórien and the Ents of Fangorn Forest, "the various races of people in Middle-earth are rooted to and unimaginable—both to themselves and to us—without their natural contexts."[8]

Of all these races, perhaps the most beloved race in Tolkien's fiction is the Hobbits (probably because they alone were created out of whole cloth by him, whereas the other races—Elves, Dwarves, etc.—have precedents in ancient and medieval literature). What seems to be most attractive about hobbits for modern readers, living as they likely are deracinated in urban or suburban environments where technological devices are ubiquitous, is that they have a deep and long-lasting fellowship with the earth and their land:

> Hobbits are an unobtrusive but very ancient people, more numerous formerly than they are today; for they love peace and quiet and good tilled earth: a well-ordered and well-farmed countryside was their favorite haunt. They do not and did

---

[7] "They [Dwarves] are a tough, thrawn race for the most part, secretive, laborious, retentive of the memory of injuries (and of benefits), lovers of stone, of gems, of things that take shape under the hands of the craftsmen rather than things that live by their own life. But they are not evil by nature, and few ever served the Enemy of free will, whatever the tales of Men may have alleged." *RK*, Appendix F, 1132.

[8] Curry, *Defending Middle-earth*, 51.

not understand or like machines more complicated than forge-bellows, a water-mill, or a hand-loom, though they were skillful with tools.[9]

Note here that hobbits are not lovers of nature in the Rousseauian sense of lovers of wild and untamed forest, untouched by civilization; they love a "well-ordered and well-farmed countryside"—a land that is shaped and used by them, but in loving fellowship with it, such that the land can be said to shape and use them as much as they shape and use it. Hobbits also are not Luddites—haters of all technology; they are actually quite ingenious with tools and machines, but prefer them to be on a scale accessible to average human understanding, where the user is not mystified by their operation (as many users of contemporary technological devices are, treating these devices almost as magical fetishes). In other words,

> The Hobbits are, of course, really meant to be a branch of the specifically *human* race (not Elves or Dwarves)—hence the two kinds can dwell together (as at Bree), and are called just the Big Folk and the Little Folk. They are entirely without non-human powers, but are represented as being more in touch with "nature" (the soil and other living things, plants and animals), and abnormally, for humans, free from ambition or greed of wealth. They are made small (little more than half human nature, but dwindling as the years pass) partly to exhibit the pettiness of man, plain unimaginative parochial man—though not with either the smallness or the savageness of Swift, and most to show up, in creatures of very small physical power, the amazing and unexpected heroism of ordinary men "at a pinch."[10]

The hobbit is there to hold a mirror to us, in our smallness and pettiness to be sure, for Tolkien does not idealize the hobbits; they can be parochial and small-minded. But they also show us what a genuine fellowship of human beings with the earth and land would look like and how this is indeed possible.

9 *FR*, I, prologue, 1.
10 *Letters*, 158, note.

In stark contrast with the hobbits' love for and deep fellowship with their land, the Shire, are the effects produced by Sauron's Ring. As Rose Zimbardo notes, the Ring is a nihilating force; all who wear it lose some of the being peculiar to their kind and thus can no longer live among their fellow creatures.[11] Thus, Frodo, who bears the Ring through most of *The Lord of the Rings*, has lost some of his hobbit nature and can no longer live with any ease or fellowship among his fellow hobbits; he must therefore take the ship over the sea to the Undying Lands. The destructive aspect of the Ring also extends into the realm of relationships between individuals and between whole peoples: "the estrangement that divides all those who oppose him"[12] manifests the power of the Dark Lord.

To illustrate this point—that what is destructive about the Ring is its nihilating power, its power to dissolve natures into interchangeable parts and thus destroy all fellowship between beings—Tolkien includes in *The Fellowship of the Ring* by way of counterexample the character of Tom Bombadil. Tom Bombadil is probably one of the most fascinating and oddest characters in what is, by any standard, a very odd book. What makes him strange is that, strictly speaking, his presence does not advance the plot of *The Lord of the Rings*, nor does he have any role to play in the further action of the book (thus Peter Jackson left him out of his film adaptations entirely). Nevertheless, Tolkien retained Tom (Tolkien had already made him the central figure of several poems that he had composed earlier, well before he began *The Lord of the Rings*), because he thought that he pointed to something crucial:

> I kept him in, and as he was, because he represents certain things otherwise left out. I do not mean him to be an allegory—or I should not have given him so particular, individual, and ridiculous a name—but "allegory" is the only mode of exhibiting certain functions: he is then an "allegory," or exemplar, a particular embodying of pure (real) natural science: the spirit that desires knowledge of other things, their history

---

11 Zimbardo, "Moral Vision," 73.
12 *FR*, II, 6, 348.

and nature, because they are "other" and wholly independent of the enquiring mind, and entirely unconcerned with "doing" anything with the knowledge: Zoology and Botany not Cattle-breeding or Agriculture. Even the Elves hardly show this: they are primarily artists. Also T. B. exhibits another point in his attitude to the Ring, and its failure to affect him.... The power of the Ring over all concerned, even the Wizards or Emissaries, is not a delusion—but it is not the whole picture, even of the then state and content of that part of the Universe.[13]

For all his expressed dislike of allegory, Tolkien here admits that Tom Bombadil is an allegorical figure that communicates something very important. In essence, Tom is an allegory of pure natural science: science that seeks knowledge of natural things for their own sakes and not for doing anything with them. It is a science that knows things as "'other' and wholly independent of the enquiring mind" and thus of knowing the ends and purposes of things and the value that they have in themselves. Tom represents a recovery of what the medieval scholastics would have called "speculative science" (as opposed to "productive science")[14]: a science in which the intellect is conformed to the intelligible forms or species of things, i.e., to the truth of things, rather than making things in conformity to what we think them or want them to be.[15] In other words, it is a knowledge that both presupposes and perfects a deep fellowship with all living things (indeed, as we saw in chapter 3, genuine knowledge is itself a sort of fellowship between mind and thing). Tolkien adds that the power of the Ring over even the wisest and most powerful is not a delusion: the Ring inevitably taps into a desire in fallen rational beings to do something with the knowledge of natural beings instead of knowing and loving them as they are in their truth, which is the precondition for having fellowship with them.

13 *Letters*, 192.
14 For the notion of the "speculative intellect" or the *intellectus speculativus* as opposed to the productive intellect, see Aquinas, *S.Th*. I, 79, 11; *De ver.*, 3, 3.
15 This aspect of Tom Bombadil, as an image of pure speculative knowledge, is reflected, I think, in the fact that he is, strictly speaking, superfluous to the plot of *The Lord of the Rings*, and is thus not *productive* even in a literary sense.

Tom Bombadil does not seem to be one of those fallen creatures; the Ring leaves him completely unmoved and unaffected. When he asks Frodo for the Ring, Frodo, to his surprise, hands it over willingly. Frodo and the hobbits are even more surprised when Tom, after putting the Ring on his finger, does not disappear. He then plays jokingly with the Ring, with Tolkien giving us a comic vision of his round, blue eye peeking through the circle of the Ring and then seemingly making it disappear himself. Finally, when Frodo with great suspicion takes the Ring back and puts it on, to see whether it is truly the One Ring, he disappears in the sight of the other hobbits, but not to Tom.[16] The Ring has no power over Tom. Why is this the case?

Tolkien, of course, leaves it to the reader to pick up clues from the story and dialogue. Perhaps the first clue comes from Tom's spouse, Goldberry, who, when asked by Frodo who (or what) Tom is, replies that "He is." When Frodo looks puzzled at her statement, she continues, "He is, as you have seen him ... he is the Master of wood, water and hill."[17] This does not mean, as Tolkien explained in a letter to a reader who objected that the statement "He is" is too similar to God's declaration to Moses from the burning bush, "I am, Who am," and thus an analogue to God or even some sort of divine being. It simply means that Tom exists in the same way that he understands all the other flora and fauna of his little land (including the Old Forest) to exist: simply in and for themselves, without any desire to do anything. Far from being a selfish or narcissistic preoccupation with himself, Tom's mode of existence is actually quite the opposite: it is that of total *gelassenheit* or a "letting-go"[18] of things to be themselves as their created natures were

---

16 As Bernthal remarks concerning this episode in *The Fellowship of the Ring*: "Evil wants itself to be taken very, very seriously, and The Ring wants to be taken seriously as a dangerous instrument of power, but the idea of putting the world within the confines of a ring and thereby controlling it is just ridiculous to Tom, who sees it against a vast backdrop of joyful Creation and finds its pretensions ridiculous." Bernthal, *Tolkien's Sacramental Vision*, 137.

17 FR, I, 7, 124.

18 This term can be found most prominently in the work of the German medieval Dominican mystical theologian, Meister Eckhart (c. 1260–1328). For Eckhart, we know God, self, and world only to the degree that we let go of all

intended to be. Tom's existence is utterly free because he is free from all possession, including all self-possession. Frodo asks, "Then all this strange land belongs to him?" and Goldberry explains:

> No indeed! ... That would indeed be a burden.... The trees and the grasses and all things growing or living in the land belong each to themselves. Tom Bombadil is the Master. No one has ever caught Tom walking in the forest, wading in the water, leaping on the hill-tops under light and shadow. He has no fear. Tom Bombadil is master.[19]

All living things, for Tom, "belong to themselves": in a paradox worthy of a medieval mystical theologian, Tom is "master" of the wood and forest precisely to the degree that he tries not to own them or exploit them.[20] He has no fear of the Old Forest or of anything else in his little land precisely because he is their master in this sense: he simply lets them be (much like God-Ilúvatar creates by "letting things be"). Thus, Tom is constantly singing, and when he speaks, he speaks in poetry or rhythmical prose, as if recalling the Great Music of Creation in his own little corner of Middle-earth. Even the hobbits start to sing more than they speak: "The guests became suddenly aware that they were singing merrily, as if it was easier and more natural than talking."[21] There is in Tom's little realm no separation between literal meaning and metaphor and thus no separation between prose and poetry and, most importantly, between words and things. Tom lives this primal unity. Hence, Tom's

---

attachments to the world, time, and most of all ourselves, with all our ideas and images of God and creatures, and let God's creative power work in and through us and his creatures unobstructed. For a brief overview of Eckhart's thought, see my article on Meister Eckhart: Robert Dobie, "Meister Eckhart: From Latin Scholasticism to German Mysticism," in *A Companion to World Literature: Volume 2, 601 CE to 1450*, ed. Ken Signeurie and Christine Chism (Hoboken, NJ: Wiley-Blackwell, 2020), 897–908.

19 FR, I, 7, 124.

20 Here we also find a strong analogy with how Niggle comes to experience time and eternity in "Leaf by Niggle": in the Workhouse-Infirmary, Niggle learns to "let go" of time; by doing so, he paradoxically becomes "master of his own time" and, as such, enters into eternity (about which more in chapter 7).

21 FR, I, 7, 125.

songs have power over the trees, beasts, and elements in his land. The words with which Tom describes Farmer Maggot could also apply to him: "There's earth under his old feet, and clay on his fingers, wisdom in his bones, and both his eyes are open."[22]

As Alison Milbank comments, "Tom Bombadil is the unfallen 'master of wood, water, and hill' precisely because he does not own them. Rather he receives everything as a gift and is himself a gift-giver."[23] Tom receives and relates to the natural world as a gift, as something created and given in love. That is why the Ring has no power over him: Tom's fellowship with all living things prevents him from fetishizing the Ring, from seeing it as something cut off from and independent of the world in which it has arisen. Devoid of any possessiveness, Tom is his own master and thus cannot be possessed by the Ring (or anything else).

Nevertheless, there is also a sense in which Tom Bombadil is outside the fellowship of the hobbits and later the Nine Walkers. Fellowship demands a self-reflexive creature who is subject to individuation and time and conscious of the division between self and other.[24] Tom is not such a creature. Paradoxically, then, Tom Bombadil would not make a good guardian of the Ring. After it is proposed at the Council of Elrond that they give the Ring to Tom Bombadil for safekeeping, Gandalf replies in opposition to this idea:

> Say rather that the Ring has no power over him. He is his own master. But he cannot alter the Ring itself, nor break its power over others.... He might do so [take and keep the Ring], if all the free folk of the world begged him, but he would not understand the need. And if he were given the Ring, he would soon forget it, or most likely throw it away. Such things have no hold on his mind. He would be a most unsafe guardian; and that alone is answer enough.[25]

22 *FR*, I, 7, 132.
23 Alison Milbank, "'My Precious': Tolkien's Fetishized Ring," in The Lord of the Rings *and Philosophy: One Book to Rule Them All*, ed. Gregory Bassham and Eric Bronson (Chicago: Open Court Publishing, 2003), 42.
24 Zimbardo, "Moral Vision," 75.
25 *FR*, II, 2, 265.

Tom represents what an unfallen fellowship with natural things would look like; but, of course, we, both the inhabitants of our primary world and the inhabitants of Tolkien's secondary world (Elves, Men, Hobbits, and Dwarves), live in a fallen world where such an easy fellowship with natural things is not to be had. This is why Tom Bombadil appears and then disappears from the narrative of *The Lord of the Rings*: he gives us a glimpse of an unfallen fellowship with natural beings, but precisely because of this, he cannot play any further role in the destruction of the evil that the Ring both causes and represents, for after the Fall, genuine fellowship is something that must be recovered, and then only after much self-denial and suffering.

Nevertheless, even among the fallen peoples of Middle-earth, there are still varying degrees of relationship with the natural world that manifest a relatively easier fellowship with natural things than do human beings in our primary world. We described the Hobbits' easy relationship with their land earlier. Also, the Elves, despite their revolt against the Valar and their vengeance-filled wars against Morgoth (and then Sauron), still retain, among all the peoples of Middle-earth, something of this free and easy fellowship with the land and the things living in and on it. The reader sees this fellowship between nature and rational beings in the Fellowship's visit to the Elven kingdom of Lothlórien, which is a land of unsurpassed natural beauty in which the Elves seem to live in utter harmony with their surroundings. Such is the intimate fellowship between the land and the Elves that it is impossible to tell who made whom. There is such a unity and oneness between the Elves and the land, particularly the extraordinarily beautiful Mallorn trees, that there seems to be a direct communication between them—a sort of unity of word and thing, meaning and being that in chapter 3 we saw Tolkien defend as what is most fundamentally given in our experience of being. That is why Sam then remarks that the Elven land is wonderfully quiet—there is no bustling about to do something, because the Elves do not understand natural things primarily by their use or utility. Moreover, another result of this is that time seems to stand still (much more about this in the chapter on eternity), and there is, in Lothlórien, a "magic" that is "right down deep, where I can't lay my hands on it,"[26] precisely because everything else in Lothlórien presupposes this intimate fellowship.

Sam, who in a great Tolkienian paradox constantly excuses himself for his lack of clarity and articulation but nevertheless expresses more directly and clearly than any other character what is essential, says of being in Lothlórien: "It's like being at home and on holiday at the same time, if you understand me."[27] These two things, being at home and being on holiday, we normally think of as very distinct, even mutually exclusive experiences, yet as Sam intuits, they come together in Lothlórien precisely due to this intimate fellowship between the Elves and the land. It is like being at home because of the free and easy way that the Elves relate to their land not only as a living being but a living being they know well and love. At the same time, it is like being on holiday, because the fellowship that the Elves have with their land is not oriented toward use or work, but toward an enjoyment of the land for its own sake, much like how we experience the world when on vacation or "holiday."

The reader notices that Sam refers to a "magic" that the land has that goes "down deep." It is clear from what Sam says that magic, in Tolkien's fiction, is not, as we have noted before, in its primary sense a matter of technical mastery or technical workings that are opaque to our intelligence. This might be the case for the magical machines of Saruman or Sauron, but not of the magic of the Elves. This magic is nothing other than the result of a deep fellowship of the Elves with the elements and living things of their land that is, it is true, combined with a technical mastery or, perhaps better, craftmanship. To Pippin's question about the cloaks they are receiving as gifts, "Are these magic cloaks?" one of the Elves responds: "They are Elvish robes certainly, if that is what you mean. Leaf and branch, water and stone: they have the hue and beauty of all these things under the twilight of Lórien that we love; for we put the thought of all that we love into all that we make."[28] What the elf means by putting "the thought of all that we love

---

26 *FR*, II, 7, 361.
27 *FR*, II, 7, 361.
28 *FR*, II, 8, 370.

into all that we make" is elusive. But from what we read elsewhere we can surmise that the elf here is referring to a nearly complete unity of intelligence—knowing the inherent natures and ends of things—and will—a deep love and valuing of those natures and a will and knowledge to complete and perfect what already lies in the natures and natural ends of things. Precisely because of this unity of love and intelligence, they can make things that respond in fellowship to human ends and desires, provided they are natural and therefore good. Thus, as Alison Milbank describes Sam's handling of the rope that the Elves gave him as a gift,

> With or without literary parallels, the rope has a fullness of presence in this scene. It is prompt when needed, beautiful and useful. Sam accords the rope full appreciation: "It looks a bit thin, but it's tough; and soft as milk to the hand. Packs close too, and as light as light. Wonderful folk to be sure!" ... Sam refers here to the elvish makers of his rope and he begins to undo the fetishism of things by restoring the relation of object to maker, and the fixed object to potency and use.[29]

Far from fetishizing things, true magic, unlike technology, makes clear their origins and returns them to the world of living fellowship among all beings, living or otherwise.[30] Milbank remarks, however, that this is also true in a way for Hobbits too, who, although their fellowship with nature is not as deep or magical as that of the Elves, is still much more so than that of modern human beings to their world. Whereas Elves illustrate a fellowship with the world of nature in all its mystery and remoteness, Hobbits give us a lively picture of genuine fellowship with the ordinary things and features of domestic life:

> Hobbits in the story seem to have been invented precisely in order to appreciate this ordinary domestic world of objects, just as the proper end of the ents is to love trees. In one sense,

---

29 Milbank, "'My Precious': Tolkien's Fetishized Ring," 39.
30 Although, as Milbank notes, Tolkien sometimes draws a difference between "magic" and "enchantment": in the latter we see things as they really are, whereas magic fixates and distracts us. Milbank, "'My Precious': Tolkien's Fetishized Ring," 42.

the whole complex net of invented languages and creatures, histories and mythologies exists in order that, like Sam, we can see the ordinary world in an unfetishized manner. This is the "recovery" of vision that Tolkien himself states is the purpose of fantasy or fairy-tale.[31]

As Merry, while recovering from his wounds in the Houses of Healing, puts it to Pippin in a light-hearted fashion typical of the Hobbits:

> It is best to love first what you are fitted to love, I suppose: you must start somewhere and have some roots, and the soil of the Shire is deep. Still there are things deeper and higher; and not a gaffer could tend his garden in what he calls peace but for them, whether he knows about them or not. I am glad that I know about them, a little. But I don't know why I am talking like this. Where is that leaf? And get my pipe out of my pack, if it isn't broken.[32]

All genuine fellowship among rational beings, among individuals as well as among different peoples and races, begins in Tolkien's world with a genuine fellowship with the land in which one lives; without such roots, any genuine fellowship already becomes a matter of domination and control and not true fellowship and friendship. As Craig Bernthal asserts, "The Shire, Rivendell, Lothlorien, Gondor, and Rohan tell us much about their inhabitants. By knowing geography, we come to know people whose selves grow organically from their native soil."[33] Now, one should note carefully that Tolkien is not promoting some sort of "blood and soil" mysticism: as the elf Gildor says to Frodo early on in *The Fellowship of the Ring*, "'It is not your own Shire.... Others dwelt here before hobbits were; and others will dwell here again when hobbits are no more. The wide world is all about you; you can fence yourselves in, but you cannot for ever fence it out'."[34] The Shire was not and will not be home to the Hobbits forever, no matter how deep their

31 Milbank, "'My Precious': Tolkien's Fetishized Ring," 43.
32 *RK*, V, 8, 870.
33 Bernthal, *Tolkien's Sacramental Vision*, 5.
34 *FR*, I, 3, 83.

connection to the land. Even the land of Lothlórien is fated to pass away into oblivion, for once the Ring of Sauron is destroyed, the power of the Elven ring that preserved Lothlórien from decay will fade and be lost.[35] The remorseless destruction by time of earthly attachments, no matter how right and good, is inevitable in a fallen world: "*The Lord of the Rings*, then, is an ethical text that teaches us to give up dominatory and fixed perceptions in order to receive the world back as gift."[36] We ultimately have fellowship with the land when we cease to try to possess it. Nevertheless, love for and intimate fellowship with the land of one's ancestors and birth is a necessary pre-condition for genuine fellowship among the inhabitants of that land.

Recovery of Society

The recovery of fellowship cannot for Tolkien occur in a vacuum, for fellowship by its very nature relates us to others. This insight is not, of course, original to Tolkien, but is a very old one going back to Plato and Aristotle, for whom the human being is a "political animal" or ζῷον πολιτικόν. Nevertheless, the power of Tolkien's fiction comes from actually showing how fellowship and virtue develop in a social order and how a good social order is one that arises from and is in continuity with fellowship with nature. A good social order, in turn, encourages and nurtures fellowships of various kinds among all rational beings in society.

In fact, we have a picture of such an idyllic society right at the beginning of *The Lord of the Rings* in the prologue, "Concerning Hobbits." The Shire has hardly any government to speak of: "Families for the most part managed their own affairs. Growing food and eating it occupied most of their time. In other matters, they were, as a rule, generous and not greedy, but contented and moderate, so that estates, farms, workshops, and small trades tended to remain unchanged for generations."[37] The only offices in the Shire that had any real function were the "shirriffs" (only twelve for the whole Shire!) and

---

35 *FR*, II, 7, 365.
36 Milbank, "'My Precious': Tolkien's Fetishized Ring," 44.
37 *FR*, prologue, 9.

the postmaster. The mayor at Michel Delving was a purely ceremonial figurehead, and the "Thain" of the Tooks and the "Master of Brandy Hall" of the Brandybucks were, in a way, clan chieftains whose remit only extended to their families, even if their authority and influence extended informally beyond their little realms.

Thus, you have a picture in the Shire of a polity that is half democratic, half aristocratic. It was democratic insofar as families and communities were left free to run their own affairs, pursuing a sort of Chestertonian-Bellocian distributism,[38] but it was "aristocratic" insofar as this freedom paradoxically rested upon and assumed a social order and hierarchy that was understood to be natural, rooted in the land, and therefore beyond personal whims or choices: "They attributed to the king of old all their essential laws; and usually they kept the laws of free will, because they were The Rules (as they said), both ancient and just."[39] This fact perhaps explains why Tolkien's sociopolitical views are impossible to categorize, since he rejects as deeply flawed and misleading almost all modern political ideologies. As he says in his letters concerning democracy,

> I am *not* a "democrat" only because "humility" and equality are spiritual principles corrupted by the attempt to mechanize and formalize them, with the result that we get not universal smallness and humility, but universal greatness and pride, till some Orc gets hold of a ring of power—and then we get and are getting slavery.[40]

What modern democrats mean by "equality" and "rights" is really the tyrannizing leveling of a vast societal Machine. The society (if one can

---

38 This was a politico-economic position that the early 20th century Catholic writers G. K. Chesterton and Hilaire Belloc proposed as a *via media* between capitalism and socialism. Unlike socialism, distributism sanctions and even encourages private property; but unlike capitalism, which tends to form ever larger corporations and monopolies, it asserts that society should ensure that private property be "distributed" as widely as possible among the population, making each individual family master of its domain. Hence, the name, "distributism."

39 *FR*, prologue, 9.

40 *Letters*, 246.

call it that) of the Orcs in Mordor and elsewhere illustrates more closely in Tolkien's fiction these modern notions of equality: "The Orcs that Frodo and Sam encounter in Mordor use the most modern idiom in the book: theirs is distinctly the speech of twentieth-century soldiers, but also of government or party functionaries, minor officials in a murderous bureaucracy."[41]

Far from presenting a Manichean vision of the "good peoples" of Middle-earth up against the totalitarian wickedness of Mordor and Isengard, however, Tolkien makes it clear that all the societies of Middle-earth have been to some degree corrupted. A Fall or a falling off, a decline, is seen throughout Tolkien's works—in civilizations, in nature, and in individuals (Denethor, Boromir, Gollum).[42] The depopulated nature of Middle-earth at the end of the third age is worth noting: almost all the lands of the former northern kingdom of Arnor are deserted of people, excepting rare pockets like the Shire and Bree. Even Middle-earth's strongest and most populous and urban kingdom, Gondor, is described by Tolkien as being in steep demographic decline, with many empty, derelict mansions dotting the cityscape of Minas Tirith.[43] By contrast, if the Shire is idyllic, it is because the hobbits not only have children, but are obsessed with genealogy and family trees.[44] Indeed, it is no accident that a family's genealogy is described as a "tree," as it denotes rootedness in the land and a natural intergenerational fellowship that, Tolkien implies, is the only firm basis for a good society. In Tolkienian fantasy, the recovery of society is a recovery not just of fellowship among our fellow rational creatures who exist in the present and the begetting of future generations, but of a fellowship with the dead, with past generations—a sort of "democracy of the dead," as Chesterton called the honoring of tradition.[45] By contrast, in declining

---

41 Anna Vaninskaya, "Tolkien and His Contemporaries," in *A Companion to J. R. R. Tolkien*, ed. Stuart Lee (Hoboken, NJ: Wiley-Blackwell Publishing, 2020), 363. It is also interesting to note that the troops of Mordor also have numbers, which is a typical feature of totalitarian, bureaucratic societies.

42 Holmes, "*The Lord of the Rings*," 142.

43 Stanton, *Hobbits, Elves and Wizards*, 40.

44 FR, prologue, 7.

45 Chesterton, *Orthodoxy*, 53.

societies, the begetting of children is ignored or even scorned. As Faramir says of ancient Gondor,

> Death was ever present, because the Númenóreans still, as they had in their old kingdom, and so lost it, hungered after endless life unchanging. Kings made tombs more splendid than houses of the living, and counted old names in the rolls of their descent dearer than the names of sons. Childless lords sat in aged halls musing on heraldry; in secret chambers withered men compounded strong elixirs, or in high cold towers asked questions of the stars. And the last king of the line of Anárion had no heir.[46]

Genealogy in Gondor, unlike in the Shire, becomes a sterile antiquarianism, and fellowship with past and potential future generations is replaced by a vain quest for interminable life and an equally vain attempt to know "scientifically" the future. In healthy and happy societies, by contrast, fellowship with nature is most manifested in the enthusiastic begetting of children and in the welcoming of children not as burdens but as gifts. It means that the past is also living, and our ancestors are treated as if they were fellow living family members.

This interlinking of generations, the intimacy of the family and its loves, fellowship, and history, is prior to any "politics," defined as the acquisition and use of power for societal ends (be they for the common good or, more commonly, for the good only of those wielding that power). Tolkien greatly disliked political readings of the *Lord of the Rings*, precisely because he was trying to recover an experience of fellowship among individuals and peoples that is prior to and more basic than the exercise of political power:

> I dislike the use of "political" in such a context; it seems to be false. It seems clear to me that Frodo's duty was "humane" not political. He naturally thought first of the Shire, since his roots were there, but the quest had as its object not the preserving of this or that polity, such as the half republic, half

---

46 *TT*, IV, 5, 678.

aristocracy of the Shire, but the liberation from an evil tyranny of all the "humane"—including those, such as "easterlings" and Haradrim, that were still servants of the tyranny.[47]

Indeed, the great bane of modernity is its inevitable tendency to reduce everything, not only society but even personal and intimate interpersonal relationships, to politics, rather than treating the former as prior to and more fundamental than the latter. Since, as we have seen, modernity views all reality as a Machine, devoid of any inherent meaning or purpose, all meaning and purpose can only come from human agents; since these agents are interpreted mechanistically, they can only be motivated, as in Thomas Hobbes, by power, particularly political power. Denethor is Tolkien's warning against such a view:

> Denethor was tainted with mere politics: hence his failure, and his mistrust of Faramir. It had become for him a prime motive to preserve the polity of Gondor, as it was, against another potentate, who had made himself stronger and was to be feared and opposed for that reason rather than because he was ruthless and wicked. Denethor despised lesser men, and one may be sure did not distinguish between orcs and the allies of Mordor.... He had become a "political" leader: sc. Gondor against the rest.[48]

This exclusively political view of things leads Denethor to extreme pride, as he is convinced that he is the only one who can save Gondor: "Yet the Lord of Gondor is not to be made the tool of other men's purposes, however worthy. And to him there is no purpose higher in the world as it now stands than the good of Gondor; and the rule of Gondor, my lord, is mine and no other man's, unless the king should come again."[49]

Tolkien contrasts Denethor's mere politics with the wisdom of the Elves, who were willing to destroy their own polities in order to preserve Middle-earth: "Elrond cannot be said to have a political duty

---

47 *Letters*, 240–41.
48 *Letters*, 241.
49 *RK*, V, 1, 758.

or purpose."⁵⁰ What is true of Denethor is *a fortiori* true of Sauron: Denethor, of course, is not an evil character in the sense that, although he despairs, he never, like Saruman, allies with Sauron nor ever contemplates betraying his country. Nevertheless, it is even more the case that Sauron is a "political animal," as Scott Davison notes: "The clearest illustration of the nature of evil comes from Sauron himself. Gandalf says that Sauron calculates everything with reference to his desire for power. This focus on domination is so powerful that it even colors his fears about the One Ring, as Gandalf makes clear: 'That we should wish to cast him down and have *no* one in his place is not a thought that occurs to his mind'."⁵¹

I think one can sum up Tolkien's attitude toward politics as one analogous to ancient philosophers' attitude about wealth: just as that person is genuinely rich who has the fewest wants and therefore does not have to think about money more than is necessary, so a society is free to the degree that its people do not have to think about politics more than is necessary. A society in which everything is political, down to the most intimate or even casual human interactions, is a totalitarian society, for such a society views itself as a Machine that can only be ruled by force, fear, or manipulation. The conversation between the orc commanders Shagrat and Gorbag in the pass of Cirith Ungol illustrates very well the distorted politics of totalitarian societies⁵²: every decision taken by higher-ups is about selfish power and domination. Moreover, everything is shrouded in secrecy and is opaque to everyone else. This gives the evil of the Machine great power, for it applies its power unpredictably, ruthlessly, and without scruple. As Stratford Caldecott notes, however, this is also the source of evil's great weakness:

> Evil rules by fear and greed, and it is weaker than it realizes, because the enemy is divided each one against his neighbor, looking ever for his own advantage. Friendship is stronger, because individuals work together for a common cause. In

---

50   *Letters*, 241.

51   Scott A. Davison, "Tolkien and the Nature of Evil," in Bassham and Bronson, The Lord of the Rings *and Philosophy*, 107.

52   *TT*, IV, 10, 738.

the end, this is why Aragorn makes a more powerful king than Sauron. People follow him and support him because they love him.[53]

Good societies are bound by a fellowship of friendship and love, bound to a love of the land and country in which they take root, which is prior to politics; bad societies are bound together only by force, fear, rootlessness, and propaganda. Not only do totalitarian societies ignore or discourage fellowship among their members, with nature, and with the land, but they actively seek to destroy such fellowships, for all relations must be reduced to the calculus of political power. It is also not just present fellowship that these societies seek to destroy, but all fellowship with the past, for, as we saw Chesterton assert, only our fellowship with past generations binds human beings in love and friendship with present and future generations. It is no accident, therefore, that totalitarian societies reserve a special hatred for the past, which goes well beyond a justified recognition of past injustices and rightful attempts to rectify them, to a condemnation of past generations *in toto* and the erasure or rewriting of historical memory. Any fellowship with the past is an obstacle to the complete destruction and rebuilding of society along utopian lines in the present.

Even an idyllic society like the Shire can be corrupted quite easily, as Saruman himself discovered, since mere politics promises, like Sauron's Ring, a power that is very seductive but ultimately enslaving. As Farmer Cotton relates to the Four Travelers (Frodo, Sam, Merry, and Pippin) concerning the devastation visited by the Ruffians under the command of Sharkey (who turns out to be Saruman) on the Shire since they had been gone,

> Take Sandyman's mill now. Pimple knocked it down almost as soon as he came to Bag End. Then he brought in a lot o' dirty-looking Men to build a bigger one and fill it full o' wheels and outlandish contraptions. Only that fool Ted was pleased by that, and he works there cleaning wheels for the Men, where his dad was the Miller and his own master. Pimple's idea was to

53 Caldecott, *The Power of the Ring*, 168.

grind more and faster, or so he said. He's got other mills like it. But you've got to have grist before you can grind; and there was no more for the new mill to do than for the old. But since Sharkey came they don't grind no more corn at all. They're always a-hammering and a-letting out a smoke and a stench, and there isn't no peace even at night in Hobbiton. And they pour out filth a purpose; they've fouled all the lower Water, and it's getting down into the Brandywine.[54]

The natural fellowship hobbits had with the Shire has been replaced by the power politics of the totalitarian leader—in this case, Saruman or "Sharkey"—who returns to wreak his vengeance on the vulnerable hobbits. Where the hobbits were once their own masters, they are now slaves to the Machine and to those who control it. It is no accident that this totalitarian rule by "Sharkey" also devastates the land ("Sharkey" has in particular a special animosity toward trees and has as many cut down as possible—not for lumber or firewood but for mere spite), for a totalizing political worldview cannot understand or engage in any sort of fellowship with natural things. Of course, as Sam realizes, the devastation is worse to the degree that what it destroyed was good.[55]

In sum, Tolkien wishes to show through his fantasy that the true, ultimate, and most important things for living a good and happy life are precisely those things which escape political calculation. Indeed, all political calculation, even—or especially—the cleverest, fails and founders precisely because it cannot comprehend that what is most important escapes politics:

> Here we meet, among other things, the first example of the motive (to become dominant in Hobbits) that the great policies of world history, "the wheels of the world," are often turned not by the Lords and Governors, even the gods, but by the seemingly unknown and weak—owing to the secret life in creation, and the part unknowable to all wisdom but One, that resides in the

54 *RK*, VI, 8, 1013.
55 "'This is much worse than Mordor!' said Sam. 'Much worse in a way. It comes home to you, as they say; because it is home, and you remember it before it was all ruined'." *RK*, VI, 8, 1018.

intrusions of the Children of God in the Drama. It is Beren the outlawed mortal who succeeds (with the help of Luthien, a mere maiden even if an elf of royalty) where all the armies and warriors have failed: he penetrates the stronghold of the Enemy and wrests one of the Silmarili from the Iron Crown. Thus he wins the hand of Luthien and the first marriage of mortal and immortal is achieved.[56]

It is this "secret life of creation" or the "secret fire" that is the real driver of events in history, and it is the only real source of their power, significance, and meaning, because it transcends both nature and time.

It is the humble and those held of no account—those who are outside the play of power-politics—that truly move the events of history. This is because, paradoxically, it is not a finite or created power that moves history; for this infinite, creative power to move history it must also, paradoxically, find in rational agents those who, like Frodo (until just before the end) and the rest of the Fellowship, renounce power. In this context, then, it is not surprising that when Tolkien writes a letter to his son Christopher during the darkest days of World War II (1943), he makes this statement:

> My political opinions lean more and more to Anarchy (philosophically understood, meaning abolition of control not whiskered men with bombs)—or to "unconstitutional" Monarchy. I would arrest anybody who uses the word State (in any sense other than the inanimate realm of England and its inhabitants, a thing that has neither power, rights, nor mind); and after of chance of recantation, execute them if they remained obstinate!

It is rather interesting that in this tongue-in-cheek comment, Tolkien lumps anarchy together with unconstitutional monarchy, but his meaning becomes clearer as he continues:

> Anyway the proper study of Man is anything but Man; and the most improper job of any man, even saints (who at any rate

---

56 *Letters*, 149.

were at least unwilling to take it on), is bossing other men. Not one in a million is fit for it, and least of all those who seek the opportunity. And at least it is done only to a small group of men who know *who* their master is. The medievals were only too right in taking *nolo episcipari* as the best reason a man could give others for making him a bishop.[57]

There can be no fellowship and no just social order without a personal virtue that values things other than or higher than power, yet modern states and systems of government and social organization are established on the assumption that such virtue is unnecessary or is even a bit of backwardness to be stamped out—the Machine will function regardless of the virtues and vices of its members (or even *because of* the vices of its members). Thus, Tolkien says, it is far better to have an "unconstitutional" monarch who would rather go hunting or collect stamps than be governed by a democratic politician in a system of government that encourages and even requires that those who rise to the top be those individuals with the most ambition and hunger for power. It is no accident then, that Tolkien portrays his ideal society, the Shire, as a quasi-anarchic polity where the king is distant yet respected and everyone acquires the virtues necessary to manage his or her own affairs competently and independently. Hence, as Tolkien says, to understand man, we must recover value that is rooted in a realm of meaning and being higher and greater than the finite, temporal, material, human world.

---

57 *Letters*, 63–64.

CHAPTER SIX

The Recovery of Virtue

Virtue, according to the Aristotelian-Thomistic tradition, is a habit of character that allows an agent to fulfill easily and consistently ends or goals that are natural to it. Hence, on the traditional understanding, even nonrational beings can have virtue by analogy: a plant has virtue insofar as it has the power to bring about an effect specific to its nature, such as healing (and in his fiction Tolkien uses "virtue" in this older sense). Human beings have virtue in its primary sense, however, insofar as they can acquire habits (which are neither from nature nor contrary to nature) that allow them to perform actions that are in accordance with reason, for rational activity is the natural end or goal of human activity. Thus, to use a common example, a human being with the virtue of courage has the habit or disposition of being able to control feelings of fear—heeding fear when it is reasonable to do so, but overriding it when it is not. Depending on whether someone habitually acts in accordance with reason, i.e., has virtue, they develop a good or bad character.

As we saw in the chapter "The Recovery of Nature," however, the notion that natural things have inherent goals and ends is one that was banished from modern thought, not because it was false or incoherent, but because it did not fit into the mechanistic view of the world that modern philosophers and scientists presupposed and wanted to advance. Hence, modern moral theories like utilitarianism or Kantian deontology seek to determine what is good or bad either based on whether it gives quantifiable pleasure ("the greatest pleasure for the greatest number," as in utilitarianism) or based on maxims that can be universalized without qualification (such as in Kant's notion of the categorical imperative, wherein one should "act only according to that maxim whereby you can also will that that maxim become a universal law"). Both modern ethical theories assume that natural things, including human beings, are devoid of natural ends and goals, and that any moral judgment is therefore grounded in subjective (even if perhaps universal) judgments either of pleasure and pain (whether for oneself or for the "greatest number") or of universal, logical consistency. And yet, as Tolkien's fiction shows, these ethical philosophies are ultimately the philosophies of Saruman and Sauron: for Saruman, social utility and order are the only goods that in turn justify any means to pursue them; on the other hand, Sauron is the abstract, universal eye that calculates everything in accordance with power and domination—a universal will to be sure, but one devoid of any fellowship with the natural world or embodied rational beings. In such schemes, there is no room for virtue, only a more or less refined enjoyment of pleasure or the exercise of bloodless, abstract reason.

Indeed, one can go even further and assert that not only is the concept of virtue barely understood by modern men and women: it is positively hated or feared. As the early twentieth-century phenomenologist Max Scheler argued, modern value systems are structured by *ressentiment*. The man or woman of *ressentiment* is unable to value anything as such, i.e., as having any inherent goodness, beauty, or greatness. Everything is valued only in opposition to an ideal that one hates because it seems unattainable: "The formal structure of *ressentiment* expression is always the same: A is affirmed, valued, and praised not for its own intrinsic quality, but with the unverbalized intention of denying, devaluating, and denigrating B. A is 'played off' against B."[1] Nietzsche already saw *ressentiment* as the foundational principle of modern morality, which he identified with Christian morality, and its supposed resentment against the vitality and power of the strong explicitly valued in all the old pagan scales of value. Scheler however argues that Nietzsche confused a decadent, pseudo-Christian, nineteenth-century universalist humanitarianism with genuine Christian love, which far from exalting weakness or lowliness as such, rather manifests true self-mastery and thus true power in its ideals of self-sacrifice and self-abnegation. Indeed, modern secular humanitarianism reserves special hatred and *ressentiment* for genuine Christian values and virtues, for the latter are not in the end egalitarian and levelling but rather noble and ennobling. There is, paradoxically, no one more humble and yet more noble and thus more liable to being resented than the saint.[2]

[1] Max Scheler, *Ressentiment*, trans. Lewis B. Caser and William W. Holdheim (Milwaukee, WI: Marquette University Press, 2007), 42.

[2] The phenomenon of *ressentiment* also explains, I think, the extreme distaste and even disgust that Tolkien's work aroused and still arouses in the intellectual establishment (well detailed by Shippey, *Author of the Century*). This extreme revulsion by many literati at Tolkien's fantasy goes well beyond mere dislike or difference of taste: these critics seem to take afront that Tolkien's Middle-earth exists at all. For these critics, real works of literature are about exposing all noble ideals and virtues as so many mystifications of power and privilege. In approaching literature this way, modern literary criticism falls into contradictions: it levels all value and greatness to such an extent that it denies any inherent, artistic value to the very literary works that form its subject matter—they are mere products of power, after all; at the same time, it exalts the literary class as a quasi-Gnostic elect that is able to reveal the true meanings of these works (if "truth" has any meaning here). Tolkien's fantasy, by contrast, reveals to the reader that nobility and virtue are, in fact, the *only things* that lend reality to human actions insofar as they perfect properties inherent in our nature and in the nature of the things we act upon. As such, Tolkien's fantasy also grounds and recovers the inherent value of literature to recover and acquire what perfects us as human beings, which is probably why readers some years ago consistently voted *The Lord of the Rings* the best book of the twentieth-century. It restores the value of literature as a resource for the recovery of meaning and wisdom for the perfection of one's character. Furthermore, Tolkien's fiction shows how, because the perfections of virtue transcend power relationships, they ironically are made most manifest in the humble and those held of little account (like the Hobbits) by the world.

Perhaps most interestingly, Scheler's analysis of *ressentiment* as the root of modern morality and value systems illuminates why modern men and women put an inordinate value on the Machine and why they are so heavily invested in a mechanistic understanding of reality:

> Guided by *ressentiment*, the modern world view reverses the true state of affairs. It "sells short," as all thinking geared to declining life, and seeks to understand the living by analogy with the dead. It interprets life as such as an accident in a universal mechanical process, the living organism as a fortuitous adaptation to a fixed dead milieu.[3]

The attraction of a mechanistic universe is not merely that it seems to give us unlimited power through technology, but even more fundamentally that it banishes virtue and even value from the natural world and, by extension, from the human world, since we are part of that world; it relieves the man and woman of *ressentiment* of the obligation to pursue or, even worse, acknowledge superior human excellence or virtue. By contrast, Tolkienian fantasy presents us with a world free of ressentiment and therefore full of genuine nobility and virtue that is yet tempered by the humble and the ordinary.

The Virtue of Pity (and Friendship)

True virtue for Tolkien begins paradoxically by knowing our limits, both our personal limits and the limits imposed by the kinds of beings we are. This is the case with all the most admirable characters in his fiction: "These characters [Galadriel, Bombadil, Sam] know their own limits. Why be moral? Plato asks. And Tolkien answers, 'To be yourself'. What kind of life should I choose? A life that is in accord with my abilities. If you need a Ring of Power to live your life, you have chosen the wrong life."[4] That is, Tolkien's good or heroic characters know that they are severely limited in what they

---

3 Scheler, *Ressentiment*, 122–23. See a similar analysis by Hans Jonas in "Gnosticism, Existentialism and Nihilism," 7–37.

4 Eric Katz, "The Rings of Tolkien and Plato: Lessons in Power, Choice, and Morality," in The Lord of the Rings *and Philosophy: One Book to Rule Them All*, ed. Gregory Bassham and Eric Bronson (Chicago: Open Court Publishing, 2003), 20.

can do, but they respond by seeing this fact as an opportunity to develop the goodness inherent in their natures and character. The temptation becomes strong to use the Ring to master events and make up for these limitations; just as the temptation is strong for us to use power—technological, material, or political—to master events or our own defects, real or imagined. Tolkien's heroes know that only by living in accord with the powers natural to them as whatever being they are (Elf, Hobbit, Man, Woman, etc.) can they truly be themselves and therefore truly be good. To quote Eric Katz again, "To resist the Ring is to remain oneself, to be the person you are without any extraordinary powers. All who come in contact with the Ring (except, it appears, Bombadil) lose themselves (at least momentarily) in the desire to be greater than they are."[5] If you need the help of technology, its devices, surgeries, drugs, and prosthetics (i.e., rings of power) to be who you are, then you are on the path to nihilistic self-destruction, not self-fulfillment.

In short, Tolkien's fiction focuses on the fact that much of what the tradition calls "virtue" is recovered in the face of events that seem beyond any individual or even any particular society's control. The great attraction of Tolkien's fantasy is that it addresses one of the most pressing questions of life: What do I do in the face of seemingly insurmountable odds, i.e., when most people around me and even all of society seem set against what I understand to be true and good? In the following passage, Frodo expresses the sentiment many of us have had:

> "I wish it need not have happened in my time," said Frodo.
> "So do I," said Gandalf, "and so do all who live to see such times. But that is not for them to decide. All we have to decide is what to do with the time that is given to us."[6]

Later in *The Lord of the Rings*, Gandalf reminds the reader yet again: "It is not our part to master all the tides of the world, but to do what is in us for the succour of those years wherein we are set, uprooting the evil in the fields that we know, so that those who live after may have clean earth to till. What weather they shall have is not ours to rule."[7] A very large component in the recovery and the

---

5 Katz, "The Rings of Tolkien and Plato," 19.
6 *FR*, I, 2, 51.
7 *RK*, V, 9, 879.

development of virtue, Tolkien implies, is precisely the abandonment of any notions of worldly success and thus all feelings of *ressentiment*; to be virtuous is to do what is right and good now for its inherent value, regardless of the results or any comparison to others' standing. The paradox here is that only by abandoning success or achievement according to the standards of what counts as power and control are we in accord with the natural ends and purposes of things. As Stratford Caldecott remarks, Tolkien threads a mean between the postmodern Nietzschean idea that we are creators of ourselves and the premodern idea that we are purely the creatures of family or tribe: "To be most authentically myself is to be for others. It is by giving myself away that I find myself, along with my real destiny."[8] To put it another way, an action or choice is only truly good to the degree that one chooses what is true or good for itself; such a choice often demands a renunciation of power. As Faramir, a paragon of nobility and uprightness in *The Lord of the Rings*, says when he suggests that he feels deceived and lied to by Frodo and Sam: "I would not snare even an orc with a falsehood."[9] Such is the power of truth that it must be chosen even if it seems, in the short term, to be greatly to one's disadvantage.[10]

Thus, several times in *The Lord of the Rings*, Tolkien emphasizes the virtue of pity.[11] Pity has no purpose or end outside of the act of valuing the life in front of one for itself, regardless of use or advantage—or even at the cost of any advantage to oneself. As Gandalf explains to Frodo regarding Bilbo's pity toward Gollum, even though he acknowledges that any calculating person would expect that Gollum would betray Bilbo and later Frodo, "It was Pity that stayed his [Bilbo's] hand. Pity, and Mercy: not to strike without need. And he has been well rewarded.... Be sure that he took so little hurt from the evil, and

8   Caldecott, *The Power of the Ring*, 172.
9   *TT*, IV, 5, 664.
10   Probably the most problematic feature of Peter Jackson's cinematic adaptation of the book is its drastic change in the character of Faramir: the movie makes him into a man of *ressentiment*, which is precisely the opposite of his character in the book.
11   For the centrality of the virtue of pity for Tolkien in his fiction (and the influence the nineteenth-century novel *John Inglesant* had on his conception of pity) see Ordway, *Tolkien's Modern Reading*, 241ff.

escaped in the end, because he began his ownership of the Ring so. With Pity."[12] The fact that Bilbo valued the life of Gollum before any mechanistic calculations of pleasure and pain or of use or disadvantage, meant that the Ring could not completely bring Bilbo under its sway of manipulation and calculation (and more importantly, it perfected a good in Bilbo himself that resisted the effects of the Ring).

That genuine pity acts for the sake of the other only as other (and therefore not because it makes the one showing pity feel good) points to another factor that Tolkien highlights in his fantasy: that genuine virtue and goodness are a matter of responsibility. That is to say, we develop virtue precisely to the degree that we confront rightly and with courage events and situations that we don't want but that demand from us a response. That we confront such situations has nothing to do with any inherent goodness or badness on our part: "You may be sure that it was not for any merit that others do not possess: not for power or wisdom, at any rate. But you have been chosen, and you must therefore use such strength and heart and wits as you have."[13] Paradoxically, what makes the good life or, better, what develops the virtue that is the necessary condition for living the good life, lies not in the plans and projects we have for ourselves and their fulfillment; rather, it lies in confronting and overcoming obstacles that we do not choose. As the Austrian psychiatrist Victor Frankl observed concerning the experiences he and his fellow prisoners in Nazi death camps underwent during World War II, "We stopped asking ourselves what we wanted out of life and started to ask what life demanded from us."[14] Spiritual self-mastery and, from that, a meaningful life come from our *response-ability*, our ability to respond with grace and composure to the tasks that life puts before us.

Gandalf understands this truth very well, which is why he refuses the Ring when Frodo offers it to him. As Gandalf explains to Frodo, "The way of the Ring to my heart is by pity, pity for weakness and desire of strength to do good. Do not tempt me! I dare not take it, not even to keep it safe, unused. The wish to wield it would be too great for my

---

12   *FR*, I, 2, 59.
13   *FR*, I, 2, 61.
14   Viktor Frankl, *Man's Search for Meaning*, trans. Ilse Lasch (Boston: Beacon Press, 2006), 97.

strength."¹⁵ Gandalf's goodness lies in large part in his ability to see his own weakness, to know that the greater his power—and his power is greater than that of most in Middle-earth—the greater the temptation for him to use (or misuse) the Ring.

So yes, the Ring has a great power to dominate and control not only its wearers but even those close to it. For Tolkien, the greatest peril always lies within the individual. As Sam says to Faramir when the perilous nature of Lothlórien is mentioned among them, "It strikes me that folk takes their peril with them into Lórien, and finds it there because they've brought it. But perhaps you could call her [Galadriel] perilous, because she's so strong in herself."¹⁶ This fact leads to a further paradox: that self-knowledge strangely gives an advantage and power over those, like Saruman and Sauron, who calculate everything only in terms of power. As Christopher Garbowski observes,

> [T]he best characters either realize that evil is not only in the "other" but also a potential within themselves, or they learn this at some point in the narrative. Instead of leading to pessimism, however, it is one of their strengths. It gives them an advantage of moral imagination over monological evil: whereas the profoundly evil forces cannot conceive of an action that is not based on self-interest, in this case the disposal of the One Ring, the good characters can imagine themselves as evil, which influences their strategy.¹⁷

Good characters can easily imagine what evil characters will or might do, because they recognize the potentiality for evil in themselves. The reverse is not the case for evil characters. They are creatures of *ressentiment*, for whom virtue is just an illusion of fools, a mask for power, or something that is simply incomprehensible.

Therefore, the recognition of one's limits is the precondition for genuine virtue. This recognition of limits also means that the virtuous person understands that he or she is already in a web of relationships, with the self, other rational creatures, and the natural world. For Tolkien,

15 *FR*, I, 2, 61.
16 *TT*, IV, 5, 680.
17 Garbowski, "Evil," 428.

the essence of virtue, then, is in the making of a gift of oneself, for the natural end or goal of human virtue is fellowship, both with other human beings and with the created world. Stratford Caldecott, along with many other close readers of Tolkien, has noticed the importance of gifts in Tolkien's fiction. The gifts of Galadriel are particularly central to the eventual success of the Fellowship in *The Lord of the Rings*, although this is not immediately evident. To quote Caldecott, "Gifts, of course, are used to signify friendship, and true love is often described as a 'gift of self'." The gifts of Galadriel are no ordinary gifts: as we saw earlier, the cloaks and rope that she gives the members of the Fellowship have a magical quality. The phial of light that she gives to Frodo contains the original light of the Two Trees of Valinor, thus connecting the Fellowship back to the very beginning of the creation of Arda: "Thus her [Galadriel's] gifts of friendship connect directly with a greater tapestry of story linking all their lives with the fair Light and Life in Arda as a whole."[18] Gifts bind the characters in love and friendship. It is not just the Elves that give gifts, but one of the most attractive virtues of the Hobbits is their love of giving gifts. Hobbits are hospitable and delight in parties and in presents, "which they [give] away freely and eagerly [accept]."[19] Furthermore, gifts bind giver and receiver in a bond of fellowship that is not based on calculation: "Rings are gifts that bind the wearer to the giver in those ancient tales. And if one receives gold objects as gifts from the true owner, no harm ensues to the wearer."[20]

Even more, the gift also binds the giver and receiver to the gift of creation, because creation itself is a gift. This is evident in the phial, mentioned above, that Galadriel gives to Frodo; it is not just a pretty jewel but a jewel that contains the primal light of Creation. It is a gift, therefore, that not only binds Frodo in fellowship to Galadriel, but it, along with the other gifts of Galadriel to the Fellowship, confirms and strengthens the fellowship among its members and finally binds the Fellowship to the created world and its Creator. The phial of Galadriel makes the world in all its beauty and strangeness visible; the Ring by contrast makes the wearer invisible and the world vague and murky.

18 Caldecott, *The Power of the Ring*, 170.
19 *FR*, I, prologue, 2.
20 Milbank, "'My Precious': Tolkien's Fetishized Ring," 40.

As Peter Kreeft points out, the "Ring cuts us off from community, and contact ... the Ring makes us unreal by isolating us."[21] When the members of the Fellowship receive the gifts of Galadriel, they implicitly accept one another and the world itself into a wider fellowship as gift. Even Boromir, who falls to the temptation of the Ring, receives in the end the gift of redemption through a noble death.

This is perhaps why the recovery of fellowship is also a recovery of genuine friendship. Indeed, the nature and power of friendship are central themes of *The Lord of the Rings*. Seeing the formation of unlikely friendships within the Fellowship is one of the more satisfying features of the story. The most unlikely friendship that forms is between the Elf, Legolas, and the Dwarf, Gimli. In their friendship is not only an ancient enmity between two peoples healed, but also the elemental forces that they represent. There is also the friendship between Aragorn and Gandalf and between Merry and Pippin: both pairs are at various points crucial to the success of the quest. The different races of the Fellowship and the pairs within it (Frodo and Sam, Merry and Pippin, Legolas and Gimli, Aragorn and Gandalf) show us "that we begin to become heroes simply by being friends, by being loyal to each other through the trials that afflict us and holding tight to the things and people that are worthy of love."[22] Or, as Leslie Donovan points out, "when characters join together and cooperate with each other, they succeed; but when they reject cooperation, tragedy ensues."[23] Friendship or fellowship even contains a power greater than wisdom itself, as Gandalf remarks to Elrond when he hesitates to allow Merry and Pippin to join the Fellowship: "I think that in this matter it would be well to trust rather to *friendship* than to great *wisdom*,"[24] for genuine friendship and fellowship connect us, as we saw in the last chapter, to an even deeper wisdom embedded in creation itself.

Then there is the friendship between Frodo and Sam. It is, in the end, Sam's love for Frodo, his hobbit humility, and his already-close

---

21 Kreeft, *The Philosophy of Tolkien*, 181.
22 Caldecott, *The Power of the Ring*, 169.
23 Donovan, "Middle-earth Mythology," 100.
24 *FR*, II, 3, 276, emphasis added.

fellowship with the earth (and with the land of the Shire in particular) that allow him to resist the power of the Ring and save the Quest. After Sam takes the Ring from Frodo, thinking his master dead from Shelob's sting, he imagines himself to be a mighty hero, striding across Middle-earth and converting Mordor into a giant beautiful garden. But then Tolkien describes what stops Sam's vain fantasies:

> In that hour of trial it was the love of his master that helped most to hold him firm; but also deep down in him lived still unconquered his plain hobbit-sense: he knew in the core of his heart that he was not large enough to bear such a burden, even if such visions were not a mere cheat to betray him. The one small garden of a free gardener was all his need and due, not a garden swollen to a realm; his own hands to use, not the hands of others to command.[25]

Why doesn't Sam abandon Frodo? Jorge Gracia answers: "Because his first and foremost attachment is not to an object, but to a person. His goal is not possession, but fellowship."[26] Sam and characters like him do not fetishize the world; they love things for the relations that they have to other persons and to living things. That is perhaps why the Ring has little power over Sam. In carrying his master, Frodo, on his back on the last stretch toward the doors of Sammath Naur on Mount Doom, he not only does not feel the weight of the Ring, but feels Frodo to be no burden at all:

> As Frodo clung upon his back, arms loosely about his neck, legs clasped firmly under his arms, Sam staggered to his feet; and then to his amazement he felt the burden light. He had feared that he would have barely enough strength to lift his master alone, and beyond that he expected to share in the dreadful dragging weight of the accursed Ring. But it was not so. Whether because Frodo was so worn by his long pains, wound of knife, and venomous sting, and sorrow, fear, and

---

25 *RK*, VI, 1, 901.
26 Jorge J. E. Gracia, "The Quests of Sam and Gollum for the Happy Life," in Bassham and Bronson, *The Lord of the Rings and Philosophy*, 67.

homeless wandering, or because some gift of final strength was given to him, Sam lifted Frodo with no more difficulty than if he were carrying a hobbit-child pig-a-back in some romp on the lawns or hayfields of the Shire.[27]

The intimate fellowship of friendship between Frodo and Sam breaks the power of the Ring, whose own power lies in division.[28] And yet, with great irony, that power of division turns upon Sauron to his own undoing, as all the Orcs in the Tower of Cirith Ungol end up killing off one another and therefore allowing Sam to rescue Frodo and escape with Sauron's Ring. Here we find the antithesis of the love and friendship between Frodo and Sam. Indeed, with regard to Frodo and Sam, there is an irony in the fact that the servant is carrying the master. Far from obliterating social ranks and distinctions their friendship and fellowship depend precisely upon these distinctions if there is to be genuine service and sacrifice. Virtue consists in performing your role in society with skill and excellence and not in destroying it; doing so leads to the pride of a Saruman or Sauron. In recovering friendship and fellowship, we also recover virtue.

Thus, unlike the modern *Übermensch*, the sovereign individual, free of all ties to other people, society, or even nature and thus free to live by his or her own rules, we human beings are, for Tolkien, in many respects no different from any other living thing in the created world. We are gardeners of our character, but we are also dependent on seed, soil, and conditions that we have not chosen:

> A man is not only a seed, developing in a defined pattern, well or ill according to its situation or its defects as an example of its species; a man is both a seed and in some degree also a gardener, for good or ill. I am impressed by the degree in which the development of "character" *can* be a product of conscious intention, the will to modify innate tendencies in desired directions; in some cases the change can be great and permanent.[29]

27 *RK*, VI, 3, 941.
28 "Indeed in nothing is the power of the Dark Lord more clearly shown than in the estrangement that divides all those who still oppose him." *FR*, II, 6, 348.
29 *Letters*, 240.

We are free, Tolkien here says, to mold our character for better or worse; good character is molded in responsibility to one's spouse, one's friends, one's country, and the entire created order, for that in turn is ordered in responsibility toward its Creator. Life is constituted precisely by this interweaving of two strands: free choice and unalterable fate.

The Recovery of Love, Marriage, and Sexuality

Although seemingly peripheral to the story of *The Lord of the Rings*, marriage actually occupies a central place in Tolkien's working out of his epic. The male-female dynamic in Tolkien's stories is found deep down in the intertwining fates of Elves and Men. Love of Elves and Faerie is intimately related to the love between man and woman[30] and, ultimately, what unites man and woman, Man and Elf, is fruitfulness.[31] Marriage in Tolkien's world is rooted in fellowship with creation insofar as its inherent purpose is procreative: as the place where new human life comes into the world and is nurtured, marriage has a meaning in itself apart from any accidental emotional attachments. In that sense, marriage is a sacrament: a visible, material, and effective sign of grace that, as we saw in the chapter on the recovery of language, unites the literal biological need with a wider world of interpersonal, intelligible meaning, a meaning that points both to the transcendent act of world-Creation and to the act of sub-creation.

It appears, then, to be no accident that Tolkien's deepest and most intimate thoughts on virtue come in the context of a letter he wrote to one of his sons on the nature of marriage. On the one hand, marriage demands the cultivation of the pagan virtues of self-mastery and loyalty; on the other hand, marriage also demands the Christian recognition that we are fallen beings and that marriage demands sacrifice: "This is a fallen world. The dislocation of sex-instinct is one of the chief symptoms of the Fall. The world has been 'going to the bad' all down the ages."[32] What are the consequences of this? Tolkien explains that

---

30 Caldecott, *The Power of the Ring*, 127.
31 Caldecott, *The Power of the Ring*, 130.
32 *Letters*, 48.

> the essence of a *fallen* world is that the *best* cannot be attained by free enjoyment, or by what is called "self-realization" (usually a nice name for self-indulgence, wholly inimical to the realization of other selves); but by denial, by suffering. Faithfulness in Christian marriage entails that: great mortification. For the Christian man there is *no escape*.[33]

The Ring of Sauron, like modern conceptions of marriage, promises a cheap self-realization—one bought without self-denial, suffering, or mortification. It promises a mechanistic (i.e., technological, medical, therapeutic, etc.) solution to problems without the hard work of developing personal virtue. Furthermore, for Tolkien, as we have seen above, virtue is recovered precisely in response to tasks or events whose consequences are not only unknown to us but that often demand of us things, like suffering and self-denial, that we do not want. Marriage is the paradigmatic case for this reality: while in most cases today, we are free to choose our mate, we are completely in the dark about whether that choice will be a good or bad one, the consequences joyful or heartbreaking. Even in the best of marriages, hardship, illness, and death always lurk at the door. Tolkien observes:

> Only a *very* wise man at the *end* of his life could make a sound judgment concerning whom, amongst the total possible chances, he ought most profitably to have married! Nearly all marriages, even happy ones, are mistakes: in the sense that almost certainly (in a more perfect world, or even with a little more care in this very imperfect one) both partners might have found more suitable mates. But the "real soul-mate" is the one you are actually married to. You really do very little choosing: life and circumstances do most of it (though if there is a God these must be His instruments, or His appearances).[34]

This is why Christian marriage is a training school for life: we become virtuous to the degree that we pick up our cross and complete the quest

---

33 *Letters*, 51.
34 *Letters*, 51.

of our lives by loving those we are called to love with courage and joy, even (or especially) when they stop loving or disappoint us.

As Stratford Caldecott observes, "just as evil is always an inverted mockery of the good, so the One Ring is an inverted mockery of the wedding ring signifying friendship. Sauron's Ring represents *the destruction, the antithesis, of friendship.*"[35] Now, it is well known that many contemporary critics disliked (or rather, despised) as old-fashioned, even Victorian, what they took to be Tolkien's views on women and sexuality. As many Tolkien scholars have shown, this view is unfair and demonstrates often a simple inability to read what Tolkien wrote. The role of women in Tolkien's work is complex. As Sandra Miesel notes, an egalitarian spirit prevails between the sexes in Tolkien's work: "Gender roles are flexible: no thought or skill is limited to one sex ... Females keep records; males usually cook. Nerdanel, daughter and wife of great smiths, mastered that predominantly masculine craft."[36] Tolkien's saying "where will wants not, a way opens"[37] provides a key to the specific and unique virtues of women in his fiction: heroism, like in Aragorn letting Frodo and Sam continue on their quest and going after Merry and Pippin, lies in letting go. As Adam Roberts argues, "This mode of relinquishing, Tolkien is saying, is as great an act of heroism as storming into battle brandishing your sword."[38] The power of the feminine in Tolkien's work is linked specifically to this power, which is as great as if not greater than the assertion of strength, for it is essentially what allows the Fellowship to destroy the power of the Ring.

So while there is an egalitarian spirit between the sexes in Tolkien's world, male and female are not interchangeable, like parts in a machine. As Kreeft points out, the character of Eowyn, who, as a female warrior, breaks various stereotypes of woman (and is therefore a very popular character), is not an exception to this fact.[39] She is actually a character

---

35 Caldecott, *The Power of the Ring*, 170.
36 Miesel, "Life-giving Ladies," 149.
37 *RK*, V, 3, 1052.
38 "Passivity in the novel is a passion. That is the heart of the matter." Adam Roberts, "Women," in *A Companion to J. R. R. Tolkien*, ed. Stuart Lee (Hoboken, NJ: Wiley-Blackwell Publishing, 2020), 481.
39 Kreeft, *The Philosophy of Tolkien*, 106–7.

who eventually comes to understand the unique nature and power of the feminine. Hence, in the end, Tolkien has Eowyn say: "I will be a shieldmaiden no longer, nor vie with the great Riders, nor take joy only in the songs of slaying. I will be a healer, and love all things that grow and are not barren."[40] Notice here the end of her statement to Faramir, her soon-to-be husband: she wishes to realize the true and therefore good end or goal of the union between man and woman, which is to be fruitful, like natural things, and not barren, like artificial things or the Machine. "Femininity means fruitfulness: it gives life and makes life worth living."[41] We should also point out that Tolkien balances this statement of Eowyn with one very like it by Faramir: "Let us cross the River and in happier days let us dwell in fair Ithilien and there make a garden. All things will grow with joy there."[42] That is, fruitfulness is not just a task for women but for men as well in loving union with their female spouses. As Sandra Miesel concludes, "Eowyn outgrows her hero-worshipping crush for a genuine love. She and her husband ... will rule a deserted region as prince and princess. The lily finally gets to bloom in a real garden where both courage and nurturing skills count."[43]

Therefore, the many critics who faulted and still fault Tolkien for a lack of any explicit sexual activity in his works, particularly *The Lord of the Rings*, are missing a very important point, which Alison Milbank rightly highlights: "Critics have often noticed the lack of sexual activity in *The Lord of the Rings*. This, I believe, can be explained through the corrosive power of the Ring, which takes the focus away from the romantic quest and subsumes to itself the power of the erotic."[44] We have had occasion to mention several times how the Ring can be seen as a fetish: "Relationships between things are substituted for those between people, and those commodities acquire an idolatrous character as fetishes: they are totally of our own creation but we fail to recognize

---

40 *RK*, VI, 5, 965.
41 Miesel, "Life-giving Ladies," 151.
42 *RK*, VI, 5, 965.
43 Miesel, "Life-giving Ladies," 143.
44 Milbank, "'My Precious': Tolkien's Fetishized Ring," 35.

this."⁴⁵ As a fetish, the Ring of Sauron reduces all relationships to ones of power, and since power can be exercised absolutely only on beings lacking free will, it must reduce all creatures to things devoid of will or even life. But even here, Millbank notes, we see an impoverishment even of the notion of a "thing." The meaning of "thing" in Old English and Old Norse had a wider meaning of "matter of concern, discussion" or "contested matter" (similar to *res*—as in *res publica*, or "matter of public concern," in Latin). Thus, "things" as they were originally understood were phenomena charged with meaning and significance. When in thrall to fetishized objects, however, we go to the opposite extreme of holding them as inert or as of no account once their aura disappears.⁴⁶ The origin of a thing in a world of life and meaning is forgotten, and the fetish begins to have control over the one who possesses it; in other words, it is the possessor who becomes possessed.

In sum, the Ring of Sauron functions as a sexual fetish in the tales of Middle-earth. A sexual fetish is any object of sexual desire that directs the sexual act away from its natural *telos* or end, which is procreation (really a species of sub-creation), and thus perverts it. It leads to sterility and to a dead and barren world, which is precisely the world of the Machine.⁴⁷ While the Ring is undestroyed, the desires of rational creatures are diverted away from marriage and procreation, not just for the named characters in the story, but also for the whole of Middle-earth, which is, as noted above, in a state of precipitous demographic decline at the beginning of *The Lord of the Rings*. Hence, once the Ring has been returned to its origin, it is de-fetishized and, as a result, we see a great bursting forth of fertility and life in Middle-earth.⁴⁸ The final chapters of *The Lord of the Rings* record a whole series of marriages—between Aragorn and Faramir and Eowyn, Sam and Rosie

---

45 Milbank, "'My Precious': Tolkien's Fetishized Ring," 37.

46 Milbank, "'My Precious': Tolkien's Fetishized Ring," 38.

47 Sandra Miesel argues that, in many ways, the supreme female evil of Middle-earth that is even greater than Ungoliant and Shelob is Sauron's Ring, since both are all-devouring, seeking to return all to a womb-like darkness. Miesel, "Life-giving Ladies," 148.

48 Milbank, "'My Precious': Tolkien's Fetishized Ring," 41.

Cotton[49]—which had to be long postponed due to the power of the Ring to fetishize human relations and even biological activity and divert them into sterile and ultimately useless passions.[50] Even the earth shares in this great burst of fertility at the end of the story, as Sam sows the acorn and the dust of Galadriel throughout the Shire, leading to a magnificent growth in trees, flora, and even a great baby boom of hobbit children. The northern lands of the former kingdom of Arnor start once again to be populated under the authority of the new United Kingdom under King Elessar (Aragorn).

In the end, however, this fruitfulness is not possible without *sacrifice*, and sacrifice is not possible without *courage*. In fact, Tom Shippey goes so far as to say, "courage is perhaps the strongest element in the Tolkienian synthesis of virtue."[51] While the pagans understood the former—facing fate with courage—they did not know the joy of the happy ending, which is the promise that the life, death, and resurrection of Christ gives the Christian. As Tolkien writes to his son in his letter on marriage cited above,

> Out of the darkness of my life, so much frustrated, I put before you the one great thing to love on earth: the Blessed Sacrament.... There you will find romance, glory, honour, fidelity, and the true way of all your loves upon earth, and more than that: Death: by the divine paradox, that which ends

---

[49] Although, as if to emphasize this very point, the two characters in the story that carried the Ring for any length of time, Bilbo and Frodo, are and remain unmarried bachelors, without children and therefore without any direct heirs. Samwise Gamgee and Rosie Cotton do end up having twelve children, but Sam wore the Ring very briefly and, moreover, due to his stout, plain "hobbit-sense," did not seem to have been deeply affected by it, at least not with regard to the begetting of children.

[50] Sandra Miesel notes that the three major female characters of the *Lord of the Rings*—Arwen, Galadriel, and Eowyn—balance each other out. Each in her own way brings renewal and fruitfulness. There is the mirroring of high and low in the marriages of Aragorn and Sam. Finally, each character marries and then plants a new tree as an *axis mundi*: "Thus *The Lord of the Rings*' female characters do loom larger in symbolic space than in wordage occupied." Miesel, "Life-giving Ladies," 143–44.

[51] Shippey, *The Road to Middle-earth*, 154.

life, and demands the surrender of all, and yet by the taste (or foretaste) of which alone can what you seek in your earthly relationships (love, faithfulness, joy) be maintained, or take on that complexion of reality, of eternal endurance, which every man's heart desires.[52]

For Tolkien, marriage is a training ground for virtue insofar as it cultivates in us a spirit of self-sacrifice and patient endurance. Paradoxically, this is what makes true marriage the locus of great joy and models us on our Savior: it is through self-sacrifice and patient endurance that abiding love, meaning, and hope can be found. This truth is what the rare yet significant marriages between mortal Men and immortal Elves in Tolkien's legendarium point to: the true meaning of marriage lies in the intersection between time and eternity, the mortal and immortal, for true marriage is a death to self that leads to true immortality. This is shown by the fact that these unions ultimately bring about the defeat of evil as embodied by Morgoth and Sauron.

Perhaps the most important such union in Tolkien's legendarium is that of the mortal man Beren and the immortal elven maiden Lúthien, for it illustrates this deeper, metaphysical significance of marriage, a significance that goes beyond the merely biological or psychological. The romance of Beren and Lúthien is central to the tales of the *Quenta Silmarillion*: through the love of Beren and Lúthien for each other, they are able to defeat Morgoth and recover the Silmarils, thus saving Middle-earth from near total domination by him. Nevertheless, a doom hangs over their love: Beren is destined to die and Lúthien destined to live more immeasurable ages without him. What is to be done? Tolkien has the Vala, Manwë, give Lúthien a choice:

> Because of her labours and her sorrow, she should be released from Mandos, and go to Valimar, there to dwell until the world's end among the Valar, forgetting all griefs that her life had known. Thither Beren could not come. For it was not permitted to the Valar to withhold Death from him, which is

[52] *Letters*, 53–54.

the gift of Ilúvatar to Men. But the other choice was this: that she might return to Middle-earth, and take with her Beren, there to dwell again, but without certitude of life or joy. Then she would become mortal, and subject to a second death, even as he; and ere long she would leave the world for ever, and her beauty become only a memory in song.[53]

Lúthien, of course, makes the second choice: to return to Middle-earth with Beren and share a mortal life and suffer a second death with him. The parallels with the Christian teaching about Christ here are obvious: by taking on human nature, Christ, though divine and immortal, took on our humanity and mortality in order save us from sin and death. What is interesting here is that Tolkien links the Incarnation with marriage: what Christ represents is a sort of divine marriage not only between God and humanity but also between the immortal and the mortal, eternity and time. The question remains, why should Lúthien make that choice? I think that the answer lies in Tolkien's characterization of Death as "Ilúvatar's gift to Men": the gift of Death is an integral aspect of understanding the world as gift, as creation. This, unfortunately, means giving up "certitude of life and joy."

As Tolkien remarks at the very end of the chapter on Beren and Lúthien in the *Quenta Silmarillion*, "So it was that alone of Eldalië she has died indeed, and left the world long ago. Yet in her choice the Two Kindreds have been joined; and she is the forerunner of many in whom the Eldar see yet, though all the world is changed, the likeness of Lúthien the beloved, whom they have lost."[54] By her choice, her act of faith, Lúthien changes not only her own fate, but also the fate of the Two Kindreds, Men and Elves, by uniting them in a common destiny that transcends time. Marriage in Tolkien is an image of how the mortal can be taken up into the immortal and how time can be taken up into eternity. Through both procreation and self-sacrifice, it orients the husband and wife to what is beyond the present moment—to what is even beyond one's present, mortal life. It is an intimation of eternity entering into and transforming time.

53 *QS*, xix, 187.
54 *QS*, xix, 187.

CHAPTER SEVEN

The Recovery of Eternity

When *The Lord of the Rings* was first published, Tolkien complained that most readers missed the deepest and most important theme of his work. Yes, the theme of power and domination is important for the story. The story also provides, he continues,

> the theme of a War, about something dark and threatening enough to seem at that time of supreme importance, but that is mainly "a setting" for characters to show themselves. The real theme for me is about something much more permanent and difficult: Death and Immortality: the mystery of the love of the world in the hearts of a race "doomed" to leave and seemingly lose it; the anguish in the hearts of a race "doomed" not to leave it, until its whole evil-aroused story is complete.[1]

---

[1] *Letters*, 246; see also *Letters*, 284.

Central to the development of this theme, Tolkien asserts, is the contrast he draws between mortal Men, doomed to die, and the race of Elves, doomed not to leave Middle-earth, but to linger until the world ends. Thus, as Tolkien insists in another letter, he is not writing an allegory about power and domination. What he does think his fiction provides is applicability and, in particular, it allows us to apply it to our foremost concern as human beings, death:

> There is *no* "symbolism" or conscious allegory in my story. Allegory of the sort "five wizards=five senses" is wholly foreign to my way of thinking. There were five wizards and that is just a unique part of history.... That there is no allegory does not, of course, say there is no applicability. There always is. And since I have not made the struggle wholly unequivocal: sloth and stupidity among hobbits, pride and [illegible] among Elves, grudge and greed in Dwarf-hearts, and folly and wickedness among the "Kings of Men," and treachery and power-lust even among the "Wizards," there is I suppose applicability in my story to present times. But I should say, if asked, the tale is not really about Power and Domination: that only gets the wheels going; it is about Death and the desire for deathlessness. Which is hardly more than to say it is a tale written by a Man![2]

In this chapter, therefore, we shall look at what Tolkien has to say about death and immortality and, even more so, on two phenomena closely, even essentially, related to them: time and eternity. Time and the nature of time is a continual, if unstated, preoccupation of the characters in Tolkien's fantasy, and, I think, of Tolkien himself (like his alter-ego, Niggle). Men and Elves are deeply conscious of time, but for opposite reasons: the former because theirs is limited and the latter because theirs is relatively unlimited. It is this clash of opposing concerns that not only allows Tolkien to illuminate the nature of time but also allows us to pose and even answer the question of whether there is something beyond time itself and whether we as human beings have a share in the eternal and the immortal.

2 *Letters*, 262.

Time and Mortality

As we saw in chapter 2, the Ring of Sauron has several distinguishing properties, but some are more superficial and some more essential than the others. Perhaps the most superficial property of the Ring is that it turns its wearer invisible. Even more deeply, the Ring, as we have seen before, alters the perception of the wearer, dulling, for example, sight, but enhancing hearing, or making certain things closer and other things more distant.[3] The Ring also, of course, gives its wearer great power over others, being able to command obedience and fear in them. But the deepest and the most essential property of the Great Ring of Power, that property from which all the others flow, is that it alters and distorts time: it not only distorts one's sense of time, however, but it actually draws out ontologically the temporality inherent in the nature of the wearer; it has a real effect on one's very being. As such, the power of the Ring resides in its being able to grant a sort of limitless temporal existence; but this, Tolkien explains in his letters, is really a sort of counterfeit immortality:

> As for "message": I have none really, if by that is meant the conscious purpose in writing *The Lord of the Rings*, of preaching, or of delivering myself of a vision of truth specially revealed to me! I was primarily writing an exciting story in an atmosphere and background such as I find personally attractive.... Though it is only in reading the work myself (with criticisms in mind) that I became aware of the dominance of the theme of Death.... But certainly Death is not an Enemy! I said, or meant to day, that the "message" was the hideous peril of confusing true "immortality" with limitless serial longevity. Freedom from Time, and clinging to Time. The *confusion* is the work of the Enemy, and one of the chief causes of human disaster. Compare the death of Aragorn with a Ringwraith. The Elves

---

[3] Thus, some of the attributes of the Ringwraiths are the following: they have certain sensory capacities and limitations. They love the darkness. They produce terror simply by being what they are. They give forth a certain noxious or poisonous exhalation. See Stanton, *Hobbits, Elves and Wizards*, 28.

call "death" the Gift of God (to Men). Their temptation is different: towards a faineant melancholy, burdened with Memory, leading to an attempt to halt Time.[4]

The great temptation, the source of all other temptations, according to Tolkien, is to confuse limitless duration with true immortality or, put another way, limitless, serial time with eternity. Freedom from time (essentially eternity as we shall see) is radically different from clinging to time (a distinction that is the key to Niggle's rehabilitation). This confusion is, of course, a result of the Fall and original sin, as Tolkien notes elsewhere in his letters.[5] It is a confusion that is, therefore, common to all rational creatures in our fallen world, even Hobbits like Bilbo. As Bilbo explains to Gandalf before his long-expected eleventieth birthday, "I am old, Gandalf. I don't look it, but I am beginning to feel it in my heart of hearts. *Well-preserved* indeed! ... Why, I feel all thin, sort of *stretched*, if you know what I mean: like butter that has been scraped over too much bread. That can't be right. I need a change, or something."[6] Here the reader can see that the Ring has been at work on even a simple and honest Hobbit like Bilbo. It is already stretching out the natural limit of his mortal existence, and the result is not more life but less, not a deeper connection and fellowship with his fellow hobbits but a greater and greater disconnect and lack of fellowship with them.[7] As Gandalf explains to Frodo,

> A mortal, Frodo, who keeps one of the Great Rings, does not die, but he does not grow or obtain more life, he merely continues, until at last every minute is a weariness. And if he often uses the Ring to make himself invisible, he *fades*: he becomes in the end invisible permanently, and walks in the twilight under the eye of the Dark Power that rules the Rings.[8]

4 *Letters*, 267.
5 "The chief form this would take with them would be impatience, leading to the desire to force others to their own good ends, and so inevitably at last to mere desire to make their own wills effective by any means." *Letters*, 237.
6 *FR*, I, 1, 32.
7 Thus, as Rose Zimbardo observes, "The Ring, then, takes its wearer not only out of the community of positive being, but out of the cycle of time to which all being is subject." Zimbardo, "Moral Vision," 74.
8 *FR*, I, 2, 47.

The stretching out of one's natural span of life leads not to an increase in being and life, but to a decrease, and eventually to a sort of nihilation of one's inherent nature. When one's inherent nature is hallowed out and destroyed, all fellowship with those of the same nature—or any nature—is destroyed as well.

That eternity should not be confused with limitless duration is an argument that Thomas Aquinas makes in the *Summa theologiae*.[9] Time, he argues, is not simply a part of eternity as a minute is a part of an hour and an hour a part of a day; nor is eternity distinguished from time in that the latter has a beginning and end while the former does not. This distinction, Aquinas asserts, is simply accidental. Rather, the difference between time and eternity lies in the fact that in eternity there can be no parts according to which there can even be a before and after.[10] For Thomas, eternity and time are functions of the kinds of substances of which they are predicated: a substance that is utterly one, simple, and immutable is also eternal (hence, question 10 of the *Summa* logically follows question 9, "On the Immutability of God"); a substance that is composed of parts (material, spatial, or metaphysical, such as form and matter) and has an origin, development, and end is by consequence temporal.

This understanding of time is quite different from the modern one proposed by Isaac Newton, and adopted uncritically by Immanuel Kant, and through him much of contemporary philosophy, which understands time as extraneous to the things that supposedly exist "in it"; by contrast, Aquinas argues that it is rather time that exists as a property "in" various kinds of substances that, due to their inherent natures, also have an inherent temporality. For if every natural thing has an inherent end or goal, then the realization of that end or goal presupposes change or the actualization of potentiality, which is the precondition for any temporality; if its end or goal were fully actualized and completely coincidental with its substantial being, then it would

---

9   *S.Th.* I, 10, 4.

10   Thus, even the motion of the heavens is not, strictly speaking, eternal, since even if, as Aquinas supposed per the best the scientific knowledge of the time, the heavenly bodies moved without ceasing, there are still parts to their motions, since these can have, at least in principle, a beginning and end at some point designated arbitrarily in either space or time.

exist "in" eternity, for all potential for development has been exhausted, and so, therefore, has its temporality. Thus, Aquinas argues in reply to the third objection that since eternity is the measure of all time, so it must not be qualitatively different from time:

> Just as eternity is the proper measure of existence itself, so is time the proper measure of motion. Thus to the degree that some existence recedes from the permanence of existing and is subject to change, to that degree it recedes from eternity and is subject to time. Therefore, the existence of corruptible things, because it is liable to change, is measured not by eternity, but by time. Time, then, measures not only what is changeable in act, but also those things that are liable to be changed (*transmutabilia*). Thence, not only does it measure motion, but rest also; which is of that which is by nature liable to be moved, but is not in fact moved.[11]

Thus, as Aquinas makes clear, the more a created being, by the very nature of its substance, falls away from God's immutable substance, to that degree it is in time, since motion is contained in its very ontological structure. This is why it is also incorrect to think of eternity as some sort of static "now" (*nunc*); this notion presumes the standpoint of a being moving temporally from past, through the present, into the future, with a "now" that is inherently insubstantial and fleeting: "Eternity, however, remains the same both in the subject [the existing thing] and in reason [our concept of it]. Thus eternity is not the same as the 'now' of time (*Aeternitas autem manet eadem et subiecto et ratione. Unde aeternitas non est idem quod nunc temporis*)."[12] Eternity denotes a property of a substance that is in perfect actualization and fulfillment; we cannot, therefore, compare its "now" with the "now" of a temporal substance which has not yet reached its end and is thus not yet in perfect fulfillment. Hence, its "now" is largely empty and fleeting, and when we talk of the "now" of eternity, we can only do so in a sense analogous to the "now" of our experience of the temporal present.

[11] *S.Th.* I, 10, 4 ad 3.
[12] *S.Th.* I, 10, 4, ad 2.

As the passage from the *Summa* cited above indicates, time does not exist as time in things alone, apart from any consciousness; beings are temporal insofar as they can found or cause an experience of time in the mind—in consciousness. Here we have a close analogy to the problem of universals that we saw in chapter 3: just as the universal as universal—as a concept that can refer to many particular things—exists only in the mind, but nevertheless refers to a real, common or shared nature in particular things, so time—as measured by "before" and "after"—exists only in consciousness; yet that time-consciousness is founded upon and caused by the temporality inherent in the natures of things. Fr. Norris Clarke puts this well when he explains:

> [T]ime is some real process of successive change, held together and recognized as such in the unity of an act of consciousness. It is thus a creative synthesis of real and mental being; its foundation is real being, but it exists formally and explicitly as time only as a mental being, a being in consciousness—something we humans have produced in creative cooperation with the real world. In brief, one hour of time cannot exist as a real being outside the mind because all its parts cannot exist all at once: at any moment all its past ones are gone and the future ones not yet present. It can be present as a unity only in a conscious mind.[13]

Time, therefore, arises from the unity of consciousness with temporal being; eternity arises from the complete unity of consciousness with fulfilled or perfect being.

Thus, if we were to stretch out our present life into an infinite series of "nows," it would not approach any nearer to eternity, no matter how long it was stretched out; such limitless duration would not be a boon but a great curse, a torment. As Bill Davis says of the Ringwraiths, "The Ringwraiths are horrific because they are undead: they are not dead, and for them *not* dying is a curse."[14] Hell, therefore,

---

13   W. Norris Clarke, SJ, *The One and the Many: A Contemporary Thomistic Metaphysics* (Notre Dame, IN: University of Notre Dame Press, 2001), 163–64.

14   Bill Davis, "Choosing to Die: The Gift of Mortality in Middle-earth," in

is strictly speaking not eternal, but rather characterized by infinite duration: "in hell there is no true eternity, but rather time, according to the Psalm 80:16: *Their time will be forever* [*erit tempus eorum in saecula*]."[15] As was indicated above, the notion that every thing has a nature, i.e., a natural form, which has inherent properties that develop toward an inherent end or goal, is crucial to the distinction between time and eternity and its proper understanding—a proper understanding that is absent in modern thought, because modern philosophy has eliminated the notion of things having inherent natures and ends, and therefore an inherent temporality (thus, in place of multiple "times" or "temporalities," modern thought knows of only one, abstract, featureless "time"). As Bill Davis explains further,

> While we are tempted to think that living is always better than dying, Tolkien follows the philosopher Aristotle in thinking that only *natural* existence is a good thing. Continuing to exist in any other way—any *unnatural* way—is worse than death. Like every natural thing, Ringwraiths have a *nature*, a way they are supposed to be. Even though the Ring dominates them, they are still by nature men. The way a thing is supposed to be—its nature—determines not only the limits of what it can do, but also how it finds fulfillment. A flower finds its fulfillment in blossoming and providing seeds for reproducing itself. A beaver dams a river, builds a lodge, and mates. Men by nature develop civilizations and reproduce; and they die when their time is spent.[16]

The Lord of the Rings *and Philosophy: One Book to Rule Them All* (Chicago: Open Court Publishing, 2003), 125. Tom Shippey gives a fascinating account of the etymology of the word "wraith" and all of its associated meanings, which include "writhe" and "wreath." The common meaning seems to be of something that is "twisted" or "bent," with ancillary meanings being "unsubstantial" and "shadowy." Thus, Shippey says, "There is a terrible 'applicability' about the idea of wraiths, which many if not most of Tolkien's readers have been well able to follow." Shippey, *The Road to Middle-earth*, 150.

15 *S.Th.* I, 10, 3, ad 2.
16 Davis, "Choosing to Die," 125–26.

Thus, to draw one's life out beyond its natural limit is not a good, but a great evil. To quote Bill Davis again, "for the Ringwraiths, unending existence is a fate worse than death; it involves the perpetual pain of having their natures frustrated."[17] That is why, Tolkien states in many places, death is, for beings of our nature, a gift and a boon, for without it our natures would remain perpetually unfulfilled and thus unprepared for the eternity in which they would stand complete and, literally, time-less.[18]

Indeed, Tolkien boldly calls a "Satanic lie" the insinuation by Sauron that the Men of Númenor could become immortal simply by invading and conquering Valinor or the Undying Lands:

> This was a delusion of course, a Satanic lie. For as the emissaries from the Valar clearly inform him [Ar-Pharazôn, king of Númenor], the Blessed Realm does not confer immortality. The land is blessed because the Blessed dwell there, not vice versa, and the Valar are immortal by right and nature, while Men are mortal by right and nature. But cozened by Sauron he dismissed all this as a diplomatic argument to ward off the power of the King of Kings. It might or might not be "heretical," if these myths were regarded as statements about the actual nature of Man in the real world: I do not know. But the view of the myth is that Death—the mere shortness of human life-span—is not a punishment for the Fall, but a biologically (and therefore also spiritually, since body and spirit are integrated) inherent part of Man's nature. The attempt to escape it is wicked because "unnatural," and silly because Death in that sense is the Gift of

---

17   Davis, "Choosing to Die," 126.

18   The great insight of twentieth-century existentialism was its exposition of the necessity of the phenomenon of death for our own self-definition: without death, our choices, plans, and projects would lack any existential weight—they would be always provisional and thus meaningless. Of course, existentialists like Sartre and Heidegger ruled out *a priori* any rational exploration of what might await us after death or beyond time, but they nevertheless recognized this crucial aspect of death as necessary to our self-definition as full human beings. See Peter Kreeft, *Love Is Stronger than Death* (San Francisco: Ignatius Press, 1992), chapter 3.

God (envied by the Elves), release from the weariness of Time. Death, in the penal sense, is viewed as a change in attitude to it: fear, reluctance. A good Numenorean died of free will when he felt it to be time to do so.[19]

A mortal cannot become immortal merely by changing place; immortality demands a fundamental change in the type of being one is. Death is not a mere temporal end, but a fulfillment of our nature. Now, Tolkien is aware that this view of death is different from the biblical account in Genesis, where death is asserted to be a punishment for the Fall. Hence, the mention of whether his view is heretical or not, at least as regards the primary world. And yet, it is evident that Tolkien only thought the contradiction with Scripture to be apparent: something can be both a punishment and a remedy at the same time.[20]

But I think the most important thing to note about this passage is the importance Tolkien gives to the contrast between the experience that Men have of time and death and that which the Elves have of their time in Middle-earth and their (qualified) immortality. If we think of death as a curse, Tolkien seems to say, then look at the Elves and think about the implications of their being unable to die. As we saw with Tolkien's description of the Ringwraiths, to live forever in serial time, cut off from any fellowship with other beings, rational or nonrational, would be torment—a literal Hell. As Tolkien remarks concerning Frodo and his traveling over the sea to the Undying Lands to heal, even he, Frodo, must die: "Frodo was sent or allowed to pass over Sea to heal him—if that could be done, *before he died*. He would have eventually to 'pass away': no mortal could, or can, abide for ever on earth, or within Time."[21] It is essential to human nature that an individual human nature, being a composite of body and soul, must die, and as Jonathan McIntosh observes, Tolkien's meditations on Elven immortality and human

---

19   *Letters*, 205, note.

20   More precisely, as Stratford Caldecott notes, Tolkien seemed to work around this apparent conflict by saying that his myths look at death from an Elvish perspective, whereas the Bible was revealed specifically to fallen, mortal human beings. Caldecott, *The Power of the Ring*, 116.

21   *Letters*, 328.

mortality can be seen as an attempt to recover "a proper understanding of human nature as a true union and mutual belongingness of body and soul."[22] Tolkien himself remarks, "Elves are certain aspects of Men and their talents and desires, incarnated in my little world."[23]

So, Tolkien asks us to reflect upon what would it mean for human beings, although fallen (as the Elves are in his mythology), to be by nature immortal (or, more accurately, to have lifespans coterminous with the duration of Middle-earth itself)? What would be their experience of time and eternity?[24] In *The Fellowship of the Ring*, Tolkien has Legolas put the Elven experience of time more concretely and succinctly:

> Legolas stirred in his boat. "Nay, time does not tarry ever," he said; "but change and growth is not in all things and places alike. For the Elves the world moves, and it moves both very swift and very slow. Swift, because they themselves change very little, and all else fleets by: it is a grief to them. Slow, because they need not count the running years, not for themselves. The passing seasons are but ripples ever repeated in the long long stream. Yet beneath the Sun all things must wear to an end at last."[25]

Since the Elves are by nature relatively unchanging,[26] at least with regard to their substance (whereas they do change with regard to

---

22 McIntosh, *The Flame Imperishable*, 201. As Carl Hostetter remarks in his appendices to *The Nature of Middle-earth*, Tolkien's philosophical anthropology is thoroughly Catholic, even Thomist: "That is, it is the nature of incarnate persons, both Elves and Men, to be a unity of body and spirit, such that if either is lost or separated, the incarnate person is incomplete, and has suffered a grievous loss and disruption to its nature. Neither the body nor the material world are inherently inferior to the spirit, or something that a spirit has a duty to seek to escape." *NME*, 404. See also Fimi, *Tolkien, Race and Cultural History*, 10.

23 *Letters*, 189.

24 Elizabeth Whittingham, in her examination of the evolution of Tolkien's mythology over his life, points out that Tolkien's thinking on death and immortality underwent substantial revision during his life, especially beginning in the late 1950s. Whittingham, *The Evolution of Tolkien's Mythology*, 129.

25 *FR*, II, 9, 388.

26 As Tolkien points out in *The Nature of Middle-earth*, Elves do change, but extremely slowly, at a rate of some 144 human years to one Elf year.

their accidents, i.e., in place, time, and in certain qualities), the world seems to move swiftly; at the same time, from their own experience, the world hardly seems to change at all, since all things that change are insubstantial compared to their own nature.[27]

We can, therefore, see the Elves as Tolkien's analogue to the angels, something that Tom Shippey has noted, although as Shippey points out, the Elves are incarnate and, to a degree, fallen angels.[28] Of course, unlike the fallen angels of the Bible, the Elves of Tolkien's mythology are capable of repentance and redemption, for as incarnate beings, they have a special love for living things, the lands in which they live, and Middle-earth as a whole, which is a sort of saving grace (not to mention that they have the whole lifetime of Middle-earth to repent and thus have a mode of temporality[29]): "They [the Elves] have a devoted love of

---

27 What Legolas is here describing, it could be argued, is a mode of time that Thomas Aquinas calls *aeviternity*, which is a mode of temporality between eternity and time. This is the mode of temporality Aquinas argues belongs to the angels, since the angels, as immaterial and thus immortal beings, cannot be said to experience time as such; however, just as the heavenly bodies can have time "attached" or "joined" (*adiunctam*) to them even though they are unchanging and everlasting in their substance, so the angels can have temporal events joined to them through the exercise of their intellect and will. Aquinas sums up the difference between the three modes of time (time, aeviternity, and eternity) in this way: "And so time has a before and after; *aevum*, however, does not have a before and after, but these can be conjoined to it; eternity, however, has neither a before nor after, nor is it compatible with such." *S.Th.* I, 10, 5.

28 Shippey, *The Road to Middle-earth*, 239–40.

29 Elves, of course, can die in the sense that the union between their body and soul may be sundered. However, they do not leave Arda, but go to the Halls of Mandos, where they may be reincarnated (though they may choose not to be). Now, Christian doctrine strictly rules out reincarnation, since every individual is a unique creation in whom body and soul are essentially united, i.e., two principles of one living substance. But Tolkien dismisses any suspicion of heterodoxy by arguing that, by entertaining a race of beings that reincarnates, we may better understand what it means for human beings to die and to leave the "circles of the world": "'Reincarnation' may be bad *theology* (that surely, rather than metaphysics) as applied to Humanity; and my *legendarium*, especially the 'Downfall of Númenor' which lies immediately behind *The Lord of the Rings*, is based on my view: that Men are essentially mortal and must not try to become 'immortal' in the flesh. But I do

the physical world, and a desire to observe and understand it for its own sake and as 'other'—sc. as a reality derived from God in the same degree as themselves—not as a material for use or as a power-platform."[30] Still, the Elves are fallen and Tolkien explains why they are fallen and the consequences of their Fall:

> But the Elvish weakness is in these terms naturally to regret the past, and to become unwilling to face change: as if a man were to hate a very long book still going on, and wished to settle down in a favourite chapter. Hence they fell in a measure to Sauron's deceits: they desired some "power" over things as they are (which is quite distinct from art), to make their particular will to preservation effective: to arrest change, and keep things always fresh and fair.[31]

In a sense, the consequences of the Fall for Elves is the inverse of that for Men; whereas Men seek to extend serial time or duration as long and far out as possible, the Elves seek to arrest time altogether. This is perhaps why, as I mentioned in the previous chapter while discussing marriage, the occasional, rare unions of Men and Elves in his stories (Beren and Lúthien, Tuor and Idril, Aragorn and Arwen) are so central: they unite the two modes of time and allow the reader a glimpse of what is beyond time, i.e., eternity. By willingly taking on a mortal nature, Lúthien and Arwen manifest a hope that death is not a merely temporal end, but a consummation of one's created nature—the final unfolding of what one in fact always was and is. The essence of mortal Men is, while they live, stretched and scattered as it were in time, but is then finally gathered up into completion in death.

But, perhaps Tolkien's deepest reflections on time, eternity, death, and immortality are found in the *Athrabeth Finrod Ah Andreth*, a short Platonic dialogue between an Elf, Finrod, and a mortal woman,

---

not see how even in the Primary World any theologian or philosopher, unless very much better informed about the relation of spirit and body than I believe anyone to be, could deny the *possibility* of re-incarnation as a mode of existence, prescribed for certain kinds of rational incarnate creatures." *Letters*, 189.

30 *Letters*, 236.
31 *Letters*, 236.

Andreth.[32] In this work, Tolkien has a male Elf and a mortal woman discuss the disparate fates of their kinds, one doomed to age and die, and the other doomed not to age but to remain in this world for however long it lasts. Andreth raises the question whether Men were really originally doomed to die by nature, or whether this has been the result of some Fall: "They say plainly that Men are *not* by nature short-lived, but have become so through the malice of the Lord of the Darkness whom they do not name."[33] The question is raised because Andreth is mourning the loss of her lover, the brother of Finrod and therefore an Elf, not to death, for as an Elf he cannot die, but to the loss of her own beauty in old age and her own eventual death.[34] This sadness points to a deeper shadow that lies upon them: as good and as beautiful as Arda is, it cannot satisfy the longings of the human heart for pure goodness and joy. Andreth notes that the Elves do not understand "the saying that goes among Men: *too often seen is seen no longer*. And they wonder much that in the tongues of Men the same word may mean both 'long-known' and 'stale'." The "staleness" of things from which we need recovery is an essential consequence of our own temporarily and, more specifically, of our clinging to time. Andreth laments:

> "We have thought that this was so only because the Elves have lasting life and undiminished vigour. 'Grown-up children', we, the guests, sometimes call you, my Lord. And yet—and yet, if nothing in Arda for us holds its savour long, and all fair things grow dim, what then? Does it not come from [the] Shadow upon our hearts? Or do you say that it is not so, but this was ever our nature, even before the wound?"
>
> "I say so, indeed," [answers] Finrod. "The Shadow may have darkened your unrest, bringing swifter weariness and soon turning it to disdain, but the unrest was ever there, I believe. And if this is so, then can you not now perceive the disharmony

---

32 Published posthumously by Christopher Tolkien in *Morgoth's Ring*.
33 *MR*, 309.
34 Whittingham, *The Evolution of Tolkien's Mythology*, 160–61.

that I spoke of? If indeed your Wisdom had lore like to ours, teaching that the *Mirröanwi* are made of a union of body and mind, of *hröa* and *fëa*, or as we say in picture the House and the Indweller."³⁵

As Finrod here implies, the human heart had a yearning for what is infinite and timeless well before the Fall; the latter simply made that unrest and longing even greater. Nevertheless, this yearning implies there is something eternal in human nature, something rooted in what is beyond time.³⁶ Thus, Andreth talks of an ancient "hope" or "Estel"—"hope" in the sense of "trust" (in Eru). Andreth explains: "They say that the One will himself enter into Arda, and heal Men and all the Marring from the beginning to the end. This they say also, or they feign, is a rumour that has come down through the years uncounted, even from the days of our undoing."³⁷ Here, of course, Tolkien is making an almost direct reference to the Incarnation, where the Creator himself will enter into his creation. Here, Tolkien comes closest in his fictional work to making his own Christianity explicit.³⁸ But how, Tolkien asks, can this entering of Eru into creation be possible?

> "He is already in it, as well as outside," said Finrod. "But indeed the 'in-dwelling' and the 'out-dwelling' are not the same mode."
>
> "Truly," said Andreth. "So may Eru in that mode be present in Eä that proceeded from Him. But they speak of Eru Himself *entering into Arda*, that this is a thing wholly different. How could He the greater do this? Would it not shatter Arda, or indeed all Eä?"

35 *MR*, 316.
36 "If humans invent Elves and fountains of youth to escape from death, then Elves may invent the idea of the 'Gift' as an escape from deathlessness. The Númenoreans then inherit this perspective.... The conclusion: whether death is a penalty or a gift may depend on whether such a gift is accepted. Submission to the will of God transforms the curse of death into an opportunity for hope, while clinging to life in rebellion against God ends in despair." Freeman, *Tolkien Dogmatics*, 319.
37 *MR*, 321.
38 Whittingham, *The Evolution of Tolkien's Mythology*, 159.

> "Ask me not," said Finrod. "These things are beyond the compass of the wisdom of the Eldar, or of the Valar maybe. But I doubt that our words may mislead us, and that when you say 'greater' you think of the dimensions of Arda, in which the greater vessel many not be contained in the less."[39]

Eru/Ilúvatar is related to his creation as the author is to the places and people in his works and, as such, he is both in his creation and also outside of it. Still, how the Creator may actually enter into his creation as a character within it is indeed strange and even impossible to imagine. Nevertheless, this very thing that is impossible to imagine is precisely what the Christian Gospel not only imagines but claims actually to have happened. Why does the Creator do this—enter into his creation? Tolkien hints at an answer in his own commentary to the *Athrabeth*: "To be perpetually 'imprisoned in a tale' (as they said), even if it was a very great tale ending triumphantly, would become a torment."[40] The goal, then, of the author entering his creation is to give those characters true and eternal life, by bringing them out of the tale into fellowship with the author. The author willingly enters the time of the story to bring its characters to share in the life of the author, which is, compared to the time of the story, eternal. The characters in the story, however, cannot know that this is the case from within the story itself; the story can only refer to itself. Knowledge of this higher end or fulfillment can only come, as mentioned above, from a sort of revelation. As Verlyn Flieger puts it, "The unknown must be accepted in faith. This is exactly the point. The ability to let go, to trust, is the ability to rely on faith. To cling to the known, the tangible—even if it is a Silmaril—is to be bound. Tolkien's deathless Elves are in his world exemplars of bondage to unending life."[41] Indeed, the very fact that death is a problem within the story points to something beyond the story.

This is why in Tolkien's mythology the existence of the Elves, as beautiful and full of light as it often is, is also strongly tinged with regret and sadness. Condemned to the circles of this world, they can never

---

39 *MR*, 322.
40 *MR*, 332.
41 Flieger, *Splintered Light*, 144.

know intimate fellowship with their Creator; they can never escape the Story. Thus, even the Undying Lands in the far West are only an image of eternity and full communion and fellowship and not the substance of these themselves. As Tolkien remarks in rough notes published near the end of the *Athrabeth*,

> [T]he mythical idea underlying is that for mortals, since their "kind" cannot be changed for ever, this is strictly only a temporary reward: a healing and a redress of suffering. They cannot abide for ever, and though they cannot return to mortal earth, they can and will "die"—of free will, and leave the world. (In this setting the return of Arthur would be quite impossible, a vain imagining.)[42]

Here, Tolkien alludes to an important feature of his stories concerning the Men of Númenor: although mortal, when they did die (at least before their open rebellion against the Ban), they did so of their own free will, choosing when and where to die (without doing violence to themselves, i.e., committing suicide). Hence, for the Númenóreans, death was originally understood as a gift to be voluntarily assumed.[43] Tolkien remarks that this is also the case for mortals of the Undying Lands, where, despite their name, no mortal can abide forever:

> Frodo was sent or allowed to pass over the Sea to heal him— if that could be done, *before he died*. He would have eventually to "pass away": no mortal could, or can, abide for ever on

---

42 *MR*, 366.

43 In a letter, Tolkien asserts that unfallen Man would have died of his own free will, much like Mary was assumed body and soul into heaven: "It was also the Elvish (and uncorrupted Númenórean) view that a 'good' Man would or should *die* voluntarily by surrender with trust *before being compelled* (as did Aragorn). This may have been the nature of *unfallen* Man; though compulsion would not threaten him: he would desire and seek to be allowed to 'go on' to a higher state. The Assumption of Mary, the only *unfallen* person, may be regarded as in some ways a simple regaining of unfallen grace and liberty: she asked to be received, and was, having no further function on Earth. Though, of course, even if *unfallen* she was not 'pre-Fall'. Her destiny (in which she had cooperated) was far higher than that of any 'Man' would have been, had the Fall not occurred." *Letters*, 286, note.

earth, or within Time. So he went both to a purgatory and to a reward, for a while: a period of reflection and peace and a gaining of a truer understanding of his position in littleness and in greatness, spent in Time amid the natural beauty of "Arda Unmarred," the Earth unspoiled by evil.[44]

If mortal men were permitted into the Undying Lands, this would not be a blessing but a curse, the reason for which Tolkien makes clear: the fleeting nature of the existence of mortal men and women would become even more unbearable as everything in the Undying Lands would not decay.[45] It is significant here that Tolkien describes the Undying Lands as a sort of purgatory, only here "purgatory" designates a place of healing and reflection in the original sense of a place of "purgation" or "purification" (very different from the prison house in which Niggle must do his own convalescence).

Nevertheless, whatever the nature of purgatory, Tolkien seems to think that some sort of summing up and reckoning of the balance is necessary in order to enter into eternity, for entry into eternity presupposes that each individual human life is its own story that has a beginning, middle, and end, and only when all the loose ends of the story are tied up and all narrative debts paid off can it fully take life in the mind of its Author. I agree with Stratford Caldecott that Tolkien looked at death from the larger "backdrop of the greater mystery of existence itself." To notice loss and fading is a "Nostalgia for something real."[46] A no more powerful expression of this sense of hope within great loss can be found in the final words between Arwen and Aragorn in "The Tale of Aragorn and Arwen." As Arwen says to Aragorn,

> There is now no ship that would bear me hence, and I must indeed abide the Doom of Men, whether I will or I nill: the loss and the silence. But I say to you, King of the Númenóreans, not till now have I understood the tale of your people and their fall. As wicked fools I scorned them, but I pity them at last. For

44 MR, 366.
45 MR, 428.
46 Caldecott, *The Power of the Ring*, 119.

if this is indeed, as the Eldar say the gift of the One to Men, it is bitter to receive.

Aragorn replies:

> So it seems.... But let us not be overthrown at the final test, who of old renounced the Shadow and the Ring. In sorrow we must go, but not in despair. Behold! we are not bound for ever to the circles of the world, and beyond them is more than memory. Farewell![47]

Time inevitably leads to sorrow, but in that sorrow lies hope, because it indicates that we are made by our very nature for what is eternal.

Eternity

As we saw earlier, Tolkien follows Aquinas in insisting that time and eternity are qualitatively different, that eternity is not simply infinite duration. This is because, as we saw above, time and eternity are not abstractions independent of existing substances. Rather, Aquinas argues that time is a property of substance and therefore a thing's mode of time is a function of the nature of the substance of which it is a property: "Time is not number as abstracted apart from what is numbered.... Number, however, in the numbered does not exist in the same way in all things, but diversely in diverse things."[48] Thus, different natures will have different modes of time, as we saw Tolkien explore in his fiction in the different modes in which Elves and Men experience time. The mode of temporality of any being takes its unity from the underlying subject of which it is an accident: "Therefore time is referred to that movement, not only as a measure is to the thing measured, but also as accident is to the subject, and thus receives its unity from it."[49] Indeed, Tolkien makes this quite explicit in his letters, where, while discussing the downfall of Númenor, he says:

---

47 *RK*, Appendix A, 1063.
48 *S.Th.* I, 10, 6.
49 *S.Th.* I, 10, 6.

The view is taken (as clearly reappears later in the case of the Hobbits that have the Ring for a while) that each "Kind" has a natural span, integral to its biological and spiritual nature. This cannot really be *increased* qualitatively or quantitatively; so that prolongation in time is like stretching a wire out ever tauter, or "spreading butter ever thinner"—it becomes an intolerable torment.[50]

Because we human beings (and other incarnate rational beings) have a natural span, we also have a natural temporality. How, then, can we know what eternity is and, if we are natural, incarnate minds for whom temporality is the mode natural to us, how can we actually come to participate in an eternity that is, in a sense, above our nature?

To get an answer we must, again, turn to Thomas Aquinas. Aquinas cites with approval Boethius's definition of eternity from *The Consolation of Philosophy*[51]: "Eternity is the simultaneously total and perfect possession of unending life (*aeternitas est interminabilis vitae tota simul et perfecta possessio*)."[52] What does this definition mean? Let us examine it part by part: eternity is a "possession"; a possession of what? It is a possession of "life." What kind of life? Unending life, *idest principio et fine carens* (that is lacking any beginning or end). And since it has no beginning or end, eternity *successione caret, tota simul existens*: it possesses this life completely (*tota*) and perfectly, without any deficiency. How can this be? As Aquinas remarks, since we exist in time, we cannot but conceive of eternity as a succession of discrete nows; it follows that we can only conceive of eternity by removing this sort of composition of nows. Let us look at our own lives: our lives as we experience them are already stretched out through a series of moments. This means that at any particular time, we never are in a complete and perfect possession

50 *Letters*, 155, note.

51 A work that would have been well known to Tolkien as it was enormously popular during the Middle Ages and was translated into old English as early as the time of King Alfred. Indeed, it was an essential influence on a Middle English text that Tolkien himself had edited, the *Ancrene Wisse*. See *Ancrene Wisse: The English Text of the Ancrene Riwle* (London: Oxford University Press, 1962).

52 *S.Th.* I, 10, 1.

of our life: our lives are, in a sense, already stretched out (thus, if not for death, we would become Wraiths!). Our nature is never complete and perfect at any particular time, no matter how advanced in life, because our past is no longer and our future still remains unactualized (however little of it may be left). As Tolkien observes in a note included in *The Nature of Middle-earth*,

> [That] which distinguishes the living from the unliving is that the living employ Time in their realization. In other words it is a part of their nature to "grow," using such material as is needed or is available to them for their embodiment. So that a living pattern does not exist fully at any one moment of time (as do unliving patterns); but is complete only with the completion of its life. It cannot therefore rigtly be seen instantly, and is only imperfectly envisaged even with the help of memory. Only those who conceived its pattern and whose sight is not limited to the succession of time can, for instance, see the true shape of a tree.[53]

It is an essential feature of living, material beings that their inherent ends and goals unfold through time. But this would not be the case for our nature in eternity. Once our nature enters eternity, past, present, and future are "enfolded" into one complete nature; and the complete and perfect possession of this life is substantial life and thus exists in an "eternal now." But this "eternal now" can only be conceived of in a manner analogous to the "now" of time: like the "now" of time, the eternal "now" is a sort of presence, but unlike the temporal "now," it is not fleeting and insubstantial nor is it static and "frozen" like the "now" of time in "stop-motion" photography: "Two things are to be considered in time: that is, time itself, which is successive, and the temporal now, which is imperfect. He [Boethius] therefore says the 'total simultaneously' so as to remove time, and 'perfect' so as to exclude the temporal now."[54]

But how is this "complete and perfect" possession possible? It is possible, at least partly, through the intellect: as Augustine argued well

---

53 *NME*, 251.
54 *S.Th.* I, 10, 1 ad 5.

before Aquinas, the human mind is itself stretched out over past, present, and future, and this stretching out is essential to the nature of human consciousness.[55] Human consciousness actualizes the inherent temporality of things as time-consciousness, and yet, by doing so, reveals what things are in their eternal nature by gathering into consciousness all the features of the thing that are never present at one moment. Even more, it reveals that the human consciousness presupposes the existence of an eternal nature, since, as Augustine argues, consciousness of past, present, and future is a constant attempt in time to approximate the fullness of the eternal now. Time then, in its natural span, is a participation in eternity insofar as the human gathers the natures of things (including that of the human person) from their scattered state in time and sees them in the timeless unity of their natures. Aquinas remarks:

> Certain things participate in the form of eternity all the more insofar as they have unchangeability either according to their existence, or further according to their operation, such as the angels and the blessed who take delight in the Word: for to the degree that they have this vision of the Word, the saints do not have "unstable thoughts" as Augustine says in XV *De Trinitate*. Hence, those seeing God are said to have eternal life, according to John 17:13: *This is life eternal, that they may know, etc.*[56]

---

[55] The various texts gathered together in *The Nature of Middle-earth* show that Tolkien had a distinctly Augustinian understanding of time-consciousness and its relation to the things we know and experience: "Thus the Incarnate may distinguish, say, a mountain from the land about it, giving it a name, such as *Dolmed* [one of the Blue Mountains]. But what are the bounds of Dolmed? Some may say 'here it begins' or 'here it ends'; but others may say otherwise; and if the bounds are agreed, it will be by custom or convention of people, not by the nature of the land. Neither would its bounds in Time be clear, so that one of the Incarnate living many ages might say 'now Dolmed has begun to be' or 'now it has ceased'. For this aggregation of materials upon the surface of Arda has no inner individuality distinguishing it from the adjacent material. The distinction is applied by minds receiving the impression of a shape that can be held in memory; and it is by memory alone that it is name-worthy." *NME*, 252. Cf. Augustine's *Confessiones*, XI, 23, 30: *video igitur tempus quondam esse distentionem*.

[56] *S.Th.* I, 10, 3.

Thus, according to Augustine and Aquinas, although we are essentially finite and therefore temporal beings, we may come to participate in eternity through coming to know the divine Word, Christ, who not only is substantial and eternal Life and Intellect, but who reveals eternity through time in his own Story or Gospel. Although by nature temporal, human consciousness can, by fellowship with the divine Mind or *Logos*, participate in eternity. In such a fellowship, time no longer matters (much like what we saw happen to Niggle in "Leaf by Niggle"). To enter into eternity, in short, means letting go of even ourselves and our grasping after time, for as Kreeft remarks, "the road to immortality is the death of the ego."[57] We enter eternity only to the degree that we let go of time, which does not annihilate time, let alone freeze it in some static state, but which allows us to become masters of our time rather than allowing time to become masters of us.[58] Thus, eternity is not some mental abstraction, but an essential property of a fully living, intelligent substance or *Person*, to whom we relate as persons in fellowship and not as we would to an abstract idea or principle.

This glimpse of eternity is not directly possible for embodied (let alone, fallen) beings like us. As Ralph Wood remarks concerning Tolkien's approach to truth, Tolkien "assumes no timeless and spaceless 'foundation' on which his imaginative world might be erected. For him, transcendent reality is to be found in the depths of this world rather than in some arcane existence beyond it."[59] This is in marked contrast to the pure, "will-less, painless, timeless subject of knowledge" assumed by Descartes to be the privileged arbiter of knowledge and truth.[60] Again, "eternity" is not a mere idea or abstraction of an absolute

---

57 Kreeft, *The Philosophy of Tolkien*, 98.

58 This is the great insight also of Meister Eckhart, for whom to the degree that we become "poor in spirit" and let go of time, to that degree we enter into the eternal "now" (*nû*) of God and allow God's Son, Jesus Christ, to be born within us. See, Sermon 52, "beati pauperes spiritu," *Die deutschen werke*, ed. Josef Quint, vol. 2 (Stuttgart: Kohlhammer Verlag, 1936), 486–506.

59 Ralph C. Wood, "Tolkien and Postmodernism," in *Tolkien among the Moderns*, ed. Ralph C. Wood (Notre Dame, IN: University of Notre Dame Press, 2015), 260.

60 This is how Nietzsche characterizes the pure subject of pure science

thinking subject: "Until the end, we cannot stand *sub specie aeternitatis* to see the final outcome. Yet we can know indeed what kind of story we are enacting.... What we learn from Tolkien is that this infinitely larger story encompasses all the smaller stories, that it retrieves all things worthy from them—even from the story of modernity and its hypermodernist legacy. All the perversions and distortions of the one true Story can be redeemed."[61] Eternity and eternal things can better be seen and understood not through abstract, scientific reason, but through narrative and myth. This is again why divine revelation comes to human beings in the form of a Story, not a scientific treatise; only through story can we approach eternity by seeing it unfold in time. By hearing, reading, and ultimately participating in that Story can our temporal lives be given eternal meaning and even eternal life.

Thus, as Stratford Caldecott remarks, for Tolkien, "The real desire for immortality ... is healthy; it is a desire to overcome the process of decline itself. It is a desire not to extend but to *transcend* time."[62]

---

that we find in Descartes and the whole modern philosophical tradition that flows from him. The Cartesian ego is a being cut off not only from the body but from life, struggle, and power, and therefore from everything that gives life—including scientific knowledge—meaning. See his *Genealogy of Morality* III, n.12. The edition quoted here is translated by Maudemarie Clarke and Alan J. Swensen (Indianapolis: Hackett Publishing, 1998).

61 Wood, "Tolkien and Postmodernism," 274–75.

62 Caldecott, *The Power of the Ring*, 113. That this was a topic of great importance to Tolkien is shown by the extensive treatment he gives to the matter of time and memory in his posthumously published *Notion Club Papers* (briefly discussed in chapter 3). As we have already indicated, the members of *The Notion Club* are fascinated by questions of whether something like ancestral memory or time travel—not through machines *à la* H. G. Wells, but through dreams and visions—is possible. One of these characters, Ramer, expresses directly and concisely the very question that was perhaps on Tolkien's own mind: "Being an *incarnate* mind, I am conditioned by Time and Space, even in my curiosities; though being a *mind*, I want to get beyond the range of my own body's senses and history." *SD*, 178. Is time travel possible through the mind alone, he asks— through dreams, perhaps, or some deep memory? Perhaps his own legend of Númenor (Anadûnê—the island of the Adûnâi) is simply a memory of the lost island-civilization of Atlantis. Or is it the other way around? "And the Adûnâi held that men so blessed might look upon other times than those of the body's life;

And Tolkien tries to awaken this healthy desire for immortality and true eternity by exploring various "temporalities" in both the various races and the various places they inhabit. Thus, myth and fantasy can explore ways in which another way of looking at death is possible, where death is not simply a rude and meaningless disruption and ending of our projects and possibilities as it is for modern men and women, but the very fulfillment of our nature as human beings. It is interesting and notable how, for example, throughout *The Lord of the Rings*, the various characters experience distortions of time in various places that one can only describe as varieties of "time wells."[63] These distortions of time in the realm of Faerie (or "Elven time") are actually not original to Tolkien; they have precedents in medieval literature (in the Middle-English poem *Sir Orfeo*, for example, which was a favorite of Tolkien's).[64] It is in the Elven realms of Middle-earth in particular that the characters—and the readers along with them—feel this change in time. For example, as the Fellowship enters Lórien, all relations to time change for its members:

> As soon as he [Frodo] set foot upon the far bank of Silverlode a strange feeling had come upon him, and it deepened as he walked on into the Naith: it seemed to him that he had stepped over a bridge of time into a corner of the Elder Days, and was now walking in a world that was no more. In Rivendell there was memory of ancient things; in Lórien the ancient things still lived on in the waking world. Evil had been seen and heard there, sorrow had been known; the Elves feared and distrusted the world outside; wolves were howling on the wood's borders; but on the land of Lórien no shadow lay.[65]

It should be noted here that, as this passage makes clear, the change in time-consciousness that Frodo experiences is essentially connected with travel back in time to the "Elder Days," to a "memory of ancient

---

and they longed ever to escape from the shadows of their exile and to see in some fashion the light that was of old." *SD*, 373.

63 David M. Miller, "Narrative Pattern in *The Fellowship of the Ring*," in *A Tolkien Compass*, rev. ed., ed. Jared Lobdell (Chicago: Open Court, 2003), 102.

64 Shippey, *Author of the Century*, 89.

65 *FR*, II, 6, 349.

things." In Lórien, the past is in fact present: "It seemed to them that they did little but eat and drink and rest, and walk among the trees; and it was enough."[66] Because the past is present, there is no shadow on the land: past has not faded into mere memory.[67] Rather, like Niggle, Frodo and his companions are, as in Rivendell, in another place where Elven time obtains, freed from the demands of time, from the relentless pressure that comes from a nature that is unfulfilled and unactualized:

> [S]uch was the virtue of Rivendell that soon all fear and anxiety was lifted from their minds. The future, good or ill, was not forgotten, but ceased to have any power over the present. Health and hope grew strong in them, and they were content with each good day as it came, taking pleasure in every meal, and in every word and song.[68]

In such places where time is transcended, at least partially, one is simply free to be, because all that one does and all that one is is for its own sake. As Stratford Caldecott astutely observes, "True freedom ... consists in the power to *be*, which is a power that is spread over time. Thus Frodo's past self comes to the rescue of his present." He is referring here to how Frodo's past acts of mercy and generosity toward Gollum rescue him in the end from himself.[69] As was argued above, who and what we are cannot be fully revealed until the whole series of our temporal existence is folded up into our eternal nature, which, far from being static and dead, is dynamic and indeed our only fully real life.

---

66 FR, II, 7, 358.

67 Shippey also argues that Lothlórien is an image of the earthly Paradise encountered by the poet of *The Pearl* (and *Sir Orfeo*). The members of the Fellowship enter a mythic time that has strong associations with Old England (the Angle), and the crossing of the rivers Nimrodel and Silverlode point to the river in *The Pearl* (as well as to the ones in ancient mythology). "His dreamer's state of liminal uncertainty, in which he is both aware of the physical and literal world, and conscious of some deeper symbolic meaning, is exactly the state of mythic or magic timelessness which I believe Tolkien aimed from time to time to reach." Shippey, *Author of the Century*, 200.

68 FR, II, 3, 274.

69 Caldecott, *The Power of the Ring*, 206.

Our present temporal existence is a shadow that is spread over time—it is only fidelity to what our eternal nature is, which is fidelity to what is good and true for all times and all places and which is also a fidelity to, as we shall see, a providential care inherent in things, that we, like Frodo, are rescued or saved from our own sins and mistakes.

It is also notable that while in Lórien we see a deep connection between a mode of time that approaches eternity and a heightened perception or appreciation of the natures of things, of wood, water, air, and artifacts: "As Frodo prepared to follow him [Haldir up the tree], he laid his hand upon the tree beside the ladder: never before had he been so suddenly and so keenly aware of the feel and texture of a tree's skin and of the life within it. He felt a delight in wood and the touch of it, neither as forester nor has carpenter; it was the delight of the living tree itself."[70] For when time is altered, slows down, and approaches eternity, the eternal natures of things reveal themselves more fully to consciousness and they acquire a life of their own, for they ultimately live first and foremost in the eternal, divine Mind who created them. This is the case for another time well in the *Lord of the Rings*: the Old Forest and the little realm of Tom Bombadil, where the hobbits experience a mode of time ("eternity" or "aeviternity"?) very much like "Elven time." As Michael Stanton observes, the House of Tom Bombadil seems to have a warping effect on our normal perceptions of time, allowing visions and dreams and, through dreams, sight into the

---

70 *FR*, II, 6, 351. "We say that unliving things or patterns do 'exist fully at any one instant of time', meaning, for instance, that IRON is always IRON, just so and nothing more nor less, whenever observed or considered. So long, that is, as its characteristic inner pattern is maintained. If this is or could be changed, it would not be IRON, or a portion of IRON, 'growing' and working out the full pattern of IRON according to iron-nature. It would rather be that iron was changed into something else, and became another *nassë*, whether by force externally applied to it, or by its own instability. Though in the case of certain *nassi* that appear 'by nature' to be thus 'unstable', breaking up or changing their inner patterns normally under like conditions, it may be thought that we have an adumbration in a lower order of the normal nature of a higher order. For such adumbrations are to be seen in all orders. Nonetheless they are only 'adumbrations' and not the same processes. Just as the apparent growth of crystals foreshadows but does not forestall the growth of plants." *NME*, 251.

past and future.⁷¹ Tom himself, in his hypnotic stories, takes the hobbits to places beyond memory and beyond waking thought:

> When he caught his words again they found that he had now wandered into strange regions beyond their memory and beyond their waking thought, into times when the world was wider, and the seas flowed straight to the western Shore; and still on and back Tom went singing out into ancient starlight, when only the Elf-sires were awake.⁷²

While in the house of Tom Bombadil, Frodo has dreams of events both present yet far away (Gandalf held captive by Saruman on the top of Orthanc) and future (a premonition of his sailing into the West).⁷³ The warping of time around the house of Tom Bombadil goes beyond the hobbits' dreams and Tom's stories: one can trace the correspondences with the various Ages of Middle-earth very closely even in the encounter with the Barrow Wights and their treasure: "In scattering the treasure, destroying the barrow, and banishing the wight, Bombadil anticipates the destruction of Barad-dûr and the windy dissolution of Sauron (mimicked later in the defeat and death of Saruman in the Shire)."⁷⁴ When the hobbits are finally shaken from the trance induced by the Wights into which they had fallen in the Barrows, Merry remembers the men of Carn Dûm coming upon them.⁷⁵

These time distortions in Tolkien's fantasy are, I would submit, a large part of its power to enchant and the foundation for its numinous quality. These distortions in time not only do not detract from the concreteness and reality of his secondary world, but actually enhance that reality and solidity precisely because such distortions in time are grounded in a living time, which in turn is an expression of real, eternal, living natures that are expressions of a real, living Mind whose creative activity is the foundation of the world. As Erazim Kohak puts it, "The

---

71 Stanton, *Hobbits, Elves and Wizards*, 169.
72 *FR*, I, 7, 131.
73 *FR*, I, 8, 135.
74 As the willow represents the First Age, so the wights represents the Second, etc. Miller, "Narrative Pattern," 103.
75 *FR*, I, 8, 143.

ultimate sense of being is the ingression of the Idea of the Good, of beauty, truth, goodness, of holiness, justice, tenderness, love, into matter and time, becoming actual within them and bestowing meaning upon them."[76] Kohak continues:

> For *being is not time*. It is value, the ingression of eternity into time. Certainly time is not a mere illusion, a veil of *maya*. It is as time that eternity is present. Love becomes present only in a life shared; life becomes actual only as the series of acts which, individually, seem mundane; a melody becomes actual only as a sequence of notes—and the good *ab solo* only as a history of relative value. Still, love is more than the seasons shared, a life more than the sequence of acts and passions in which it is acted out, the good more that the values which instantiate it.... It is the intersection of eternity with time whose locus humans can be. It is the privilege and the task of humans to recognize and to act out the presence of eternity in time.[77]

To take us out of the mechanistic time of modern civilization, which is a flat and horizontal quantity, devoid of any inherent meaning or value because sundered from any meaningful connection to the time and eternity inherent in created natures, is to allow the human mind to glimpse the eternal—to hear the Great Music of Creation born out of a living, creative, and loving Mind. We can, to be sure, only hear that Great Music in time; and yet the very beauty and sadness of the Great Music is beautiful and sad only to the degree that it transcends time. This paradox points to the mystery of Providence at work in the world, which we shall treat of in our next and last chapter.

---

76 Kohak, *The Embers and the Stars*, 197.
77 Kohak, *The Embers and the Stars*, 202.

CHAPTER EIGHT

The Recovery of Hope

In what is perhaps one of the most moving passages of *The Lord of the Rings*, Sam looks up to the sky from where he and his master, Frodo, are resting in deep shadow during a pause in their grueling trek across Mordor. At first, all Sam sees is a wall of black clouds overhead, but then he notices something that surprises him and fills him with hope:

> There, peeping among the cloud-wrack above a dark tor high up in the mountains, Sam saw a white star twinkle for a while. The beauty of it smote his heart, as he looked up out of the forsaken land, and hope returned to him. For like a shaft, clear and cold, the thought pierced him that in the end the Shadow was only a small and passing thing: there was light and high beauty for ever beyond its reach. His song in the Tower [of

Cirith Ungol] had been defiance rather than hope; for then he was thinking of himself. Now, for a moment, his own fate, and even his master's, ceased to trouble him.[1]

Like the Roman philosopher Boethius, Sam acquires a true and healing perspective on his earthly concerns and troubles by contemplating the eternal and rational order of the heavens.[2] The heavens remind Sam (and Boethius, who was wasting away in prison while writing his *Consolation of Philosophy*) of the existence of a timeless goodness, truth, and beauty that transcend the earthly and time-bound, and thus are not only untouched by earthly troubles but also promise deliverance from them. Indeed, at a crucial point in *The Return of the King* during the Battle of the Pelennor Fields, all the participants, even though they are scattered on different fronts, notice something very peculiar happening. Here we see it as described from the perspective of Frodo and Sam:

> There was battle far above in the high spaces of the air.[3] The billowing clouds of Mordor were being driven back, their edges tattering as a wind out of the living world came up and swept the fumes and smokes towards the dark land of their home.

---

1 *RK*, VI, 2, 922.

2 *CP*, III, 9. Hence, Boethius crowns his own *Consolation of Philosophy* with a discussion of the nature of time and eternity. For the relation of Boethius's philosophy to the *Lord of the Rings*, see Kathleen E. Dubs, "Providence, Fate, and Chance: Boethian Philosophy in *The Lord of the Rings*," in *Tolkien and the Invention of Myth*, ed. Jane Chance (Lexington, KY: University Press of Kentucky, 2004), 133–42. In addition, as Halsall remarks, "for Tolkien, who avoided unnecessary and deliberate use of Christian language, Boethius also provided a framework in which to present his own heavily nuanced ideas about providence, free will, chance, and necessity in a philosophical perspective." Halsall, *Creation and Beauty in Tolkien's Catholic Vision*, 131. Ordway also points out that Sam's vision of the star far above in the heavens had Marian overtones for Tolkien, for whom, as a Catholic, Mary was the *stella maris* or "star of the sea." See Ordway, *Tolkien's Faith*, 150.

3 Here Tolkien is making a direct reference to Paul's letter to the Ephesians (6:12, Douay-Rhiems), where the Apostle writes, "For our wrestling is not against flesh and blood; but against principalities and powers, against the rulers of the world of this darkness, against the spirits of wickedness in the high places [ἐπουρανίοις or the "upper air/heavens"]."

Under the lifting skirts of the dreary canopy dim light leaked into Mordor like pale morning through the grimed window of a prison.

"Look at it, Mr. Frodo!" said Sam. "Look at it! The wind's changed. Something is happening. He's not having it all his own way. His darkness is breaking up out in the world there. I wish I could see what is going on!"[4]

As Matthew Dickerson remarks concerning this passage, "Tolkien shows the reader that the power that is against Sauron is the power that controls the winds and the air. This, as is evident in Sam's words, is a source of tremendous hope to the people of Middle-earth."[5] Thus hope comes in the action of *The Lord of the Rings* when it is least expected.

This raises fundamental questions: what reasonable grounds do *we* have to hope for a happy ending to the drama of our own lives? What reason do we have to think that a happy ending—fullness of life beyond time and the walls of this world—is more than wishful thinking? Here, of course, we come to the final function of fantasy: the consolation of the happy ending, which, far from being accidental, is essential to fantasy and a logical, even necessary, outcome of recovery and escape. It is consolation insofar as good fantasy shows us that, far from being a species of wishing thinking, hope for a happy ending is grounded in a true and deep understanding of reality itself.

Christian Hope, Modern Despair

Through the action of *The Lord of the Rings*, Tolkien creates a constant play between despair and hope, between seeming chaos and glimpses of an order behind the chaos, and in doing so, he is engaging very modern themes through a perennial lens. We get glimpses in the narrative of unseen forces fighting on behalf of the Fellowship (for example, Glorfindel unwittingly helping the hobbits and Strider get to Rivendell).[6]

---

4   *RK*, VI, 2.
5   Dickerson, *A Hobbit Journey*, 198.
6   *FR*, I, xii, 210.

When Tom meets the hobbits, he suggests this may not be by chance.[7] Then, once they get to Rivendell, Elrond says to them: "there are other powers and realms that you know not, and they are hidden from you. Anduin the Great flows past many shores, ere it comes to Argonath and the Gates of Gondor."[8] If the Fellowship had not taken the detour into the Chamber of Records in Moria, their escape would have been cut off.[9] The blade with which Merry killed the Witch-King of Angmar happened to be forged deep in history (and legend) precisely for that purpose.[10] Nevertheless, these are only glimpses and usually, as in the case of the sword of Merry, seen and understood only after the fact. Ultimately, hope is a sort of trust that can only take on the color of virtue when the end is not clear and, indeed, the road that one must travel is hard: "Now at this last we must take a hard road, a road unforeseen. There lies our hope, if hope it be. To walk into peril—to Mordor. We must send the Ring to the Fire."[11]

So, in a strange twist, true hope, far from denying despair, acknowledges it but then goes to show how that very despair when mastered and faced with courage can lead to a happy ending. Indeed, hope in the face of seemingly inevitable failure is, Tolkien asserts, one of the main themes of his work:

> "Lead us not into temptation &c" is the harder and the less often considered petition. The view, in the terms of the story, is that though every event or situation has (at least) two aspects:

7   FR, I, 7, 126.
8   FR, II, 2, 268.
9   FR, II, 5, 328.
10 RK, V, 6, 844.
11 FR, II, 2, 267. Michael Stanton (*Hobbits, Elves and Wizards*, 165) finds many more examples of unexpected causes of hope in book III alone of the *Lord of the Rings*: Gandalf returns and speaks hopefully about the future conduct of the campaign against Isengard, but he cautions that hope is not a certainty; when Théoden awakes and resumes his kingly mien, men feel hope for Rohan; our hope is in the east, Gandalf tells the king; at Helm's Deep, Aragorn calls for stout defense of the citadel throughout the night, saying, "day will bring hope." There are further examples at the beginning of Book V: Beregond questions if Gondor can withstand Sauron's attack, but he tells Pippin that even if they fall, "Hope and memory shall live still"; Arwen says in a message to Aragorn, *"Either our hope cometh or all hope's end."*

the history and development of the individual (it is something out of which he can get good, ultimate good, for himself, or fail to do so), and the history of the world (which depends on his action for its own sake)—still there are abnormal situations in which one may be placed. "Sacrificial" situations, I would call them: sc. positions in which the "good" of the world depends on the behaviour of an individual in circumstances which demand of him suffering and endurance far beyond the normal—even, it may happen (or seem, humanly speaking), demand a strength of body and mind which he does not possess: he is in a sense doomed to failure, doomed to fall to temptation or be broken by pressure against his "will": that is against any choice he could make or would make unfettered, not under duress.[12]

That the good of the world may sometimes depend on an individual's sacrifice, which demands more than what that individual wants to give or seemingly can give, is a phenomenon that has been recognized in myth, legend, and history from antiquity to the present. However, Tolkien asks, what is the *sense* of this sacrifice—why do we judge it to be good and even admirable and noble—if we live in a meaningless, mechanistic world? Even modern readers find the sacrifices as embodied in the characters of *The Lord of the Rings* noble and admirable; but their worldview does not allow them to make sense of this feeling (or better, intuition). In fact, Tolkien emphasizes throughout *The Lord of the Rings* the foolishness of the Quest: "The Quest was bound to fail as a piece of world-plan, and also was bound to end in disaster as the story of humble Frodo's development to the 'noble', his sanctification."[13]

12   *Letters*, 233.
13   *Letters*, 234. Tolkien quickly adds, however, that persistence is not a virtue in itself, for one can show great persistence, even courage, in an evil cause (no doubt thinking of the great courage and resilience of individual Germans during World War II, even though these "virtues" were exercised in service to an evil regime); genuine hope can only be founded on a desire for what is truly good; to work against that good despite everything is really an act of despair: "Gollum was pitiable, but he ended in persistent wickedness, and the fact that this worked good was no credit to him. His marvelous courage and endurance,

Tolkien's mention of sanctification is significant here, for it implies that genuine hope is not just based on the attainment of a future good that seems, naturally and humanly speaking, out of reach, but also on the moral, intellectual, and spiritual transformation of the one who hopes.

Again, the virtue of hope can only be hope if it operates in darkness and lack of complete knowledge; it is, paradoxically, a virtue that perfects us in our state of imperfection. It is the virtue that sustains us especially when we find ourselves in a situation where we know we are inadequate to the task demanded of us, for hope allows us to realize that the task assigned to us was not assigned at random but according to a cosmic order to which we and our talents are fitted very precisely: "There was more than one power at work," Gandalf remarks to Frodo, elaborating that there was "something else at work, beyond any design of the Ring-maker. I can put it no plainer than by saying that Bilbo was *meant* to find the Ring, and *not* by its maker. In which case you were also *meant* to have it. And that may be an encouraging thought'."[14] As Thomas Hibbs notes, "Humility here is not a matter of groveling subservience; instead, it has to do with acknowledging one's part within a larger whole, with discovering and filling one's role in a cosmic battle between good and evil."[15] Far from puffing the bearer of hope with pride, the knowledge that one has been assigned a task to which one is wholly inadequate in natural terms generates, Tolkien claims, a humility and feeling of pity that is at the root of all the other virtues: "Many that live deserve death. And some that die deserve life. Can you give it to them? Then do not be too eager to deal out death and judgment. For even the very wise cannot see all ends."[16] Since even the wise "cannot see all ends," we must trust in doing what is right and good for its own sake, here and now, and let events take their course. Here, again, is another paradox: hope is oriented to the attainment of a normally

---

as great as Frodo and Sam's or greater, being devoted to evil was portentous, but not honourable." *Letters*, 234.

14   *FR*, I, 2, 55–56.

15   Thomas Hibbs, "Providence and the Dramatic Unity of *The Lord of the Rings*," in The Lord of the Rings *and Philosophy: One Book to Rule Them All*, ed. Gregory Bassham and Eric Bronson (Chicago: Open Court Publishing, 2003), 171.

16   *FR*, I, 2, 59.

unattainable future good, yet through hope, the virtuous agent acts purely in the present and for the present. Through hope what is always and eternally good becomes present in time. The hopeful person lives purely in the present because his or her hope is rooted in the future attainment of a timeless and permanent good.

By contrast, despair "is only for those who see the end beyond all doubt"; it "arises from pride and a feeling of omniscience, and too often in the tale, as Gandalf will have occasion to mention again, sentient creatures suffer from an excess of both."[17] It is the illusion of omniscience that we can without doubt see the ends of all things with our finite intellects from our finite, temporal perspective. That is the origin of despair—an illusion that is not dispelled but actually reinforced by modern means of communication and education. With this illusion of omniscience there follows a lack of imagination: the more one presumes to know the ends of all things, the less one imagines what can escape one's knowledge. This, as we have mentioned previously, was precisely the great mistake of Sauron, who could not imagine that anyone would not use his Ring to overpower him, because the only ends he presumed to know were those based on calculations of power and intra-worldly forces:

> That we should try to destroy the Ring itself has not yet entered into his [Sauron's] darkest dream. In which no doubt you will see our good fortune and our hope. For imagining war he has let loose war, believing that he has no time to waste; for he that strikes the first blow, if he strikes hard enough, may need to strike no more. So the forces that he has long been preparing he is now setting in motion, sooner than he intended. Wise fool. For if he had used all his power to guard Mordor, so that none could enter, and bent all his guile to the hunting of the Ring, then indeed hope would have faded: neither Ring nor bearer could long have eluded him.[18]

It is instructive here that Gandalf calls Sauron a wise fool: puffed up by his superior knowledge and intellect as a Maia, Sauron lacks the

---

17 FR, II, 2, 269; Stanton, *Hobbits, Elves and Wizards*, 38.
18 TT, III, 5, 497.

imagination that could only belong to a genuine creator, to someone who can survey the entire story of things from the standpoint of eternity. That is why Gandalf goes on to say, as Stanton summarizes, that "evil lacks imagination."[19] That is its great weakness: "Sauron cannot imagine that his enemy will *not* try to defeat him by using his own weapon against him. That evil cannot comprehend this strategy illustrates that it is a good strategy."[20] Hence, it is a great part of the true wisdom of Gandalf that he takes any interest in—indeed, even admires—the Hobbits, a race of people overlooked for the most part by "the wise." Nevertheless, although as a little people the Hobbits are not of much importance, they come in the end to trouble "the counsels of the Wise and the Great,"[21] the possibility of which Gandalf has the great wisdom to foresee.

Indeed, it is a major theme of Tolkien's work that what is folly to the wise of this world is really wisdom and what is "wisdom" to the wise of this world is really folly, making much of Tolkien's work, at least in the *Hobbit* and the *Lord of the Rings*, an extended commentary on what Paul writes to the Corinthians:

> For the foolishness of God is wiser than men; and the weakness of God is stronger than men.... But the foolish things of the world hath God chosen, that he may confound the wise; and the weak things of the world hath God chosen, that he may confound the strong. And the base things of the world, and the things that are contemptible, hath God chosen, and things that are not, that he might bring to nought things that are.[22]

Thus, it is through the humble, the Hobbits, that Middle-earth is saved, and it is through the forgiveness and pity that Frodo shows throughout the Quest that not only Middle-earth is saved, but also Frodo himself:

> [A]t this point the "salvation" of the world and Frodo's own "salvation" is achieved by his previous *pity* and forgiveness of injury. At any point any prudent person would have told Frodo

---

19 Stanton, *Hobbits, Elves and Wizards*, 38.
20 Dickerson, *A Hobbit Journey*, 22.
21 FR, I, prologue, 2.
22 1 Cor. 1:25, 27–28. See also, Caldecott, *The Power of the Ring*, 53.

that Gollum would certainly betray him, and could rob him in the end. To "pity" him, to forbear to kill him, was a piece of folly, or a mystical belief in the ultimate *value-in-itself* of pity and generosity even if disastrous *in the world of time*. He did rob him and injure him in the end—but by a "grace," that last betrayal was at a precise juncture when the final evil deed was the most beneficial thing any one cd. have done for Frodo! By a situation created by his "forgiveness," he was saved from himself and relieved of his burden.[23]

Frodo's demonstrations of pity and forgiveness toward Gollum were pure acts of folly from a worldly point of view—from the viewpoint of power dynamics and critical consciousness. But Tolkien's point here is fundamental and one that we saw in the section on the recovery of virtue: that showing pity and forgiveness are acts *good in themselves*, apart from any utility or consequences, advantageous or not. Indeed, Tolkien remarks that these acts depend on an almost mystical belief in their inherent and therefore eternal value. They may be "disastrous in the world of time," but they bring salvation from the standpoint of eternity. Even more, it seems from what Tolkien says here that the very essence of grace is the breaking into time of the value of the eternal, such that the eternal value of pity and forgiveness eventually does save Frodo even in time, for it is his previous acts of pity and mercy toward Gollum that eventually save him from himself in such a way that the before and after of time no longer plays any role.

This is, of course, the essence of Christian hope, but what of Tolkien's obvious love for pagan myths and legends in which such a hope seems to be absent? Are not these stories closer to modern despair than they are to Christian hope?

I think Tolkien would answer that they are not. First of all, as has been repeatedly emphasized, Christian hope is not to be confused with blind optimism; in fact, as we have seen, the virtue of hope in the Christian sense can only manifest itself when all worldly calculations give reasons for despair. This recognition of the grim and dark (for

---

[23] *Letters*, 234. Emphases added.

the Christian, fallen) nature of the world is, as John Davenport notes, essential not only to Tolkien's vision but, Tolkien argued, to fairy-stories in general:

> The poignant emotion Tolkien finds in this moment in good fairy tales requires a tragic recognition of the evil and imperfection of our world, or even a Norse-like resignation to the fact that we cannot overcome it by our own power; yet the tale rises above this grief in a humanly impossible reprieve that is only made possible by divine grace ('by virtue of the absurd', as Kierkegaard would say).[24]

It is therefore entirely fitting that the stories of the *Silmarillion*, which form the backdrop to the events of *The Hobbit* and *The Lord of the Rings*, should have a very dark, grim, "pagan" feel, with a great emphasis on the inexorable workings out of fate.[25] This is not just a feature of the various stories of the *Quenta Silmarillion*, but also of Tolkien's creation myth itself, as Verlyn Flieger notes:

> Tolkien's mythos as a whole begins with a fall long before humanity comes on the scene and is saved (but only temporarily) twice—once by Earendil and once by Frodo. Imperfection enters the song in the very singing of creation with the disharmony of Melkor, and this Music sets the tone for all that is to follow.[26]

Looking toward the end, Tolkien also remarks how all the victories over evil in this world are never final, that evil always returns again: "Always after a defeat and a respite, the Shadow takes another shape and grows again."[27]

24 Davenport, "Happy Endings and Religious Hope," 210–11.
25 See Shippey, *The Road to Middle-earth*, chapter 7, on the dark and fatalistic vision of the *Silmarillion*. See also Helen Lasseter Freeh, "On Fate, Providence, and Free Will in *The Silmarillion*," in *Tolkien among the Moderns*, ed. Ralph C. Wood (Notre Dame, IN: University of Notre Dame Press, 2015), 51–77, on the importance of the dark fatalism of *The Silmarillion* as a necessary prelude to the more hopeful *Lord of the Rings*.
26 Flieger, *Interrupted Music*, 140.
27 FR, I, 2, 51.

This dark, pagan fatalism differs fundamentally from modern despair in that it does not presume to "know all ends." As a result, it encourages resolute courage and resignation, not vain attempts to make reality conform in all particulars to our will. In that sense, ancient pagan fatalism is actually much closer to Christian hope than modern despair, for Christian hope is the fulfillment and perfection of pagan fatalism insofar as it reveals that courage in the face of inevitable defeat is not a vain and empty gesture, but the only way to ultimate victory. Modern despair, by contrast, is a brute negation of Christian hope: it is nihilistic even to the extent of denying any inherent worth to virtue (especially that of courage). This explains why in the fairy-story the joy of the happy ending is often mixed with, and indeed often indistinguishable from, grief.[28] As Bradley Birzer remarks, St. John's vision of the apocalypse and the New Jerusalem is, for Tolkien, the fulfillment and completion of the Norse Ragnarök.[29] Thus, Plato's metaphysically tragic concept of *ananke*, or "necessity," is taken up by Tolkien as the necessary precondition for a joyful revelation or eucatastrophe. The ancient pagans recognized what modern men and women have forgotten: "The notion of submission to one's proper part within the whole means that one's ultimate destiny is not in one's own hands. It means that the assertion of human autonomy or the celebration of raw will is a dangerous illusion."[30] Thomas Hibbs continues:

> In place of Kant's isolated individual will, which in order to be free must turn from God, nature, and society, Tolkien gives us characters who can only understand themselves and their duties

---

[28] "This synthesis of the epic mode, which tends towards tragedy and sorrow, with the eucatastrophic consolation of the fairy tale, helps explain what several commentators have recognized as the paradoxical 'joy-in-sorrow atmosphere [that] pervades the *Rings*' trilogy [citing Clyde Kilby, "Meaning in *The Lord of the Rings*," in *Shadows of the Imagination*, 73]." Davenport, "Happy Endings and Religious Hope," 215.

[29] Bradley J. Birzer, "The 'Last Battle' as a Johannine Ragnarök: Tolkien and the Universal," in *The Ring and the Cross: Christianity and The Lord of the Rings*, ed. Paul E. Kerry (Madison, NJ: Fairleigh Dickinson University Press, 2011), 280.

[30] Hibbs, "Providence and the Dramatic Unity of *The Lord of the Rings*," 171.

by seeing themselves as parts of larger wholes, as members of nations and races, as participants in alliances and friendships for the good, and ultimately as part of a natural cosmos.[31]

In other words, essential to any providential understanding of events in the world is a recovery of fellowship: essential to the working of all things for the good[32] is the love and sacrifices each person makes for other persons, because fellowship is itself built in to creatures and into creation itself, "for we know that every creature groaneth and travaileth in pain until now ... waiting for the adoption of the sons of God, the redemption of our body."[33] That is why, as Peter Kreeft accurately states, "Hope's object is *persons*, and their *emeth*, their trustworthiness, and the trust, loyalty, and friendship between them ... not an idea or ideal, not even the fulfillment of the task ... Hope's object is always personal, but it is never one's self."[34] For Tolkien, it is the supreme folly to put one's trust or hope in impersonal world processes or even in science (however that is understood). It is no different than putting one's trust in a Ring of Power. Least of all can we have any trust or hope in some impersonal phenomenon called "progress." One can only have hope in our fellowship with other persons and, ultimately, in our fellowship with the Person who devised the Story of creation itself, in which we are characters beloved by the Author.[35]

---

[31] Hibbs, "Providence and the Dramatic Unity of *The Lord of the Rings*," 173.
[32] Cf. Rom. 8:28.
[33] Rom. 8:22–23.
[34] Kreeft, *The Philosophy of Tolkien*, 202.
[35] This is why I find Curry's contrast between "religion" as an "enemy of enchantment when it asserts its own sole universal truth, and thus becomes entangled in aspirations to complete control and ultimate power" and "spirituality," embodied in nature and our social lives, very curious (Curry, *Defending Middle-earth*, 157). The positing of universal and eternal truths is, for Tolkien, not the "enemy of enchantment" nor a positing of "complete control" and "ultimate power," but, to the contrary, the precondition for challenging such claims to complete control and ultimate power within the world of time. To be able to find eternal value within Creation is the greatest if not the only genuine form of enchantment there is.

Providence, Not Progress

A recovery of hope is a recovery of Providence, the notion that, for those who persevere in courage, all things are ordered to the good, for the individual, for society, and for creation itself; to put it in Tolkienian terms, "Providence" refers to the notion that all things are ordered to a happy ending. The problem is that the notion of progress has taken the place of Providence, and the recovery of the latter is all the more difficult in that, in many ways, the notion of progress apes the notion of divine Providence. It retains the notion that historical events have some sort of end point or eschaton in a perfect society or world (a utopia is a happy ending of sorts); but (as we saw in chapter 2 in Voeglin's work) it completely immanentizes or secularizes this end point, placing the eschaton of history within time (and thus rejecting any recovery or even notion of permanent value and thus of any basis for real happiness). Even more importantly, modernity makes this eschaton the product of concerted human effort, planning, and calculation. In other words, progress not only makes possible but actually demands something like Sauron's Ring of Power for its realization.

That Tolkien rejected modern ideas of progress is clear from the many comments he made on progress in his various writings, from his *Mythopoeia* to his letters. In one letter, he made clear that his rejection of notions of progress stemmed from what he saw as the truth of the Catholic Faith: "I am a Christian and indeed a Roman Catholic, so that I do not expect 'history' to be anything but a 'long defeat'—though it contains (and in a legend may contain more clearly and movingly) some samples or glimpses of final victory."[36] For Tolkien, this truth—that history is but a "long defeat"—is not just a truth *de fide*, but one supported by the very evidence of history itself. As classical Christian philosophers like Augustine and Boethius noted long ago, both a knowledge of human history and a disinterested observation of the utter impermanence of all earthly things demonstrate that all human plans, projects, and aspirations ultimately come to nothing in the world of time. The greatest empires, the most sophisticated cultures,

---

36 *Letters*, 255.

totalitarian political movements that seem to sweep all past beliefs and certainties before them, all come to nothing in the end.

I think Tolkien was very mindful of the incoherence and therefore the baleful influence of the notion of progress, mainly because it blinds us to the very real and beneficial workings of divine Providence. Divine Providence is beneficial in two ways: on the one hand, it orders objectively our actions toward the good provided we consistently choose the good (or trust that, if we are resigned, God will draw good out of evil); on the other hand, it subjectively instills in us resolution and courage. The notion of progress, by contrast, induces despair, precisely because it assumes that the perfect good can only be obtained in time and by our efforts, and yet time is the greatest destroyer of all. In many ways, Denethor illustrates the despair of the modern man or woman of progress.[37] Like Saruman, he is, in many ways, one of the most modern characters of the book. As we saw in the chapter on the recovery of fellowship, Denethor is a purely political animal, relying for success on purely political or military force and his own calculating wisdom.

Moreover, through his use of the palantir, Denethor presumes to know more than he does, for this seeing stone allows him to see what others do not see. He thinks, like most modern men and women, that he has access to superior knowledge because he has access to a superior means of communication:

> Didst thou think that the eyes of the White Tower were blind? Nay, I have seen more than thou knowest, Grey Fool. For thy hope is but ignorance. Go then and labour in healing! Go forth and fight! Vanity. For a little space you may triumph on the field, for a day. But against the Power that now arises there is

---

37 This may seem strange at first since, as Shippey notes (*Author of the Century*, 171–72). Denethor is in many ways an image of the reactionary arch-conservative, stuck irretrievably in nostalgia for the past, wanting things to be as they were in the days of his longfathers. But what this indicates is that Tolkien was also aware that the notion of progress can contaminate the political right insofar as it can become a pure negation of the political left, grounded not in a genuine appreciation for the goodness of things and the natural order but in *ressentiment*.

no victory. To this City only the first finger of its hand has yet been stretched. All the East is moving. And even now the wind of thy hope cheats thee and wafts up Anduin a fleet with black sails. The West has failed. It is time for all to depart who would not be slaves.[38]

The irony here is that the fleet sailing up the Anduin bearing the black sails and born by the wind is the corsair fleet seized by Aragon and his companions and is therefore sailing to the rescue of Minas Tirith, not its destruction. In looking into the *palantir*, Denethor saw only what Sauron wanted him to see. In fact, Sauron did not even have to show Denethor falsehoods—the corsair fleet really was sailing up the Anduin—but merely only part of the truth. All that Sauron needed to do was to play on the presumption of Denethor to know more than he really does. As Gandalf remarks of Denethor, "He was too great to be subdued to the will of the Dark Power, but saw nonetheless only those things which that Power permitted him to see. The knowledge which he obtained was, doubtless, often of service to him; yet the vision of the great might of Mordor that was shown to him fed the despair of his heart until it overthrew his mind."[39] This illusion of a knowledge more complete than it really is further led Denethor into other foolish decisions and actions concerning, for example, the defense of Gondor and Minas Tirith: "'Such counsels will make the Enemy's victory certain indeed,' said Gandalf."[40] Thus, to the good and wise counsel of Gandalf, Denethor responds with accusations that Gandalf's plan was to undermine, betray, and supplant him. But this illusion of knowledge has an even more dangerous consequence: a tendency toward nihilism, toward wanting and desiring *nothing* rather than not getting what one wants (which is, in a sense, a good description of the state of soul of the damned in Hell): "'I would have things as they were in all the days of my life', answered Denethor, 'and in the days of my longfathers before me: to be the Lord of this City in peace, and leave my chair to a son after me, who would be his own master and no wizard's pupil. But if doom denies this to

38 *RK*, V, 7, 853.
39 *RK*, V, 7, 856.
40 *RK*, V, 7, 853.

me, then I will have *naught*: neither life diminished, nor love halved, nor honour abated'."[41]

Nevertheless, one can argue that the place of free will, both its existence and integrity, is as much a problem for the notion of Providence, divine or otherwise, as it is for the notion of progress. How can free will be truly free and efficacious if all things are ordered to a particular end (the theme, along with eternity, of the last book of Boethius's *Consolation of Philosophy*, one might add)? Tolkien addresses this problem directly in his letters, but, as one might expect, he uses an analogy drawn from literary creation:

> Having mentioned Free Will, I might say that in my myth I have used "subcreation" in a special way (not the same as "subcreation" as a term in criticism of art, though I tried to show allegorically how that might come to be taken up into Creation in some plane in my "purgatorial" story *Leaf by Niggle* …) to make visible and physical the effects of Sin or misused Free Will by men. Free Will is derivative, and is only operative within provided circumstances; but in order that it may exist, it is necessary that the Author should guarantee it, whatever betides: sc. when it is "against His Will," as we say, at any rate as it appears on a finite view.[42]

Thus, in many ways, the necessity of things is a precondition for the genuine exercise of free will for Tolkien. Free will or choice makes sense only when we are paradoxically forced by circumstances to choose, for only then would any decision be non-arbitrary, meaningful, and effective. It follows, then, that, as Patricia Spacks points out, Tolkien's universe is built upon, but then goes beyond, the fatalistic, pagan world of Beowulf: "Frodo's virtue is more significant because it operates in a context of total free will: he is *not* the creature of chance and fate in the same way as Beowulf."[43] Thomas Hibbs makes this same point more fully:

41 *RK*, V, 7, 854; see also, Shippey, *The Road to Middle-earth*, 172.
42 *Letters*, 195.
43 Patrica Meyer Spacks, "Power and Meaning in *The Lord of the Rings*," in *Understanding* The Lord of the Rings: *The Best of Tolkien Criticism*, ed. Rose Zimbardo and Neil Isaacs (New York: Houghton-Mifflin, 2004), 56.

> Ultimately, however, providence involves an ordering of the entire narrative; this is evident in and through the dramatic structure of *The Lord of the Rings*. Rather than undermining freedom, providence presupposes that finite creatures are real agents, responsible in various measures for their actions. Without this, there could be no drama.[44]

There is, Spacks continues, a real sense in Tolkien's fantasy of a world where the characters have responsibility not just to themselves but to some cosmic good: "The responsibility involved here, and throughout the epic, is not simply to one's individual integrity; it is cosmic responsibility, justified by the existence of some vast, unnamed power for good."[45] Thus, when Frodo puts the Ring on when he is on Amon Hen, he finds himself balanced apparently between two opposing powers, Sauron and, as he later learns, Gandalf ("Then as a flash from some other point of power there came to his mind another thought: *Take it off! Take it off! Fool, take it off! Take off the Ring!*"). Caught in this vice between two external wills, Frodo finds his own free will: "The two powers strove in him. For a moment, perfectly balanced between their piercing points, he writhed, tormented. Suddenly he was aware of himself again, Frodo, neither the Voice nor the Eye: free to choose, with one remaining instant in which to do so. He took the Ring off his finger."[46]

Thus, Spacks asserts, "The universe of Tolkien, unlike that of the Anglo-Saxons, is ultimately affirmative."[47] The free choices of the characters, if they are for the good, result, ultimately, in what is good; but even more importantly, they result in the "spiritual growth of the chooser."[48] As Leslie Donovan observes, "One of the central lessons about the function of free will in Tolkien's mythology is that choices made on behalf of good lead to 'good results, while evil intentions are self defeating' (Loy and Goodhew 2004, 8)."[49] Thus, the pity of

---

44 Hibbs, "Providence and the Dramatic Unity of *The Lord of the Rings*," 171.
45 Spacks, "Power and Meaning in *The Lord of the Rings*," 59.
46 *FR*, II, 10, 401.
47 Spacks, "Power and Meaning in *The Lord of the Rings*," 60.
48 Spacks, "Power and Meaning in *The Lord of the Rings*," 61.
49 Donovan, "Middle-earth Mythology," 102.

Frodo toward Gollum manages to save the Quest in the end, because it is Gollum in the end who saves Frodo from himself and through his own wickedness and greed is cast into the fires of Mount Doom along with the Ring. Aragorn thinks that all his choices go ill; and yet it is his decision to rescue Merry and Pippin from the Uruk Hai rather than accompany Frodo and Sam to Mordor that brings about the fall of the traitor Saruman. Saruman himself, in his treachery, has only managed to hasten his own doom and that of Sauron by trying to kidnap the hobbits and get the Ring for himself.[50] One can easily multiply the cases where decisions that at the time seem foolish or meaningless turn out to be crucial for the success of the Quest, while many decisions by the evil characters that seem wise and even necessary at the time turn out to be for their doom.

Why should this be the case? Is this just a contrivance of the author to make good win in the end, but something that has no basis in reality? Tolkien, I claim, would think not: that good wins in the end is no contrivance of the author, but rather reflects necessarily the essential goodness of the Author of creation himself. The choice for good, Tolkien continually emphasizes, is a choice for things that are good in themselves, which is to say, for those things that are *always good*. Pity, for example, has a value that transcends the needs and circumstances of any particular moment in time; it is *always good*. Thus, to show pity is good in itself, even if in time it may seem foolish or inconsequential. But since it is an eternal value, its value or goodness is bound to manifest itself even in time. By contrast, evil actions are, in Tolkien's universe, almost always taken with a view to pure expediency, self-advantage, and what seems to work. And yet, since these decisions are not based on anything of eternal value, they eventually crumble to nothing as time does its work of destruction, whether quickly or slowly. As Gandalf says to Frodo, it "is wisdom to recognize necessity," but what kind of necessity?

> "Despair or folly?" said Gandalf. "It is not despair, for despair is only for those who see the end beyond all doubt. We do not. It is wisdom to recognize necessity, when all other courses have been weighed, though as folly it may appear to those who cling

50 *TT*, III, 5, 497; *TT*, III, 11, 599.

to false hope. Well, let folly be our cloak, a veil before the eyes of the Enemy! For he is very wise, and weighs all things to a nicety in the scales of his malice. But the only measure that he knows is desire, desire for power, and so he judges all hearts. Into his heart the thought will not enter that any will refuse it, that having the Ring we may seek to destroy it. If we seek this, we shall put him out of reckoning."[51]

Sauron cannot recognize that there are things of eternal value, despite his enormous power derived from having, as a Maia, an intelligence far superior to that of any in the Fellowship (although Gandalf is a Maia too, he has willingly taken on the limitations of a corporeal nature and therefore cannot rival Sauron directly). When Pippin looks into the *palantir*, Sauron, out of his pride and malice, thinks that Saruman has the Ring, and this sets off a series of bad decisions that prove to be devastating for Sauron: "He [Sauron] did not want information only: he wanted *you*, quickly, so that he could deal with you in the Dark Tower, slowly."[52] Thus, Tolkien cites one of his many very own proverbs: "*oft evil will shall evil mar.*"[53] Gandalf quickly realizes that the entire quest has been inadvertently saved by Pippin looking into the Palantir, even though in the short term this seems to have been disastrous.

Thus, since evil is metaphysically nothing in itself but a negation or privation of being and goodness, when it is carried to its logical term, it destroys itself. Even more, evil is a negation of eternity and eternal value, for the perfect fullness of being is also eternal being; any privation of such being from oneself by falling away from it is thus a privation of eternal being and a fall into time. Providence, by contrast, is in many ways the working out of the eternal good in time (something that is both indicated by and fulfilled in the Incarnation of Christ, of the eternal God entering historical time). Hope and providence, therefore, Tolkien wishes to show, are not mere species of wishful thinking, but rooted in the very structure of creation, which itself is a reflection in time of the eternal nature of the divine Creator. It means that choice

---

51 *FR*, II, 2, 269.
52 *TT*, III, 11, 594.
53 *TT*, III, 11, 595.

for the good is often something that is, again paradoxically, forced upon us, because the basis for reality is essentially good and overflowing with eternal value, and not some temporary and subjective wish or desire. Thus, we find Sam saying in an internal debate at the apparent death of Frodo by Shelob, "You haven't put yourself forward; you've been put forward. And as for not being the right and proper person, why, Mr. Frodo wasn't, as you might say, nor Mr. Bilbo. They didn't choose themselves."[54] He recognizes the truth: the good is always a task proposed to us by the world (and, ultimately, its Creator) and not something we determine. In other words, good choices are ones that conform to one's duties; indeed, all sense of duty is grounded in the eternal and necessary nature of the good chosen, which, in turn—and paradoxically—leads to genuine freedom.

This truth is most evident in the climax of *The Lord of the Rings*, alluded to above, where Frodo is finally overcome by the Ring and unable to cast it into the fires of Mount Doom. At the very end, Frodo says: "I do not choose now to do what I came to do. I will not do this deed. The Ring is mine!"[55] As has already been pointed out, the wording Tolkien chose to put in the mouth of Frodo is very interesting: it seems like he is asserting his own freedom and power; and yet he says, "I do not choose now." Now as Spacks remarks, "Dramatically, this final twist is quite unnecessary," but "Thematically it is essential": "Free choice of good by the individual involves his participation in a broad pattern of Good; individual acts become a part of Fate ... it is appropriate that at the last he should be merely an instrument of that essentially benevolent fate through which, as Sam realizes, 'his master had been saved; he was himself again, he was free'."[56] To view it from a different perspective, by choosing things of eternal value, free will is redeemed by events and made efficacious, whereas when one chooses things of temporary or fleeting value, one's choices are quickly invalidated and rendered impotent. Necessity results in genuine freedom because it is the necessity of an eternal value that transcends time. In other words,

---

54 *TT*, IV, 10, 732.
55 *RK*, V, 3, 945.
56 Spacks, "Power and Meaning in *The Lord of the Rings*," 64.

far from being in conflict with free will, that there is an eternal good or value is the only proper foundation for genuine freedom, because only a will rooted in the choice of eternal value escapes the necessity of brute force in time: hence the difference between Frodo's eventual surrender to the Ring and Sam's trusting acceptance of the necessity of the good.

This is why, as we have seen earlier, for Tolkien it is the humble and those held to be of no account that are the real movers of the world.[57] It is through the simple and ordinary that all that is noble and heroic takes on meaning. Tolkien is not saying that the noble and heroic are not good things; they are very good for Tolkien, and the great attraction of his stories is his vivid and moving depictions of the noble and heroic. But they take their meaning from the low and humble, because it is through them that the eternal value of the noble and heroic shines and is made manifest, just like it is through the fairy-story of the Gospel and the suffering of the Cross and the eucatastrophe of the Resurrection that all that is noble and heroic in pagan myths (and in our primary world) becomes meaningful by taking on, paradoxically, both particular, historical reality and universal, eternal value. The exchange between Aragorn and Boromir, after the latter was mortally wounded trying to save Merry and Pippin, illustrates this point very well:

> "Farewell, Aragorn! Go to Minas Tirith and save my people! I have failed."
>
> "No!", said Aragorn, taking his hand and kissing his brow. "You have conquered. Few have gained such a victory. Be at peace!"[58]

Here, Matthew Dickerson notes, Boromir is partially right: "he fails to do *anything* to save Gondor from military defeat."[59] He fails to save Merry and Pippin from capture by the Uruk Hai. But in a deeper sense, it is Aragorn who is right: Boromir is saved from the power of the Ring (as Gandalf later says of Boromir: "It [the temptation of the Ring] was a sore trial for such a man: a warrior, and a lord of men. Galadriel told

---

57 *Letters*, 160.
58 *TT*, III, 1, 414.
59 Dickerson, *A Hobbit Journey*, 152.

me that he was in peril. But he escaped in the end. I am glad. It was not in vain that the young hobbits came with us, if only for Boromir's sake."[60]). So Boromir is saved from being enslaved by the Ring; but it is providentially the hobbits Merry and Pippin, whose presence in the Fellowship was, from a purely calculating, political point of view, of questionable value at most, who become the instruments not only of Boromir's salvation but that of all of Middle-earth, insofar as their capture sets in motion a series of events that leads to the downfall of Saruman and, ultimately, his master, Sauron.

The Great Escape

After being rescued by Gandalf and the Eagles from the slopes of Mount Doom, Sam wakes up alongside Frodo in a soft bed on a sunny day in a beautiful forest setting only to see Gandalf himself, who he thought was dead. With an overjoyed shock, Sam blurts out: "Is everything sad going to come untrue?"[61] Here we have, as Shippey notes, a moment of pure eucatastrophe, a wholly unexpected, sudden, and unhoped-for turn toward pure joy.[62] But Sam's wording is curious: in the end it is not so much that sorrow and grief are false, but rather they become untrue—sadness and suffering indeed exist but belong to time and thus pass away, while joy is eternal and not only does not pass away but makes all that is contrary to itself untrue. It is myth, particularly the true myth of the Gospel, that reveals to us this fundamental truth. As Tom Shippey remarks, Tolkien's great sin against the modern literary establishment is not that he is an anti-modernist in style, but that he is

> on principle *not literary*. He used "mythical method" not because it was an interesting method but because he believed that the myths were true. He showed his characters wandering in the wilderness and entirely mistaken in their guesses not because he wanted to shatter the "realist illusion" of fiction, but because

60 *TT*, III, 5, 496.
61 *RK*, VI, 4, 951.
62 Shippey, *Author of the Century*, 207.

he thought all our views of reality *were* illusions, and that everyone is in a way wandering in a "bewilderment," lost in the star-occluding forest of Middle-earth.[63]

Tolkien wanted to show in his fiction that behind the "bewilderment" of temporal events is an eternal and meaningful pattern that works toward the good, because what is good is by its very nature eternal and unchanging. As Shippey, and before him Richard West, have shown, Tolkien creates this illusion of bewilderment through his use of interlacing technique,[64] which provides "a profound sense of reality, of that being *the way things are*. There *is* a pattern in Tolkien's story, but his characters can never see it (naturally, because they are in it)."[65]

What is remarkable and fascinating about this contrast between apparent confusion and bewilderment and underlying meaning and pattern is that Tolkien's own characters are aware of it. During a brief rest on their grueling ascent of the stairs of Cirith Ungol, Sam remarks to Frodo that perhaps they "have fallen into a tale," indeed, one of "the tales that really mattered, or the ones that stay in the mind":

---

63 Shippey, *Author of the Century*, 315.

64 "Interlacing" (*entrelacement*) is a technique whereby various strands in a story are developed separately and then cross over at various points in the narrative. Moreover, the strands are often not developed synchronously: one strand leaps ahead of the other in time so that when the reader returns to another strand, he or she has to go back in time. In *The Lord of the Rings*, we find this technique used at the start of the *Two Towers*: the Fellowship separates, with Aragorn, Legolas, and Gimli pursuing the Uruk Hai who have kidnapped Merry and Pippin; in the meantime, the reader leaves Frodo and Sam and is ignorant of what they are doing. Even within Book III, which follows the hunt of Aragorn and his companions for the hobbits, the action travels backward and forward depending on whether we are looking at events from the perspective of Aragorn or of the hobbits. Hence, the reader comes to share in the bewilderment of the characters, which only heightens a sense of tension, suspense, and realism, in addition to providing a great release of joy and insight at the end.

65 Shippey, *Author of the Century*, 107, and Richard C. West, "The Interlace Structure of *The Lord of the Rings*," in *A Tolkien Compass Revised Edition*, ed. Jared Lobdell (Chicago: Open Court, 2003), 75–91.

Folk seem to have just been landed in them, usually—their paths were laid that way, as you put it. But I expect they had lots of chances, like us, of turning back, only they didn't. And if they had, we shouldn't know, because they'd have been forgotten. We hear about those as just went on—and not all to a good end, mind you; at least not to what folk inside a story and not outside it call a good end. You know, coming home, and finding things all right, though not quite the same—like old Mr. Bilbo. But those aren't always the best tales to hear, though they may be the best tales to get landed in! I wonder what sort of tale we've fallen into?[66]

Perhaps, Sam muses, we are part of a story, one in which, he is careful to note, a good or happy end is not guaranteed, but a meaningful story nevertheless: one in which the path is "laid out," and yet in which the characters can and do make choices that lead either to eternal remembrance or to eternal oblivion (if they turn back). Frodo responds: "I wonder.... But I don't know. And that's the way of a real tale. Take any one that you're fond of. You may know, or guess, what kind of a tale it is, happy-ending or sad-ending, but people in it don't know. And you don't want them to."[67] While one is in the story (whether as character or reader, it doesn't matter), not only does one not know whether the ending is happy or sad, but one does not want the characters to know the ending, for that would deprive them not only of freedom but also of the joy of the happy ending. As Sam responds to Frodo: "Still, I wonder if we shall ever be put into songs or tales. We're in one, of course; but I mean: put into words, you know, told by the fireside, or read out of a great big book with red and black letters, years and years afterwards."[68] To this, Frodo replies: "You and I, Sam, are still stuck in

---

66 *TT*, IV, 8, 711–12.
67 *TT*, IV, 8, 712.
68 *TT*, IV, 8, 712. As Rachel Fulton Brown astutely observed in her podcast series *The Forge of Tolkien* (Episode 1: "What kind of story have we fallen into?"), it is significant that Tolkien writes that the story will be told in big books written in "red and black letters," for this refers in all probability to the liturgical books of the Catholic Church, both the *Missale Romanum* for the mass and the *Breviarium*

the worse places of the story, and it is all too likely that some will say at this point: 'Shut the book now, dad; we don't want to read any more'."[69] We may be stuck in the worst part of the story, Frodo is saying, yet take heart, the story is not over yet.

Indeed, although the story of *The Lord of the Rings* ends, and it ends with the passing of Frodo, Gandalf, Elrond, and Galadriel over the seas to the Undying Lands, Tolkien gives a strong sense that the story in some way continues and must continue. We know from *The Histories of Middle-earth* that as Tolkien continued to work on his mythology, he came to think more and more about the Final End of the Age or of the Last Things. From the very dark vision of *The Silmarillion*, at least as published by his son, Christopher, Tolkien began to think more and more of what an "Arda healed" would be like and how it would be healed.[70] Indeed, in *Morgoth's Ring*, Tolkien speculated, as we saw earlier, whether Arda would be healed or not by the very Author of the work entering into his creation himself and thus revealing to the characters within the work the Author's love for them and his desire to have them join him as real persons[71] in the eternity of the divine Fellowship.[72] In

---

Romanum. In the liturgy of the hours, the prayers are printed in black, while the rubrics (instructions for what to do) are printed in red (indeed, the word "rubric" means "red").

69 *TT*, IV, 8, 713.

70 Whittingham, *The Evolution of Tolkien's Mythology*, 191. In particular, Whittingham identifies four sources of hope that Tolkien speculates about in his later writings: 1) while Eru/Ilúvatar is remote, he is present to the world and does act; 2) Ilúvatar has the claim of sovereignty in the *Ainulindalë*; 3) as the *Athrabeth* insinuates, Ilúvatar will intervene again; 4) the day will come when Ilúvatar will provide themes for the choirs to sing in the Second Music, and this time it will be played aright. Whittingham, *The Evolution of Tolkien's Mythology*, 196–98.

71 "Real" relative to the stretched-out, temporal, and thus lesser reality we have in the Story.

72 "They still believe that Eru's healing of all the griefs of Arda will come now by or through Men; but the Elves' part in the healing or redemption will be chiefly in the restoration of the love of Arda, to which their memory of the Past and understanding of what might have been will contribute. Arda they say will be destroyed by wicked Men (or the wickedness in Men); but healed through the goodness in Men. The wickedness, the domineering lovelessness, the Elves will offset. By the holiness of good men—their direct attachment to Eru, before and

an argument very reminiscent of C. S. Lewis's "Argument by Natural Desire" (which is itself taken from classic theologians like Aquinas), Tolkien asserts that this natural desire to know and love the Author of our being and of the Story of which we are a part cannot be a vain desire, but one that is intrinsically ordered to a real object.[73] Thus, in describing the beliefs of the Elves, Tolkien writes:

> But *desires of the fëa* [soul] may often be shown to be reasonable by arguments quite unconnected with personal wish. The fact that they *accord* with "desire," or even with personal wish, does not invalidate them. Actually the Elves believed that the "lightening of the heart" or the "stirring of joy" (to which they often refer), which may accompany the hearing of a proposition or an argument, is not an indication of its falsity but of the recognition by the *fëa* that it is on the path of truth.[74]

The fairy-story, then, far from being a species of wishful thinking, gives us a glimpse of truth, because it fulfills in us a natural desire for immortality and infinite joy; it gives us a glimpse of a world that is not limited to or completely contained by the iron grip of mechanistic causation or the inevitable wearing-away of time. In thinking about the case of a sudden, miraculous cure of a boy at Lourdes while his train pulled away from the station after an apparently failed visit to the shrine, Tolkien writes in one his letters: "They [these sudden acts of miraculous grace] are intrusions (as we say, erring) into real or ordinary life, but they do intrude into real life, and so need ordinary means and other results." Tolkien continues:

---

above all Eru's works—the Elves may be delivered from the last of their griefs: sadness; the sadness that must come even from the unselfish love of anything less than Eru." *MR*, 343.

73 A natural desire for food, drink, or sex presupposes necessarily that there really exists food, drink, or sexual activity; an artificial desire, such as for a Ferrari or a pet unicorn, does not, by contrast, necessarily imply the existence of what would fulfill it. Our desire for supreme joy and immortality is a natural desire, one intrinsic to human willing and desire. Therefore …

74 *MR*, 343.

> For it I coined the world "eucatastrophe": the sudden happy turn in a story which pierces you with a joy that brings tears (which I argued it is the highest function of fairy-stories to produce). And I was there led to the view that it produces its peculiar effect because it is a sudden glimpse of Truth, your whole nature chained in material cause and effect, the chain of death, feels a sudden relief as if a major limb out of joint had suddenly snapped back. It perceives—if the story has literary "truth" in the second plane (for which see the essay ["On Fairy-stories"])—and this is indeed how things really do work in the Great World for which our nature is made. And I concluded by saying that the Resurrection was the greatest "eucatastrophe" possible in the greatest Fairy Story—and produces the essential emotion: Christian joy which produces tears because it is qualitatively so like sorrow, because it comes from those places where Joy and Sorrow are at one, reconciled as selfishness and altruism are lost in Love.[75]

The truth of the fairy-story is produced precisely by the fact that it makes the release from "material cause and effect" not only plausible but even more rational and coherent than any mechanistic view of reality. It satisfies a desire by fulfilling that desire like a "limb out of joint had suddenly snapped back." And yet, it depends upon and even must affirm the ordinary for this glimpse of truth to be possible, because it is in the ordinary and lowly that, as we have seen, eternal value and meaning are revealed.

If this is true of material cause and effect, it is true *a fortiori* of death. The fairy-story, by its leading to an inevitable happy ending, reveals that death is not the final end after all, but that temporality and death are themselves but modes in and through which the eternal reveals itself and gathers temporal being into itself. This is what makes, again, the Christian Gospel the consummate fairy-story: it reveals that out of suffering, darkness, and death there springs forth infinite joy and light, and that in fact this infinite joy and light would not be possible

---

75 *Letters*, 100.

were it not for the overcoming of the suffering and darkness of death. It is a twist or turn (strophe) that, Tolkien asserts, neither he nor the most imaginative human being could have come up with, because it is so contrary to our expectations:

> The Incarnation of God is an *infinitely* greater thing than anything I would dare to write. Here I am only concerned with Death as part of the nature, physical and spiritual, of Man, and with Hope without guarantees. That is why I regard the tale of Arwen and Aragorn as the most important of the Appendices; it is part of the essential story, and is only placed so, because it could not be worked into the main narrative without destroying its structure: which is planned to be "hobbito-centric," that is, primarily a study of the ennoblement (or sanctification) of the humble.[76]

"Hope without guarantees": that the love between Arwen and Aragorn manifests this sort of hope is therefore central to the story of *The Lord of the Rings*, even though, as Tolkien here notes, he could find no way of working it into the main narrative.[77] The love between Aragorn and Arwen is based almost entirely on the hope that there is a great escape from death. Indeed, Arwen manifests hope even more than Aragorn, because she, unlike Aragorn, freely chooses mortality and therefore stakes her entire existence on this hope. The love between Arwen and Aragorn is also for Tolkien a template for all genuine love, as all genuine love is also a love for the eternal in each and every one of us. That is, all genuine love is based on the love that the Author of all creation has for his finite and mortal creatures, for it shows how it is possible for someone to give up an immortal life so that his mortal characters might share in his own immortality as Author of the story.

---

76 *Letters*, 237.

77 In this respect Peter Jackson's film adaptations, which weave the love story of Aragorn and Arwen into the main action of the story, are quite faithful to Tolkien's intentions and restore an essential element that Tolkien regretted being unable to integrate into the body of *The Lord of the Rings* (even if this was done by Jackson primarily to attract a wider audience).

There is no character that is more changed and sanctified in the story, however, than Frodo.[78] Indeed, Frodo is so changed that paradoxically he cannot enjoy the happy ending. This fact is one of the most remarkable features of Tolkien's tale: the supposedly happy ending of *The Lord of the Rings* is far from clear and unambiguous. Anyone who has read *The Lord of the Rings* with attention and sensitivity will notice the unique mingling of sadness and joy at the end. This is as it should be, if we take Tolkien at his word in his essay "On Fairy-stories," for there he asserts that the happy ending of the fairy-story brings an experience of joy so deep that it is indeed a feeling akin to grief or sorrow. Why is this the case, and if it is so, then how can we even talk of a happy ending?

First, as Tolkien repeatedly emphasizes, the eucatastrophe or sudden turn to joy is premised on darkness and suffering: there can only be a sudden and unexpected turn to joy when all seems hopeless and lost. Frodo has suffered too much for there to be any adequate compensation for it in this world of time:

> "There is no real going back. Though I may come to the Shire, it will not seem the same; for I shall not be the same. I am wounded with knife, sting, and tooth, and a long burden. Where shall I find rest?"
> Gandalf did not answer.[79]

---

[78] One must, however, mention that the Elves too have to make a heavy sacrifice. They must make a decision between two almost equally bad alternatives: take the Ring and use it against Sauron, and by doing so plunge all of Middle-earth into evil and darkness, or destroy the Ring but see the power of the three elven rings, which were linked at their creation to the One Ring, wane and have the ineffable beauty and blessedness of the Elven realms pass away forever from Middle-earth. Galadriel puts this choice succinctly in her response to Frodo offering her the Ring: "Do you not see now wherefore your coming is to us as the footstep of Doom? For if you fail, then we are laid bare to the Enemy. Yet if you succeed, then our power is diminished, and Lothlorien will fade, and the tides of Time will sweep it away. We must depart into the West, or dwindle to a rustic folk of dell and cave, slowly to forget and to be forgotten." *FR*, II, 7. Thus, in Tolkien's fantasy, the happy ending must always be bought at the loss and fading away of much that was beautiful and good in time.

[79] *RK*, VI, 7, 989.

Frodo has been changed by the Ring not only psychically, but also ontologically (as Gandalf observes Frodo in the House of Elrond, he perceives a barely noticeable "transparency" about Frodo's very body): his very nature has been stretched out by the Ring and is therefore taken out of the natural and temporal order of the beings around him, particularly his fellow hobbits. The Ring has, in a sense, rendered him unnatural. Even more deeply, as alluded to above, Frodo's sense of time has radically changed, such that as they return to the Shire, Merry remarks how everything that they have undergone seems like a dream, but for Frodo, it feels quite the opposite: it is ordinary life in the Shire that seems like a dream:

> "Well here we are, just the four of us that started out together", said Merry. 'We have left all the rest behind, one after another. It seems almost like a dream that has slowly faded".
>
> "Not to me", said Frodo. "To me it feels more like falling asleep again".[80]

What Frodo discovers is that there is indeed a happy ending, but not for him *in time*. Responding to Sam asking whether he thought he might be happy settling back into his home in the Shire, Frodo says:

> So I thought too, once. But I have been too deeply hurt, Sam. I tried to save the Shire, and it has been saved, but not for me. It must often be so, Sam, when things are in danger: some one has to give them up, lose them, so that others may keep them. But you are my heir: all that I had and might have had I leave to you.[81]

Time now is a burden and even a torment to Frodo, just as it was to the Ringwraiths; he can therefore not go back to the way things were. Unlike the Ringwraiths, however, Frodo has been redeemed by his selfless sacrifice for others. Thus, what might be a source of torment (his ontological and temporal thinning out and transparency) now produces a greater capacity for being filled with light and infinite joy, for

---

80 *RK*, VI, 7, 997. Once again, Rachel Fulton Brown, in her podcast, *Forge of Tolkien* (Episode 10, "Falling Wide Asleep") brought my attention to this detail in the story.

81 *RK*, VI, 9, 1029.

now Frodo's being has been deepened and widened both ontologically and temporally. He is therefore able to make the journey on one of the last ships to sail to the Undying Lands in the West. Indeed, once Frodo sets sail, the reader gets a final glimpse of the final joy, light, and beauty that awaits those who courageously hope:

> And the ship went out into the High Sea and passed on into the West, until at last on a night of rain Frodo smelled a sweet fragrance on the air and heard the sound of singing that came over the water. And then it seemed to him that as in his dream in the house of Bombadil, the grey rain-curtain turned all to silver glass and was rolled back, and he beheld white shores and beyond them a far green country under a swift sunrise.[82]

Tolkien concludes that Frodo left "filled with a sadness that was yet blessed and without bitterness."[83] The infinite depths of perfect joy can only be experienced through the nihilating force of infinite sorrow. In this context it is worth repeating a passage that we cited before, from a letter that Tolkien wrote to his son Michael while the latter was having a crisis of faith:

> Out of the darkness of my life, so much frustrated, I put before you the one great thing to love on earth: the Blessed Sacrament.... There you will find romance, glory, honour, fidelity, and the true way of all your loves upon earth, and more than that: Death: by the divine paradox, that which ends life, and demands surrender of all, and yet by the taste (or foretaste) of which alone can what you seek in your earthly relationships (love, faithfulness, joy) be maintained, or take on the complexion of reality, of eternal endurance, which every man's heart desires.[84]

The great divine paradox is that only in suffering the complete loss of our finite and temporal being do our deepest desires transcend time and

---

82 *RK*, VI, 9, 1030.
83 *RK*, VI, 9.
84 *Letters*, 53–54.

take on "the complexion of reality, of eternal endurance." This is what Tolkien's sub-creation is designed to help us see and experience; indeed, this for Tolkien is the entire purpose of literature itself:

> If lit. teaches us anything at all, it is this: that we have in us *an eternal element*, free from care and fear, which can survey things that in "life" we call evil with serenity (that is not without appreciating their [evil] quality, but without any disturbance of our spiritual equilibrium). Not in the same way, but in some such way, we shall all doubtless survey our own story when we know it (and a great deal more of the Whole Story).[85]

In a way, Sam provides the needed completion of Frodo's story, for it is in Sam's return to the Shire (the final words of *The Lord of the Rings*, "I'm back") and to his family, in the renewal of the Shire through his planting of the Mallorn tree in place of the old Party Tree and his planting of trees throughout the Shire with the seeds and soil gifted to him by Galadriel, that we see the full eucatastrophic ending of *The Lord of the Rings*. With Sam, the reader attains that final serenity that good literature provides, and it is through Sam—not only for the reader but in the events subsequent to the War of the Ring themselves—that we find a survey of "our own story when we know it (and a great deal more of the Whole Story)."

---

85 *Letters*, 106–7. Emphasis added.

BIBLIOGRAPHY

Works Written, Edited, or Translated by J. R. R. Tolkien

Ancrene Wisse: The English Text of the Ancrene Riwle. Edited by J. R. R. Tolkien. London: Oxford University Press, 1962.

The Book of Lost Tales, Part One, "The History of Middle Earth, I." Edited by Christopher Tolkien. New York: Houghton-Mifflin-Harcourt, 1983.

The Book of Lost Tales, Part Two, "The History of Middle Earth, II." Edited by Christopher Tolkien. New York: Houghton-Mifflin-Harcourt, 1984.

The Hobbit: Or There and Back Again. New York: Ballantine Books, 1973.

The Letters of J. R. R. Tolkien. Edited by Humphrey Carpenter (with the assistance of Christopher Tolkien). New York: Houghton-Mifflin, 2000.

The Lord of the Rings. New York: Houghton-Mifflin, 2004.

The Lost Road (and Other Writings). Edited by Christopher Tolkien. New York: Houghton-Mifflin, 1987.

The Monsters and the Critics and Other Essays. Edited by Christopher Tolkien. New York: Houghton-Mifflin, 1984.

Morgoth's Ring: The Later Silmarillion, Part One: The Legends of Aman, "The History of Middle-earth X." Edited by Christopher Tolkien. New York: Houghton-Mifflin-Harcourt, 1993.

The Nature of Middle-earth: Late Writings on the Lands, Inhabitants, and Metaphysics of Middle-earth. Edited by Carl F. Hostetter. New York: Houghton-Mifflin, 2021.

Sauron Defeated: The End of the Third Age, "The History of Middle-earth IX." Edited by Christopher Tolkien. New York: Houghton-Mifflin-Harcourt, 1992.
The Silmarillion. Edited by Christopher Tolkien. New York: Houghton-Mifflin, 1999.
Sir Gawain and the Green Knight, Pearl, Sir Orfeo. Translated by J. R. R. Tolkien. New York: Ballantine Books, 1975.
Tree and Leaf (including Mythopoeia and The Homecoming of Beorhtnoth). New York: Harper-Collins, 2001.
Unfinished Tales: The Lost Lore of Middle-earth. Edited by Christopher Tolkien. New York: Ballantine Books, 1980.

Secondary Literature

Agóy, Nils Avar. "The Christian Tolkien: A Response to Ronald Hutton." In *The Ring and the Cross: Christianity and* The Lord of the Rings, edited by Paul E. Kerry, 71–89. Madison, NJ: Fairleigh Dickinson University Press, 2011.
Aquinas, Thomas. *Quaestiones disputatae de veritate.* Edited by Raymond Spiazzi, OP. Rome: Marietti, 1964.
———. *Summa theologiae.* Madrid: Biblioteca de Autores Cristianos, 1994.
Augustine. *Confessions, Vol. 1: Introduction and Text.* Edited by James O'Donnell. Oxford: Oxford University Press, 2012.
Baltasar, Michaela. "J. R. R. Tolkien: A Rediscovery of Myth." In *Tolkien and the Invention of Myth: A Reader*, edited by Jane Chance, 19–34. Lexington, KY: University Press of Kentucky, 2004.
Barfield, Owen. *Poetic Diction: A Study in Meaning.* Middletown, CT: Wesleyan University Press, 1973.
———. *Saving the Appearances: A Study in Idolatry.* Middletown, CT: Wesleyan University Press, 1988.
Basney, Lionel. "Myth, History, and Time in *The Lord of the Rings*." In *Understanding* The Lord of the Rings*: The Best of Tolkien Criticism*, edited by Rose Zimbardo and Neil Isaacs, 183–94. New York: Houghton-Mifflin, 2004.

Bassham, Gregory. "Tolkien's Six Keys to Happiness." In The Lord of the Rings *and Philosophy: One Book to Rule Them All*, edited by Gregory Bassham and Eric Bronson, 49–60. Chicago: Open Court Publishing, 2003.

Bassham, Gregory, and Eric Bronson, eds. The Lord of the Rings *and Philosophy: One Book to Rule Them All*. Chicago: Open Court Publishing, 2003.

Bernthal, Craig. *Tolkien's Sacramental Vision: Discerning the Holy in Middle Earth*. Kettering, OH: Angelico Press, 2014.

Birzer, Bradley J. *J. R. R. Tolkien's Sanctifying Myth: Understanding Middle-earth*. Wilmington, DE: ISI Books, 2003.

———. "The 'Last Battle' as a Johannine Ragnarök: Tolkien and the Universal." In Kerry, *The Ring and the Cross*, 259–82.

Boethius. *Philosophiae consolatio, libri quinque*. Edited by Karl Büchner. Heidelberg: Carl Winter Verlag, 1977.

Brague, Rémi. *Le propre de l'homme: Sur une légitimité menacée*. Paris: Flammarion, 2015.

———. *La sagesse du monde: Histoire de l'expérience humaine de l'univers*. Paris: Fayard, 1999.

Bratman, David. "The Inklings and Others: Tolkien and His Contemporaries." In *A Companion to J. R. R. Tolkien*, edited by Stuart Lee, 317–34. Hoboken, NJ: Wiley-Blackwell Publishing, 2020.

Brown, Rachel Fulton. *The Forge of Tolkien* (podcast). January 29, 2022, https://fencingbearatprayer.blogspot.com/2020/08/the-forge-of-tolkien.html.

Burns, Marjorie J. "Norse and Christian Gods: The Integrative Theology of J. R. R. Tolkien." In Chance, *Tolkien and the Invention of Myth*, 163–79.

Caldecott, Stratford. *The Power of the Ring: The Spiritual Vision Behind The Lord of the Rings and The Hobbit*. New York: Crossroad Publishing, 2012.

Campbell, Liam. "Nature." In Lee, *A Companion to J. R. R. Tolkien*, 431–45.

Candler, Peter M., Jr. "Tolkien or Nietzsche; Philology and Nihilism." In *Tolkien among the Moderns*, edited by Ralph C. Wood, 95–130. Notre Dame, IN: University of Notre Dame Press, 2015.

Carpenter, Humphrey. *Tolkien: A Biography*. New York: Houghton-Mifflin, 2000.
Caughey, Anna. "The Hero's Journey." In Lee, *A Companion to J. R. R. Tolkien*, 404–17.
Chance, Jane. *The Lord of the Rings: The Mythology of Power*. New York: Twayne Publishers, 1992.
———, ed. *Tolkien and the Invention of Myth: A Reader*. Lexington, KY: University Press of Kentucky, 2004.
———, ed. *Tolkien the Medievalist*. New York: Routledge, 2003.
Chesterton, Gilbert Keith. *Orthodoxy*. San Francisco: Ignatius Press, 1995.
Clarke, W. Norris, SJ. *The One and the Many: A Contemporary Thomistic Metaphysics*. Notre Dame, IN: University of Notre Dame Press, 2001.
Croft, Janet Brennan. "War." In Lee, *A Companion to J. R. R. Tolkien*, 461–72.
Curry, Patrick. "The Critical Response to Tolkien's Fiction." In Lee, *A Companion to J. R. R. Tolkien*, 369–88.
———. *Defending Middle Earth: Tolkien, Myth and Modernity*. New York: Houghton-Mifflin, 2004.
Davenport, John J. "Happy Endings and Religious Hope: *The Lord of the Rings* as an Epic Fairy Tale." In Bassham and Bronson, The Lord of the Rings *and Philosophy*, 204–18.
Davis, Bill. "Choosing to Die: The Gift of Mortality in Middle-earth." In Bassham and Bronson, The Lord of the Rings *and Philosophy*, 123–36.
Davison, Scott A. "Tolkien and the Nature of Evil." In Bassham and Bronson, The Lord of the Rings *and Philosophy*, 99–109.
Descartes, René. *Discours de la Méthode*. Paris: Bordas, 1984.
Dickerson, Matthew. *A Hobbit Journey: Discovering the Enchantment of J. R. R. Tolkien's Middle-earth*. Grand Rapids, MI: Brazos Press, 2012.
Dobie, Robert. "Meister Eckhart: From Latin Scholasticism to German Mysticism." In *A Companion to World Literature: Volume 2, 601 CE to 1450*, edited by Ken Signeurie and Christine Chism, 897–908. Hoboken, NJ: Wiley-Blackwell Publishing, 2020.

Donovan, Leslie A. "Middle-earth Mythology: An Overview." In Lee, *A Companion to J. R. R. Tolkien*, 92–106.

Dubs, Kathleen E. "Providence, Fate, and Chance: Boethian Philosophy in *The Lord of the Rings*." In Chance, *Tolkien and the Invention of Myth*, 133–42.

Duriez, Colin. "Where Two or Three Are Gathered: Tolkien and the Inklings." In *Light beyond All Shadow: Religious Experience in Tolkien's Work*, edited by Paul E. Kerry and Sandra Miesel, 153–70. Madison, NJ: Fairleigh Dickinson University Press, 2011.

Eckhart, Meister. *Die deutschen werke*. Edited by Josef Quint. 5 vols. Stuttgart: Kohlhammer Verlag, 1936.

Eden, Brad. "'The Music of the Spheres': Relationships between Tolkien's *The Silmarillion* and Medieval Cosmological and Religious Theory." In Chance, *Tolkien the Medievalist*, 183–93.

Eilmann, Julian Tim Morton. "I Am the Song: Music, Poetry, and the Transcendent in J. R. R. Tolkien's Middle-earth." In Kerry and Miesel, *Light beyond All Shadow*, 99–117.

Evans, Jonathan. "The Anthropology of Arda: Creation, Theology, and the Race of Men." In Chance, *Tolkien the Medievalist*, 194–224.

Feser, Edward. *Aristotle's Revenge: The Metaphysical Foundations of Physical and Biological Science*. Neukirchen-Seelscheid: Editiones Scholasticae, 2019.

Fimi, Dimitra. *Tolkien, Race and Cultural History: From Faeries to Hobbits*. New York: Palgrave Macmillan, 2009.

Flieger, Verlyn. "Frodo and Aragorn: The Concept of the Hero." In Zimbardo and Isaacs, *Understanding* The Lord of the Rings, 122–45.

———. *Interrupted Music: The Making of Tolkien's Mythology*. Kent: Kent State University Press, 2005.

———. "'The Lost Road' and 'The Notion Club Papers': Myth, History, and Time-travel." In Lee, *A Companion to J. R. R. Tolkien*, 161–72.

———. *A Question of Time: J. R. R. Tolkien's Road to Faerie*. Kent: Kent State University Press, 1997.

———. *Splintered Light: Logos and Language in Tolkien's World*, rev. ed. Kent: Kent State University Press, 2002.

Frankl, Viktor. *Man's Search for Meaning.* Translated by Ilse Lasch. Boston: Beacon Press, 2006.

Freeh, Helen Lasseter. "On Fate, Providence, and Free Will in *The Silmarillion.*" In Wood, *Tolkien among the Moderns*, 51–77.

Freeman, Austin M. *Tolkien Dogmatics: Theology through Mythology with the Maker of Middle-earth.* Bellingham, WA: Lexham Press, 2022.

Garbowski, Christopher. "Evil." In Lee, *A Companion to J. R. R. Tolkien*, 418–30.

Gracia, Jorge J. E. "The Quests of Sam and Gollum for the Happy Life." In Bassham and Bronson, The Lord of the Rings *and Philosophy*, 61–71.

Hadot, Pierre. *Le voile d'Isis: Essai sur l'historie de l'idée de nature.* Paris: Gallimard, 2004.

Halsall, Michael John. *Creation and Beauty in Tolkien's Catholic Vision: A Study in the Influence of Neoplatonism in J. R. R. Tolkien's Philosophy of Life as "Being and Gift."* Eugene, OR: Pickwick Publications, 2020.

Hannam, James. *God's Philosophers: How the Medieval World Laid the Foundations of Modern Science.* London: Icon Books, 2009.

Hibbs, Thomas. "Providence and the Dramatic Unity of *The Lord of the Rings.*" In Bassham and Bronson, The Lord of the Rings *and Philosophy*, 167–78.

Holloway, Carson L. "Redeeming Sub-Creation." In Kerry, *The Ring and the Cross*, 177–92.

Holmes, John R. "'Like Heathen Kings': Religion as Palimpsest in Tolkien's Fiction." In Kerry, *The Ring and the Cross*, 119–44.

———. "*The Lord of the Rings.*" In Lee, *A Companion to J. R. R. Tolkien*, 133–45.

Honegger, Thomas. "Academic Writings." In Lee, *A Companion to J. R. R. Tolkien*, 27–40.

Houghton, John William. "Augustine in the Cottage of Lost Play: The *Ainulindalë* as Asterisk Cosmogony." In Chance, *Tolkien the Medievalist*, 171–82.

Hutton, Ronald. "The Pagan Tolkien." In Kerry, *The Ring and the Cross*, 57–70.

Imbert, Yannick. *From Imagination to Faërie: Tolkien's Thomist Fantasy*. Eugene, OR: Pickwick Publications, 2022.
Jonas, Hans. *The Gnostic Religion: The Message of the Alien God and the Beginnings of Christianity*, 2nd ed. Boston: Beacon Press, 1958.
———. *The Phenomenon of Life: Towards a Philosophical Biology*. Evanston, IL: Northwestern University Press, 2001.
Kant, Immanuel. *Critique of Pure Reason*, translated by Norman Kemp Smith. New York: St. Martin's Press, 1965.
Katz, Eric. "The Rings of Tolkien and Plato: Lessons in Power, Choice, and Morality." In Bassham and Bronson, The Lord of the Rings *and Philosophy*, 5–20.
Kerry, Paul E., ed. *The Ring and the Cross: Christianity and* The Lord of the Rings. Madison, NJ: Fairleigh Dickinson University Press, 2011.
Kerry, Paul E., and Sandra Miesel, eds. *Light beyond All Shadow: Religious Experience in Tolkien's Work*. Madison, NJ: Fairleigh Dickinson University Press, 2011.
Kohak, Erazim. *The Embers and the Stars: A Philosophical Inquiry into the Moral Sense of Nature*. Chicago: University of Chicago Press, 1984.
Kraus, Joe. "Tolkien, Modernism, and the Importance of Tradition." In Bassham and Bronson, The Lord of the Rings *and Philosophy*, 137–49.
Kreeft, Peter. *Love Is Stronger than Death*. San Francisco: Ignatius Press, 1992.
———. *The Philosophy of Tolkien: The Worldview behind* The Lord of the Rings. San Francisco: Ignatius Press, 2005.
Lee, Stuart, ed. *A Companion to J. R. R. Tolkien*. Hoboken, NJ: Wiley-Blackwell Publishing, 2020.
Libera, Alain de. *La philosophie médiévale*. Paris: Presses universitaires de France, 2021.
Lobdell, Jared, ed. *A Tolkien Compass*, rev. ed. Chicago: Open Court Publishing, 2003.
———. "*Ymagynatyf* and J. R. R. Tolkien's Roman Catholicism, Catholic Theology, and Religion in *The Lord of the Rings*." In Kerry and Miesel, *Light beyond All Shadow*, 79–97.

Madsen, Catherine. "Eru Erased: The Minimalist Cosmology of *The Lord of the Rings*." In Kerry, *The Ring and the Cross*, 152–69.
McIntosh, Jonathan S. *The Flame Imperishable: Tolkien, St. Thomas, and the Metaphysics of Faërie*. Kettering, OH: Angelico Press, 2017.
Merleau-Ponty, Maurice. *Phénoménologie de la perception*. Paris: Editions Gallimard, 1945.
Miesel, Sandra A. "Life-giving Ladies: Women in the Writings of J. R. R. Tolkien." In Kerry and Miesel, *Light beyond All Shadow*, 139–52.
Milbank, Alison. *Chesterton and Tolkien as Theologians: The Fantasy of the Real*. London: T. and T. Clark, 2007.
———. "'My Precious': Tolkien's Fetishized Ring." In Bassham and Bronson, *The Lord of the Rings and Philosophy*, 33–45.
Miller, David M. "Narrative Pattern in *The Fellowship of the Ring*." In Lobdell, *A Tolkien Compass*, 93–103.
Morillo, Stephen. "The Entwives: Investigating the Spiritual Core of *The Lord of the Rings*." In Kerry, *The Ring and the Cross*, 106–18.
Nagy, Gergely. "The Silmarillion: Tolkien's Theory of Myth, Text, and Culture." In Lee, *A Companion to J. R. R. Tolkien*, 107–18.
Nietzsche, Friedrich. *The Genealogy of Morality*, translated by Maudemarie Clarke and Alan J. Swensen. Indianapolis: Hackett Publishing, 1998.
Ordway, Holly. *Tolkien's Faith: A Spiritual Biography*. Elk Grove Village, IL: Word on Fire Academic, 2023.
———. *Tolkien's Modern Reading: Middle-earth beyond the Middle Ages*. Park Ridge, IL: Word on Fire Academic, 2021.
Pearce, Joseph. "*The Lord of the Rings* and the Catholic Understanding of Community." In Kerry, *The Ring and the Cross*, 224–33.
———. *Tolkien, Man and Myth: A Literary Life*. San Francisco: Ignatius Press, 1998.
Phelpstead, Carl. "Myth-making and Sub-creation." In Lee, *A Companion to J. R. R. Tolkien*, 79–91.
Reilly, R. J. "Tolkien and the Fairy Story." In Zimbardo and Isaacs, *Understanding* The Lord of the Rings: *The Best of Tolkien Criticism*, 93–105.

Roberts, Adam. "Women." In Lee, *A Companion to J. R. R. Tolkien*, 473–86.
Rogers, Deborah C. "Everyclod and Everyhero: The Image of Man in Tolkien." In Lobdell, *A Tolkien Compass*, 67–73.
Rose, Mary Carman. "The Christian Platonism of C. S. Lewis, J. R. R. Tolkien and Charles Williams." In *Neoplatonism and Christian Thought*, edited by Dominic J. O'Meara, 203–12. Albany, NY: SUNY Press, 1982.
Saussure, Ferdinand de. *Cours de linguistique générale*. Edited by Charles Bally et al. Paris: Payot, 1964.
Scheler, Max. *Ressentiment*. Translated by Lewis B. Caser and William W. Holdheim. Milwaukee, WI: Marquette University Press, 2007.
Scheps, Walter. "The Fairy-tale Morality of *The Lord of the Rings*." In Lobdell, *A Tolkien Compass*, 41–53.
Schick, Theodore. "The Cracks of Doom: The Threat of Emerging Technologies and Tolkien's Rings of Power." In Bassham and Bronson, The Lord of the Rings *and Philosophy*, 21–32.
Scull, Christina, and Wayne G. Hammond. *The J. R. R. Tolkien Companion and Guide: Reader's Guide*. 2 vols. London: Harpers Collins, 2017.
Shippey, Tom. *J. R. R. Tolkien: Author of the Century*. New York: Houghton-Mifflin, 2000.
———. *The Road to Middle-earth: How J. R. R. Tolkien Created a New Mythology*. New York: Houghton-Mifflin, 2003.
Skoble, Aeon J. "Virtue and Vice in *The Lord of the Rings*." In Bassham and Bronson, The Lord of the Rings *and Philosophy*, 110–19.
Spacks, Patricia Meyer. "Power and Meaning in *The Lord of the Rings*." In Zimbardo and Isaacs, *Understanding* The Lord of the Rings, 52–67.
Stanton, Michael N. *Hobbits, Elves and Wizards: Exploring the Wonders and Worlds of J. R. R. Tolkien's* The Lord of the Rings. New York: Palgrave-MacMillan, 2002.
Straubhaar, Sandra Ballif. "Myth, Late Roman History, and Multiculturalism in Tolkien's Middle-earth." In Chance, *Tolkien and the Invention of Myth*, 101–17.

Tomko, Michael. "'An Age Comes On': J. R. R. Tolkien and the English Catholic Sense of History." In Kerry, *The Ring and the Cross*, 205–23.

Vaninskaya, Anna. "Tolkien and His Contemporaries." In Lee, *A Companion to J. R. R. Tolkien*, 350–66.

Veldman, Meredith. *Fantasy, the Bomb, and the Greening of Britain: Romantic Protest, 1945–1980*. Cambridge: Cambridge University Press, 1994.

Voegelin, Eric. *The New Science of Politics: An Introduction*. Chicago: University of Chicago Press, 1987.

———. *Science, Politics, and Gnosticism*. Wilmington, DE: ISI Books, 2004.

West, Richard C. "The Interlace Structure of *The Lord of the Rings*." In Lobdell, *A Tolkien Compass*, 75–91.

Whittingham, Elizabeth A. *The Evolution of Tolkien's Mythology: A Study of the History of Middle-earth*. Jefferson, NC: MacFarland, 2008.

———. "*Unfinished Tales* and the History of Middle-earth: A Lifetime of Imagination." In Lee, *A Companion to J. R. R. Tolkien*, 146–60.

Wood, Ralph C. "Confronting the World's Weirdness: J. R. R. Tolkien's *The Children of Hurin*." In Kerry, *The Ring and the Cross*, 145–51.

———, ed. *Tolkien among the Moderns*. Notre Dame, IN: University of Notre Dame Press, 2015.

———. "Tolkien and Postmodernism." In Wood, *Tolkien among the Moderns*, 247–77.

Zimbardo, Rose A. "Moral Vision in *The Lord of the Rings*." In Zimbardo and Isaacs, *Understanding* The Lord of the Rings, 68–75.

Zimbardo, Rose, and Neil Isaacs. *Understanding* The Lord of the Rings*: The Best of Tolkien Criticism*. New York: Houghton-Mifflin, 2004.

INDEX

Adam, 53
Aeviternity, 190n27, 205
Ages of Middle-earth, 121, 206; end of the ages (Last Things), 233; First Age, 49–50; Second Age, 50, 52; Third Age, 123n50
Agøy, Nils Avar, 119n36
Ainulindalë, 107, 109
Ainur, 13, 108–10, 112, 136–37
Akallabêth ("Downfall"), 52, 65
Allegory, 9–10, 140–41, 180
Amon Hen, 225
Anarchy, 157–58
Ancrene Wisse, 198n51
Angels, 114; and Elves, 190; guardian, 118
Aquinas, Thomas, 19, 71, 84–85, 89–90, 35n23, 141n14, 197, 198–201, 234. *See also* Thomism/Thomistic
Aragorn, 57–58, 101, 103, 128, 129, 130, 155, 168, 173, 176, 181, 223, 226, 236; and Arwen, 191, 196–97; and Boromir, 229
Arda, 111–12, 114, 116, 136, 137, 167, 192–93; Arda "healed," 233–34

Aristotle, 67, 88, 105–6, 149, 186; Aristotelian-Thomistic Tradition, 159; *Physics*, 105n1
Arnor, 56, 151, 176
Ar-Pharazôn, 53, 55, 187
Arthur, King, 92n41, 195; Arthurian legends, 29
Athrabeth Finrod Ab Andreth, 191–96
Auden, W. H., 10, 123
Augustine/Augustinian, 71, 74, 104, 133, 199–200, 201, 221
Authorship, 13–14, 233–34

Bacon, Francis, 67n45
Balrog, 129, 131
Barad-dûr, 206
Barfield, Owen, 80–81, 85–90, 93, 97, 98; *Poetic Diction*, 81, 85; *Saving the Appearances*, 89
Barrow Downs, 121
Barrow Wights, 206
Basney, Lionel, 100, 102
Battle of the Pelennor Fields, 210
Beare, Rhona, 59
Being, 93–95
Bëor, 53n14
Beowulf, 95, 130–32, 224

Beren and Luthien, 157, 177–78, 191
Bernthal, Craig, 97, 98, 142n16, 148
Bilbo, 57, 164–65, 182, 228, 232
Birzer, Bradley, 40, 219
Boethius, 19n49, 74n64, 198, 199, 210, 221, 224
Boromir, 151, 168; and Aragorn, 229, 230
Bratman, David, 132
Bree/Breeland/Breelanders, 58, 79n5, 130, 139, 151
Brown, Rachel Fulton, 232n68, 238n80
Butterbur, Barliman, 130

Caldecott, Stratford, 40, 60, 96, 110, 123, 130, 154, 164, 167, 173, 188n20, 196, 202, 204
Campbell, Liam, 114
Caradhras, 122, 129
Carn Dûm, 206
Catholic faith, 12, 18, 44, 221. *See also* Christianity
Celeborn, 96n53, 100, 126
Celtic, 79n5
Chesterton, G. K./Chestertonian, 37n28, 101, 151–52, 155; and Belloc, Hilaire, 150
Children of Ilúvatar, 111–12, 114, 116, 121
Christ, Jesus, 42–43, 66, 95–96, 112, 178, 201
Christianity, 115, 99, 103, 193; and myth, 111; and paganism, 44–45, 119–21, 161; and spirituality, 220n35. *See also* Catholic faith
Cirith Ungol, 154, 170, 210, 231. *See also* Watcher
Clarke, Norris, 185

Clement of Alexandria, 44n45
Coleridge, Samuel Taylor, 31n15
Consolation. *See* Eucatastrophe
Council of Elrond, 144
Creation, story of, 107–12, 218
Curry, Patrick, 121, 220n35

Davenport, John, 154
Davis, Bill, 185, 186, 187
Davison, Scott, 154
Dawson, Christopher, 104
Dead Marshes, 122
Death, 1, 10, 16–17, 41, 47–48, 152, 178, 179–80, 186–97, 235–36, 239
Democracy, 150–51; of the dead, 151
Denethor, 100, 103, 133, 151, 153–54, 222–23
Descartes/Cartesian, 66–67, 72, 83, 97, 106, 201
Dickerson, Matthew, 110, 211, 229
Distributism, 150
Dol Guldur, 127
Donovan, Leslie, 115, 235
Dragons, 130
Dunadain, 52n11, 56
Duriez, Colin, 86
Dwarves, 115, 138
Dyson, Hugo, 15

Eä, 111
Eagles, 130
Elrond, 75, 96n53, 153, 168, 212
Elves (Eldar), 41, 49–52, 54, 62, 70, 91, 115–16, 127, 133, 137–38, 145–47, 153, 188–91, 193–95, 233–34; sacrifice of, 237n78
Ents, 102, 118n35, 132–33, 138
Eomer, 101
Eowyn, 173–74, 175

Eriugena, John Scotus, 19n49, 124n54
Eru (Ilúvatar), 13, 49, 53, 54, 107–10, 111–12, 119n36, 136, 193; as author, 194, 233
Escape, 38–41
Esperanto, 77–78
Eternity, 23, 56, 184, 198–202, 204–5. *See also* Time
Eucatastrophe, 41–42, 229–30, 235, 237
Evil, 16–17, 69, 70–76, 133–34, 136, 142n16, 154, 166, 227, 240
Existentialism, 187n18

Faërie, 129–32
Fairy-stories, 25–29, 31–34, 36, 38–39, 41–43, 45, 131n78, 218, 235; "On Fairy Stories" (Tolkien), 25–29, 45, 69n50, 81, 85n19, 87, 103, 117, 235, 237
Fall, the, 47–57, 117, 145, 151, 171–72, 182, 188; of the Elves, 191; of Melkor and the angels, 111
Fangorn, 102, 122, 126, 128–29
Faramir, 100, 152, 153, 164, 166, 174, 175
Farmer Cotton, 155
Farmer Maggot, 144
Fëanor, 50
Felagund, 53n14
Fellowship of the Ring, 140, 148, 189
Fetishism, 147–48, 175–76
Film adaptations (of *The Lord of the Rings*), 18. *See also* Jackson, Peter
Fimi, Dimitra, 20n55, 80n8
Flieger, Verlyn, 23n58, 80, 90, 94, 106, 194, 218
Frankl, Viktor, 165
Free will, 224–25, 228–29

Friendship, 168
Frodo, 58, 60, 61, 75, 76, 103, 123, 126, 127, 140, 142, 143, 148, 152, 157, 173, 188, 195, 203–5, 209–11, 213, 214, 216–17, 224–25, 226, 228–30, 232, 237–39; friendship with Sam, 163–70

Galadriel, 96n53, 126, 166, 167, 176, 230, 237n78
Galdor, 72
Gandalf, 67, 70, 71, 73, 75, 76, 96n53, 98, 100, 103, 115, 128–29, 131, 132, 137n5, 144, 154, 163–66, 168, 182, 206, 214–16, 223, 225–27, 230, 237
Garbowski, Christopher, 130, 166
Gelassenheit, 142
Gender, 115, 173
Genealogy, 152–53
Genesis, Book of, 107–8, 188
Gifts, 167
Gildor, 148
Gilgamesh, Epic of, 44
Gimli, 101, 122, 128–29, 168
Glorfindel, 211
Gnosticism/Gnostic/Neo-Gnostic, 65–70, 74–76, 161n2
God, 14, 15, 70–71, 96, 142–43, 172, 191; as "author," 194; the divine Mind, 118
Goldberry, 142–43
Gollum, 57, 58, 151, 164–65, 204, 213n13, 217, 226
Gondor, 56, 100, 148, 151–53
Gorbag, 154
Gospel, 42–44, 70, 100, 104, 119, 194, 201, 229, 230, 235; of John, 117
Gothic language, 77
Grace, 35n23, 97

Gracia, Jorge, 169
Grendel, 130–31

Hadot, Pierre, 38n31
Haldir, 127
Halsal, Michael, 124n54, 210n2
Haradrim, 153
Heidegger, Martin, 187n18
Helm's Deep, 132
Hibbs, Thomas, 214, 219, 224
Histories of Middle-earth, 233
History (and myth), 31, 99–104, 117
Hobbes, Thomas, 153
Hobbit, The, 51, 59, 107, 216, 218
Hobbits, 92n41, 100–101, 115, 137–39, 147–49, 167, 216; "Concerning Hobbits," 102, 149–50
Holmes, John, 79
Hope (Estel), 193, 211; and paganism, 217–19; as a virtue, 214–15
Hostetter, Carl, 67n44, 189n22
Hutton, Ronald, 119n36

Ilúvatar. *See* Eru
Imagination (creative), 31–32, 68, 88, 215; and evil, 216
Imbert, Yannick, 45
Incarnation (of Christ), 193–94, 227
Indo-European linguistics, 78
Inklings, the, 86, 99
Interlacing, technique of, 231

Jackson, Peter, 140, 164n10, 236n77
John Inglesant, 164n11
Jonas, Hans, 162n3

Kant, Immanuel, 67n45, 183, 219; Kantian deontology, 160
Kierkegaard, Soren, 218
Knowledge, 67–69, 98
Kohak, Erazim, 93, 206–7
Kraus, Joe, 100, 103
Kreeft, Peter, 93, 97, 168, 173, 201, 220

Lang, Andrew, 26
Language ("tongue"), 30, 92–93, 96
Leaf by Niggle, 1–9, 10–12, 15, 224
Legolas, 101, 128, 168, 189, 190n27
Lembas (Waybread), 97
Lewis, C. S., 15, 39n32, 234; *The Abolition of Man*, 68
Light, 113–18, 127
Logos, 95, 107, 112, 201. *See also* Christ
"Lost Road, The," 29n8
Lothlorien/Lorien, 100, 120, 126–27, 145–46, 148–49, 166, 203, 237n78
Lourdes, Shrine of, 234

Machine, the, 17, 40, 47–48, 65–66, 86, 98, 106, 131, 133–34, 156, 162, 221
Madsen, Catherine, 120n40
Magic, 27–28, 48, 57, 62–64, 98, 145–47
Maiar, 114–15, 117, 133, 137
Manicheanism, 72, 74, 151
Manwë, 52n11, 54, 73, 130, 177
Marriage, 97–98, 171–78
Mary, Assumption of, 195n43
McIntosh, Jonathan, 43, 72, 188
Meister Eckhart, 142n18, 201n58
Melkor/Morgoth, 13, 50, 53, 55, 70, 72, 109–11, 115–16, 133, 136, 145, 177

Men, race of, 49, 51, 133, 137, 188–89, 191
Merry [Brandybuck], 91, 123, 128, 132, 148, 168, 173, 212, 238. *See also* Pippin
Michel Delving, 150
Miesel, Sandra, 119, 173, 174, 175n47, 176n50
Milbank, Alison, 72, 144, 147, 174–75
Minas Morgul, 61
Minas Tirith, 151, 223
Mirkwood, 127
Mirour de l'Omme, 31
Misty Mountains, 57, 122
Moderate realism. *See* Universals, problem of
Monarchy, 157–58
Monsters, 129–34
Mordor, 58, 59, 151, 153, 209, 212, 215, 226
Morgoth. *See* Melkor
Morgoth's Ring, 13, 72, 233
Moria, 80, 129, 212
Mortality. *See* Death
Mount Doom, 60, 169, 226, 228, 230
Müller, Max, 86–87, 99
Music, Great, 108–13, 126–27, 136, 207
Myth, 87–90; "true myth," 119–20
Mythopoeia, 15–17, 97, 221

Naedfaerae, 2n3
Naming/Nomenclature, 79–80
Nature, definition of, 105–6
Nature of Middle-earth, 199, 200n55
Nazgul, 131. *See also* Ringwraiths
Neoplatonism, 19, 108n8
Newman, John Henry, 44n45
Newton, Isaac, 183

Nietzsche, Friedrich, 161, 164, 201n60
Niggle, 1–9, 143n20, 180, 201
Nihilism, 55, 223
Nimrodel, 126
Noldor, 50
Nominalism. *See* Universals, problem of
Notion Club Papers, 29n8, 99, 202n62
Númenor, 52–56, 65, 121, 197
Númenóreans, 70, 91, 187–88; and death, 195

Oath (of the Noldor), 50
Ockham's Razor. *See* Wiliam of Ockham
Old Forest, 121, 123–26, 142, 143, 205
Old Man Willow, 125
Orcs, 111, 115, 129, 132–33, 151, 170
Ordway, Holly, 119n36, 210n2
Orthanc (Isengard), 137n6, 206

Paganism, 95, 119–20; Greek, Roman, and Norse pagans, 10
Pascal, Blaise, 22
Paul, Saint, 210n3, 216
Pearl, The, 29
Phenomenology, 21–22
Philosophy, 93
Pippin [or Peregrin Took], 91, 123, 128, 132, 148, 168, 173, 227
Pity, 164–68, 216–17, 226
Plato/Platonism, 22, 36n24, 82, 88, 94, 149, 162, 219; *Meno*, 94n48; *Phaedo*, 94n48; Platonic Forms, 127; *Republic*, 114n24; *Timaeus*, 36n24, 94

Postmodernism, 20–21, 83–84
Prancing Pony, 58
Progress, 17, 220–22
Providence, 221–27
Purgatory, 4, 10, 196, 224

Quenta Silmarillion, 49, 177–78, 218

Radagast, 137n6
Ragnarök, 219
Realism. *See* Universals, problem of
Recovery, 12–13, 21–23, 32–38, 41, 94, 126
Reilly, R. J., 125
Religion, meaning of, 135
Ressentiment, 160–62, 164, 166
Return of the King, 102, 210
Revelation, divine, 202
Rhudaur, 129
Rings of power, 51, 56, 237n78
Ring of Sauron, 56–64, 71–72, 74, 98, 100, 140–42, 144, 149, 154, 155, 163, 165–66, 167, 170, 172, 173, 175, 176, 181–82, 214, 215, 220, 228
Ringwraiths, 57–58, 75, 181, 185–87, 188, 238. *See also* Nazgul, Witch-king of Angmar
Rivendell, 92n41, 120, 203, 204, 211
Roberts, Adam, 173
Rohirrim/Rohan, 100, 148
Rousseau/Rousseauian, 125, 139
Ryle, Gilbert, 72

Sacraments/sacramental, 44, 97–98, 120–21, 123; Blessed Sacrament, 117–18, 239; of marriage, 171, 176–77
Sammath Naur, 169

Sam(wise) Gamgee, 58, 59, 61–62, 99, 123, 127, 145–46, 147, 156, 166, 169, 173, 209–10, 228–32, 240; and Rosie, 175–76
Sartre, Jean-Paul, 187n18
Saruman, 67, 70, 73, 84, 92–93, 98, 103, 115, 133, 137n6, 154–56, 160, 166, 206, 222, 226
Satan, 111
Sauron, 50–53, 55, 64, 71, 72, 98, 100, 103, 115, 127, 131, 154, 160, 166, 177, 206, 215, 216, 225, 227; eye of, 56–61, 74n63; and Morgoth, 73–74
Saussure, Ferdinand de, 83
Scheler, Max, 160–62
Scheps, Walter, 120
Science, 22, 140–41; speculative vs. productive, 141
Secret Fire (Flame Imperishable), 13–14, 109–10, 112–13
Sexuality, 173–75
Shadowfax, 136
Shagrat, 154
Shelob, 131, 169, 175n47, 228
Shippey, Tom, 2n3, 11, 58, 84, 98, 125, 176, 185n14, 190, 204n67, 222n37, 230–31
Shire, the, 120, 124, 125, 128, 148–52, 155–56, 158, 169, 238, 240; and Bree, 79n5
Siewer, Alfred, 124n54
Silmarillion, 9, 52, 91, 107, 114, 120, 123n50, 233
Silmarils, the, 50, 116, 157
Silverlode, 203
Sir Gawain and the Green Knight, 27, 131n78
Sir Orfeo, 203

Smaug, 37n27
Spacks, Patricia, 224–25, 228
Stanton, Michael, 205, 212n11, 216
Structuralism, 83
Sub-creation, 29–32, 49, 62–63, 171
Swift, Jonathan, 139

Technology, 98, 139, 163
Ted Sandyman, 99
Time, 4–5, 23, 33–34, 56, 143n20, 145–46, 180, 238; Elven, 204–5; modes of, 188–98, 203, 238; time and eternity, 182–88; time, eternity and being, 207. *See also* Eternity
Theoden, 102
Thing, meaning of, 175
Thomism/Thomistic, 19, 99, 183–85, 190n27. *See also* Aquinas
Tolkien, Christopher, 107, 117, 157
Tom Bombadil, 125–26, 138, 140–45, 163, 205–6, 212
Treebeard, 91, 132
Trees, of Valinor, 113, 117, 120; Party Tree, White Tree of Gondor, 120; Sam's Mallorn Tree, 167, 240
Trinity, Holy, 20, 118
Trolls, 132–33
Tuor and Ichil, 191
Two Towers, 231n64

Übermensch, 170
Ungoliant, 175n47
Universals, problem of, 81–85, 86, 185
Utilitarianism, 160

Valar, 49, 52, 55, 72, 91n38, 112–15, 117–18, 137, 145
Valdman, Meredith, 133n88
Valinor, 50–51, 55–56, 114, 121, 187, 196, 233, 239
Virtue, meaning of, 159, 172; and responsibility, 165
Voegelin, Eric, 70n51, 221

Waldman, Milton, 9, 47, 50, 51
Watcher: Tower of Cirith Ungol, 59n26; in the water, 129
Welsh language, 77
West, Richard, 231
William of Ockham, 82; Ockham's Razor, 83n14
Witch-king of Angmar, 131, 212
Wittgenstein, Ludwig, 22, 189n24
Wizards, 137, 141
Wood, Ralph, 201
World War I, 73
Wormtongue, Grima, 133
Wyrd, 122

Zimbardo, Rose, 136, 140, 182n7

Also available from The Catholic University of America Press

Tolkien, Philosopher of War
by Graham McAleer

The Third Spring: G.K. Chesterton, Graham Greene, Christopher Dawson, and David Jones
by Adam Schwartz

Faithful Fictions: The Catholic Novel in British Literature, second edition
by Thomas Woodman

Revelation and Convergence: Flannery O'Connor and the Catholic Intellectual Tradition
Edited by Mark Bosco, SJ, and Brent Little

Shakespeare and the Idea of Western Civilization
by R. V. Young

Christian Humanism in Shakespeare: A Study in Religion and Literature
by Lee Oser

Acts of Faith and Imagination: Theological Patterns in Catholic Fiction
by Brent Little

One Poor Scruple (Catholic Women Writers)
by Josephine Ward

The End of the House of Alard (Catholic Women Writers)
by Sheila Kaye-Smith

The Martyrdom of Maev and Other Irish Stories
by Harold Frederic

Hell and the Mercy of God
by Adrian J. Reimers

www.ingramcontent.com/pod-product-compliance
Lightning Source LLC
Chambersburg PA
CBHW032335300426
44109CB00041B/960